Give sorrow words

Much has been written about dying and bereavement in recent years, but the stress of terminal illness in childhood – as it affects both families and professionals – is only just beginning to be better understood. Dorothy Judd, a Kleinian psychotherapist, has worked with ill, disabled and dying children and here puts her clinical experience in the context of new developments in hospices and hospital care.

The book's central focus is a diary of Judd's work with Robert, a seven-year-old suffering from leukaemia. Of especial interest to mental health professionals will be Judd's account of therapeutic work in the hospital setting, away from the privacy of the consulting room. Interviews with hospice founders and with staff at Great Ormond Street Hospital for Sick Children in London, make it a most unusual book.

Give Sorrow Words – its title drawn from *Macbeth* – combines great sensitivity to the experience of terminal illness with an astute awareness of the more theoretical debates in this increasingly important area of research. The author questions whether dying should ever be prolonged, even in the interests of medical research, particularly when there is only a slim chance of survival, and when the treatment is often agonising.

Dorothy Judd is a child psychotherapist at the Tavistock Clinic, and at Kingsbury Child and Family Centre, London. She is Honorary Secretary of the Association of Child Psychotherapists. She originally trained as an art therapist.

Mrs Judd playing

Robert playing and happy

Give sorrow words:
Working with a dying child

Dorothy Judd

Foreword by Dora Black

'an association in which the free development of each
is the condition for the free development of all'

Free Association Books / London / 1989

First published in Great Britain in 1989 by
Free Association Books
26 Freegrove Road
London N7 9RQ

British Library Cataloguing in Publication Data
Judd, Dorothy
    Give sorrow words: working with a dying child.
    1. Terminally ill children. Psychological aspects
    I. Title
    155.9′37

    ISBN 1-85343-099-4
    ISBN 1-85343-098-6 pbk

A percentage of the royalties from this book are going to
The Child Psychotherapy Trust
27 Ulysses Road
London NW6 1ED

The Trust is dedicated to ensuring that more
child psychotherapists are trained to treat the
emotional problems of children and their families
within the National Health Service. This would include
the kind of work described in this book.

Typeset by Photosetting, Yeovil

Printed in Great Britain by
Billing & Sons Ltd, Worcester

To my father, Samuel Woolf,
who died in 1984,
and to the memory of 'Robert' himself

'... ne'er pull your hat upon your brows;
Give sorrow words; the grief that does not speak
Whispers the o'er-fraught heart and bids it break.'
Macbeth

Contents

Acknowledgements

Compiling these acknowledgements has been perhaps the most enjoyable part of the task of writing this book. I shall trace the help chronologically. First and foremost and woven into the whole time-span of the work involved, I would like to thank my husband, Denis, for his direct support, encouragement, and helpful comments, as well as his background support in sharing the holding of the domestic fort.

Then, my second analyst, Alex Tarnopolsky, facilitated the process of thinking about this work and the possibility of writing something about it. Shirley Hoxter was a source of inspiration to me, as tutor, seminar leader, supervisor, and workshop convenor, at different stages of my training as a child psychotherapist at the Tavistock Clinic, and subsequently as I began to work with physically ill children.

Jeanne Magagna, Sheila Miller, Margaret Rustin, Juliet Hopkins, and Jon Jureidini, all looked at earlier stages of my draft of the diary (Part Two of the book), and made very helpful comments. Later Gianna Williams helped with valuable thoughts.

A particularly significant person was Ann Scott of Free Association Books. I have been especially fortunate to have had her as my editor. Her ideas about the ways in which the diary (Part Two) could be developed into a book, as well as her encouragement and detailed comments, have been invaluable. During Ann's absence, Selina O'Grady continued confidently to nurse the book along, with great attention to detail. I am grateful, too, to Miranda Chaytor for editorial help, and to Gillian Wilce, for her very careful copy-editing.

Meira Likierman read the whole almost finished manuscript and passed on many very useful thoughts. I am particularly grateful to her for her time.

Dora Black was a source of encouragement and support throughout, in reading parts of the manuscript, allowing me to carry out some of the work, and in making herself available for interview. Thanks, too, to Grant Prentice for agreeing to my undertaking some of the clinical work, as well as to David Lee and the many nurses, doctors, and teachers in the hospital school.

Much gratitude, too, to Richard Lansdown, Mother Frances Dominica, Dorothy Jordan, and Margaret Atkin for agreeing to my interviewing them, and for permission to quote them extensively. Similarly, many thanks to Mary Sue Moore for her generous comments and insight, and to Ricky Emanuel and Peter Speck for encouragement.

I would also like to thank two colleagues, Gill Roger and Frances Gomme, for their compassionate support at different times, as well as Carolyn Lelyveld for inspiration and understanding early on. Phil Beauchamp, too, was an important and valued colleague. The ongoing work discussion group which I convene at the Tavistock Clinic has provided a valuable psychodynamic approach to illness and disability.

I am grateful to the staff of the Tavistock Joint Library for their trouble; to the typists Linda Kaufman, Jackie Lightband, Jill Fletcher, and, particularly, Linda Burkill, for their hard work.

Last but not least, there are the many children whose experiences have been the basis for all my work.

London, January 1989

Foreword

Those of us working in hospital have the task of helping children and their families cope with the effects of chronic, sometimes life-threatening illness in children, and with the pain, inconvenience and constrictive effect of the 'high-tec' treatments now available. Multiple injections and venesections, cytotoxic drugs and radiotherapy are now routine in the treatment of leukaemia and solid tumours, but radiotherapy may involve the child being placed alone in a room inside a machine for an hour. He has to remain still and is likely to feel very sick and vomit. He will be a long way from home, especially if he comes to a regional hospital for a bone marrow transplant. If his parents come in with him – and we encourage and even insist on it – they have to cope with separation from other children and home, and live in a strange artificial environment. They have to relate to many different people at a time when anxiety about their child makes it difficult to function optimally.

For the child, according to his stage of development, anxiety is moderated by the presence of his parents, but he cannot help but be aware of the danger he is in, and research has revealed the propensity of the child to protect the parents from pain and depression (Bluebond-Langner, 1978). This partial reversal of the normal state of things – the parents usually protect the child – is often self-imposed and is rarely sought for or encouraged by the parents, but it constitutes a burden on an already overstressed child. Small wonder that the level of psychological disturbance in child, parents and siblings in life-threatening illness is between 50 and 75 percent (Koocher and O'Malley et al., 1980). If the price the child has to pay for recovery is a crippled mind, then the price may be too high.

In an effort to alleviate the emotional pain for children and their families, physicians are now working closely with child psychiatrists and their colleagues in some centres to provide a psychological support and treatment service. Dorothy Judd, a child psychotherapist, came to us to help develop this service, which also involves child psychiatrists, psychologists and social workers. Sometimes we are able to work with the whole family together, at other times, individual therapy may be more appropriate. Our aim is to provide time and space for children and families to reflect on their experiences, understand what is happening, adapt to the reality of the illness and treatment, enable the expression of fear, anger, anxiety and sadness and provide a safe place and person – one who is not involved in the medical treatment, and so can be the container of unwanted and sometimes frightening feelings. In this way it may be possible to bear the unbearable – the uncertainty about the future.

Doctors and nurses who have to do painful and unpleasant procedures to children, who may have to make an apparently well child sick, sometimes also have unbearable emotions. In order to carry on, we may develop defences against this pain which may make us less sensitive to our patients' emotional experiences. Child psychiatric teams can offer to share this pain and allow it to be lived with and therefore not denied – a process which makes us all more human.

In what follows, Dorothy Judd offers us an overview of children's attitudes to death and considers the moral and ethical issues raised by treatments for life-threatening illness in children. She allows us to share her attempt to enter into the world of the dying child, to experience with Robert and his parents the bewilderment, the isolation, the mutual pretence, the pain and anxiety that serious illness brings to families. Using her sensitive personality, honed by training and experience, she is able to make a space for this boy to make some sense of his experience – to 'live until he dies', as Spinetta has put it (Spinetta and Deasy-Spinetta, 1981). At the same time her social worker colleague is helping the parents to bear the unbearable.

Robert did not win his battle with his illness. But an increasing number do, as our haematology colleagues refine and improve their treatments, using the knowledge which they gain from their experience with many children like Robert. It is our task to make sure that they and their families have as high a level of emotional care as they do of physical care. With resources dwindling within the NHS we may not be able in future to offer the help to these families they need and deserve. I hope this moving account of a talented child psychotherapist's work with one very ill boy will help those who have to make funding decisions to understand the nature of our contribution to the care of these suffering families.

Dora Black, Consultant Child Psychiatrist, Vice Chairman, CRUSE – National Association for Bereavement Care.

Preface

To begin at the beginning. The work which this book describes arose out of a workshop I attended at the Tavistock Clinic in 1985, for child psychotherapists working with physically ill and disabled children. It gave me support and some very early insight into my work as a child psychotherapist with a small number of physically disabled children, some of whom had limited prognoses, at a special school. I began to consider basic problems concerning the chronically ill, the disabled, and the dying. When are defences useful and when are they maladaptive? How can the chronically ill child work through the normal developmental phases - particularly adolescence, with its essential bids for independence and autonomy - when his illness or disability makes him dependent on adults for basic care? Beyond which point should life be sustained by medical intervention, and how do we evaluate the quality of the remaining life for a child whose death is prolonged? Arthur Hugh Clough's caveat from *The Latest Decalogue* comes to mind:

> Thou shalt not kill; but need'st not strive
> Officiously to keep alive.

This interest led me to further work, mainly with leukaemic children, in a large teaching hospital, where I was supported by colleagues and a workshop for those of us engaged in working with children facing life-threatening illness.

When I showed my account of the work with one of these children - 'Robert' (in Part Two of this book) - to Ann Scott, at Free Association Books, she expressed interest but called it 'the foothills of a publishing project'. I wasn't sure whether to feel discouraged or encouraged: only the foothills - but at least it could be considered a potential publishing project. With Ann's encouragement I developed it further.

It grew at first into many little offshoots, which somehow, almost organically, became a recognizable shape. The process was not unlike that of knitting a garment: the various parts developed, to be pieced together; details like 'pockets' were added; some mistakes were corrected and 'dropped stitches' picked up, while others remained, perhaps for ever; finally, the 'rough ends' were tidied up. Through the creative process of making this book, it felt that the painful ordeal of this particular child, and many like him, could at least lead to further thinking about crucial issues around the care of dying children.

At a more personal level, one of the underlying reasons for writing this book is that the impact of working with terminally ill children affected me deeply. Robert appeared in my life as suddenly as he departed from it: a first, brief encounter, late September, with a pert little boy with a beguiling Scottish accent, so full of life and spirit that I reeled from the first meeting. I was shocked deep inside myself to think of his diagnosis – leukaemia – and the life-threatening disease in his body, destroying his blood. He occupied a pleasant side-room off the children's ward of a large teaching hospital in the North of England. The bustle of the ward seemed to take this new patient in its stride: it was only his mother's anxious expression and startled eyes that conveyed to me the seriousness of the situation.

The smell of the ward pervaded my nostrils for hours, strangely reminding me of a combination of talcum powder and babies' faeces. Perhaps this was evoked by the atmosphere of nurturing and cleanliness, of the apparent acceptance of bodily products that accompanies the care of the ill, of a powerful maternal presence in the ward, and by the helplessness of most of the patients.

This experience touched on other, earlier, more personal losses. The process of writing, firstly, the detailed account of my contact with one dying child, and then a fuller survey of the subject, was not only a way of sorting out some of my own thoughts and feelings, but also arose out of a sense of my own finiteness. For it is partly through this sense of mortality that our creativity is galvanized; that we seek to repair, create, and recreate, phoenix-like, that which has gone – in the sense of 'happened' as well as 'lost'.

Nothing can alter the absolute loss of a child, but we need to consider the climate in which a child dies, in an attempt to allow the experience to carry its own truth. Part of this truthfulness, and of the allowing of truthfulness on the part of the child, lies in acknowledging our 'not knowing' about the meaning of death, nor when it will come, to a particular child or his family: to be able to tolerate the uncertainty that a limited prognosis brings.

In *Four Quartets* T. S. Eliot writes:

In order to arrive at what you do not know

You must go by a way which is the way of ignorance...

And what you do not know is the only thing you know...

This uncertainty, and the sense of vulnerability it brings, is hard to stay with, without what Keats (1817) calls the 'irritable reaching after fact and reason'. Perhaps Keats's own life-threatening illness contributed to his understanding of this 'negative capability', as he called it, 'when a man is capable of being in uncertainties, mysteries, doubts'.

Much of this book is factually and theoretically based, hopefully not as a way of avoiding some of the uncertainties, but as a way of providing a framework within which to reflect. I hope that alongside the research quoted and the arguments presented there is sufficient quiet and stillness, where the reader can dwell on his or her own thoughts and search for meanings.

The theoretical framework of this book is, generally, a Kleinian one: that is, I have drawn upon the writings of Melanie Klein, who, beginning in the 1920s, pioneered child analysis. Klein's perspective arises out of Freud's discoveries of the child within the adult: she developed Freud's theories further, thus encompassing the possibility of seeing the baby within the child and within the adult. At first, some of her theoretical conclusions seemed surprising even to Klein herself: 'My study of the mind of the small child brought certain facts before me which seemed strange at first sight' (1932). Therefore, some of the ideas put forward in this book may well appear strange to the reader who is new to Klein's ideas.

This perspective arises logically for me out of my training at the Tavistock Clinic, my personal analyses and supervision, as well as a continued appraisal and reappraisal of these ideas through ongoing clinical work. Inevitably, further studies by Anna Freud, Winnicott, Bowlby, Bion, and many others have helped me, in common with many other child psychotherapists, to extend the theoretical framework.

However, although theories help to form a useful structure, it is the actual work with a child from which the excitement of discovery springs – the essential 'learning from experience', as Bion (1962) calls it. Alongside this comes the inevitable frustration of not understanding, of waiting, of continuing to look at one's own internal world, and attempting to understand one's own unconscious processes.

Recently much has been written about death, dying, and bereavement, and a great deal about children, but little has been written about the issues involved in bringing these two areas together. Therefore I address children's attitudes to death and how an imminent death affects these attitudes; ways in which adults, both professionals and parents, approach the death of children; and the increasing problems which arise when death is postponed through medical intervention and children are either living with an uncertain prognosis or experiencing a protracted death. I have not focused in much detail on bereavement – on the effects of the death of a child on parents and siblings – because that is a full study in itself. As the main focus is on dying children, the book aims to encompass their preoccupations and the climate in which they find themselves.

I have attempted to marry clinical experiences with theoretical concepts, published research on children's attitudes to death, and interviews with other experienced professionals.

My main focus is children with cancer, because, after accidents, cancer accounts for more deaths in children aged between one and fourteen years than any other cause. Yet cancer can be considered rare. One in every six hundred children under the age of fifteen develops a cancer, and of these leukaemia is the most common.

The experience of working with the child whom I describe in detail in Part Two was a very intimate one, and therefore one that is not easily shared in a public way through writing and publishing the account. However, I felt that it was important to try to convey the story as I perceived it. It raises many questions about approaches to dying children, and about the support needed by the family and by the medical and non-medical professionals involved.

Besides considering the appropriate psychological approach, this story raises the question of the medical efficacy of keeping someone alive where the chances of survival are very slim. The extreme physical suffering in many cases of this type has to be borne in mind when the decision to pursue medical treatment is made. It can be argued, of course, that each case can provide new medical knowledge, leading hopefully to further improvements in the future treatment of illness.

Above all, this book raises the question of whether those involved can or should ever shift their focus from one of working towards the day when the patient will be well again to one where death is accepted more openly and the impending loss is shared among all, including the patient. I can never generalize about the approach in such a delicate and painful situation, especially where a *child* is facing death, when 'where there's life, there's hope' is a necessary and understandable dictum for all those involved. In parallel with this, however, I believe there could be a place for thinking about that which perhaps is not unthinkable.

Bion (1984) describes how the infant, as part of normal development, when overwhelmed by a state of extreme helplessness, may project a feeling that it is dying into the mother. This is part of a basic psychic interplay between mother and child; the mother helps to make the infant's unmanageable experiences more tolerable through her 'reverie', her ability to take the infant's projections and anxieties 'on board'. In time, that which is thus 'processed' by the mother can be reintrojected – that is, taken once again into the infant's psyche, to become a part of his inner world.

However, if the projection of a feeling that it is dying 'is not accepted by the mother the infant feels that its feeling that it is dying is stripped of such meaning as it has. It therefore reintrojects, not a fear of dying made tolerable, but a *nameless dread*' Bion (1984, p. 116, my italics).

If the 'nameless dread' becomes something that can be acknowledged, perhaps given a form and shape, in words, play, drawings, or in a tacit calm acceptance, then perhaps fear, despair, isolation, and depression can to some extent be alleviated. Although here Bion is writing about an infantile phantasy and not a reality of dying, the feelings aroused in a fatally ill child may well be similar.

Note on conventions

Throughout the book I use the word 'phantasy' to denote what the Kleinian psychoanalyst Susan Isaacs (1952) describes as 'the mental corollary, the psychic representative of instinct. There is no impulse, no instinctual urge or response which is not experienced as unconscious phantasy ... A phantasy represents the particular context of the urges or feelings (for example, wishes, fears, anxieties, triumphs, love or sorrow) dominating the mind at a particular moment.'

I use the word 'fantasy' to denote more conscious imaginings, on a spectrum between daydreams and hallucinations.

Unless I am referring to actual clinical material, I generally describe the infant/child as 'he', although of course I mean he or she.

The 'stage' is set in Great Britain, and sometimes more generally in the western world. I am not relating to the psychodynamics of grief and bereavement of other cultures.

I have changed as many details as possible in the case studies I have given, in order to protect the anonymity and confidentiality of those described - except where I have interviewed various professionals and gained their permission to quote them.

Part One

Framework

Chapter One

The death of a child

> Although we know that after such a loss the
> acute state of mourning will subside, we also
> know that we shall remain inconsolable and
> will never find a substitute. No matter what
> may fill the gap, even if it be filled
> completely, it nevertheless remains
> something else. And actually this is how it
> should be. It is the only way of perpetuating
> that love which we do not have to
> relinquish.
> Freud, 'Letter to Ludwig Binswanger' (1929)

Freud wrote the above on the day his dead daughter would have been thirty-six years old. At the time of her death, he had written, 'Deep down I sense a bitter, irreparable narcissistic injury' (1920b).

The death of a child is one of the most disturbing, shocking, unacceptable events that can occur. It is a death out of season. More than the death of an adult, who has at least to some extent 'lived his life', the death of a child is an outrage against the natural order of things, disrupting our sense of purpose, of future promise, of our progeny continuing after our death. For the parents of a child who dies, the loss that is mourned includes not only a shared past, but future hopes. It is 'endured, rather than overcome', by mourning (Mitchell-Rossdale, 1988).

Mother Frances Dominica (Superior General of the Anglican Society of All Saints), who founded and runs Helen House in Oxford, the first hospice in the world for children, told me (personal communication):

> I think the first thing is to be realistic, and it was important for us, soon after Helen House opened, to admit that the death of a child is an outrage. You can't explain it away, you can't make it tidy and nice, let alone give all the answers. Firstly, it's an outrage, and secondly, we don't understand why it should happen. And once you've accepted those two things, I think you're half way there.

Even to those not in the bereaved immediate family, the reverberations in the community are considerable. Feelings of shock, disbelief, and outrage are quite common among neighbours who hear about the death of a child, more so of course if the death is sudden. The security of the onlooker has been threatened.

This feeling, that the 'shadow of death' could as easily pass over one's own family, is only temporarily chastening. For those not directly involved, the event fades in a way that may be surprisingly rapid. We return to our everyday lives, where, we hope, 'death shall have no dominion' (Dylan Thomas, 1966).

ATTITUDES TO DEATH AND DYING

In considering children's attitudes to death, we need to gauge the climate and background from which they emerge. There is still the tendency today to say 'Not in front of the children' when discussing death, and an attempt to thus protect children. We need to question whether children's fears of death are a reflection of adults' inhibitions and adults' own anxieties about death, or whether children themselves have fears of death as part of normal psychological functioning.

Today in the West, paradoxically, there is a surge of public interest in the subjects of death, dying, and bereavement, but a continued denial in the everyday lives of most people. On the surface, it seems that the taboo around death, dying, and bereavement is being lifted, not only at a popular level in the media, but also at an academic and professional level (Parkes, 1972; Pincus, 1976). Bereavement counselling is now fairly widely available. There is the growth of the hospice movement over the past twenty years, with, now, the provision of over 200 hospice care services in Britain; there is also the influence of the writings of Elizabeth Kübler-Ross. The introduction of 'death education' (Willcock, 1988) in over a thousand schools in the USA, for five-year-olds and upwards, indicates a more enlightened development which Britain may follow. Dr Robert Stevenson, one of the promoters of such courses there and a national authority on death education, strikes at the heart of the taboo. He believes that silence on the subject is damaging to the child, leading to thoughts of 'What is this terrible thing I'm supposed to be afraid of, and from which I am excluded?' Inevitably, however, he has his opponents. They claim that the subject should have no place on the timetable, and they are concerned that many children will be too emotionally immature to cope adequately with the subject.

But, as I will try to convey, ours is in many ways more of a death-denying society than it was at the turn of the century. Death was then a public event and often took place in the presence of family, friends, and children. In 1900 approximately two-thirds of the people who died in western countries were under the age of fifty, and most died at home in their beds. Children learned to view death as part of the natural progression of life. Up to, and including, the First World War, death was very accessible (Ariès, 1974; Feifel, 1962; Gorer, 1965; Stannard, 1977).

As Alan Bloom (1988, p. 192) states, in writing about the early years of this century in an English village:

> Death was much more in evidence than birth. The arrival of babies was almost furtive, but the church bell tolled for every death. And you knew from the tolling whether the deceased was a man, woman or child. One ... knew when someone was very ill because straw would be spread on the road to deaden the sound of hooves and wheels for the sufferer.

When discussing this century's trend away from such acceptance of death, Dr Dora Black says (personal communication):

> As Gorer writes, there was so much slaughter, death, and horror during the First World War, that the 1920s became a death-denying society in a manic way. That merged into a period of therapeutic optimism, when penicillin was discovered. The first real drug that could *cure* anything was only discovered in 1907. Before then there were no curative drugs. Salvarsan, which affected syphilis, was the first curative drug. Before that, drugs like morphine could kill pain, but not cure; and drugs like digitalis, in the nineteenth century, could help heart disease, but not cure it.
>
> Research into drugs was held up by the First World War. Then the sulphonamides were discovered; then antibiotics, after the Second World War. So there was tremendous excitement that we could actually treat and cure diseases for the first time.

She believes that the 'combination of a heavy death toll by the end of the First World War and the medical treatment breakthroughs* led to a taboo on talking about death, for doctors considered death as a failure', and continues, 'There was also a magical feeling which still exists to some extent: I remember that my mother would never mention the word "tuberculosis" or "cancer" because to say it meant that in a sense you were giving it to someone.' These cultural taboos on talking about death shifted, if not lifted, after the Second World War, she surmises. 'Firstly, people had a more

---

* It is, however, important to make a distinction between the decrease of the infant mortality rate as a result of medical advances on the one hand, and, on the other, as a result of better diet, the availability of clean water, and the proper institution of sewage disposal. The improvement of public health in general had started before the considerable medical advances in the treatment of infectious diseases. In fact McKeown (1976), the epidemiologist, concluded that the key factors in improving health have been environmental and social, not medical. It is striking to note that over the last thirty-five years, life expectancy has increased in Britain by four years – whereas it had increased by twenty-five years over the previous sixty years (Forfar, 1984).

realistic attitude to what they could cure and what they couldn't, and this continued. Secondly, there is more openness generally about what people feel that they can talk about.'

We have, then, a commonly held belief that death was far more 'out in the open' in the nineteenth century than in the twentieth, and that nowadays, in contrast, it is something which is still generally hidden away, but that we are re-emerging from a 'dark age' of repression of the subject of death.

Although both Ariès, Gorer, and others have made invaluable contributions to the body of historical and sociological perspectives, and many of their findings are beyond dispute, an important essay by the historian David Cannadine (1981) has questioned our own romanticization and idealization of death in Victorian Britain. Cannadine examines attitudes to, and the effects of, war, death, grief, and mourning, and suggests that it is extremely difficult, if not impossible, to trace the evolution of something as private as grief.

In questioning the 'beguiling and nostalgic progression from obsessive death and forbidden sex in the nineteenth century to obsessive sex and forbidden death in the twentieth', he comments that although there may be some truth at a public level about the views held by Gorer and Ariès, research shows that at a private level the Victorian interest in sexuality was not that dissimilar from attitudes today (Marcus, 1966; Walvin, 1987) and casts similar doubt on assumptions about a disparity between modern and Victorian attitudes to grief.

Cannadine also wonders if the more elaborate mourning rituals were psychologically beneficial, or if their predominant value was one of commercial exploitation and ostentation. He suggests that the 'denial of death' which Ariès and others attach to the 1940s onwards in fact begins before 1914 – but that this was a decline in the *celebration* of death, while death continued to be *glorified*, particularly in war.

Freud, on the other hand, believed that the mass slaughter of the First World War would be bound to alter man's conventional views of death: 'Death will no longer be denied; we are forced to believe in it' (1915a, p. 291). Interestingly, the outcome of the widespread bereavement caused by the First World War seems to have been a turning away from Victorian mourning rituals and religion, and a turning instead to nationwide public construction of memorials.

Moving ahead to the Second World War, the horrifying use of the atomic bomb utterly changed man's views of his own power. Universal death was, and is, now possible. It is under this shadow of the possibility of global death that we all live. The effects on the individual of the possibility of a nuclear holocaust and of mass disasters are beginning to be looked at by psychoanalysts ('The Aftermath of Disaster – Survival and Care', Conference at Tavistock Clinic, June 1987; Segal, 1987), psychotherapists, psychologists, as well as sociologists and historians. Just as Freud (1915a) predicted that the mass slaughter of the First World War would make it impossible for us to 'maintain our former attitude towards death', so this nuclear age has an effect that must further alter our attitudes; even though, on the surface, we tend to ignore the threat on a day-to-day basis.

From a psychoanalytic view, Segal (1987) argues that all wars mobilize very primitive mental mechanisms (see below pp. 12–13) but that the existence of nuclear weapons induces these mechanisms to a far greater degree because of the threat of total annihilation that they pose. Increased threats from outside lead to increased infantile omnipotence, denial, and psychotic defences, as ways of defending against the consequences of an escalating arms race.

At a more personal level, on the other hand, dying can be judged to be easier today than it used to be, as it more usually occurs at a time which is psychologically more acceptable: old age (Cannadine, 1981). And, owing to improved pain-control and other medical interventions, it can be made more peaceful and comfortable. Derek Nuttall, Director of CRUSE – the National Association for Bereavement Care – speaking at a conference on 'Bereavement: Grief and Loss' held by the Association for Child Psychology and Psychiatry in October 1988, also pointed out that more services are available to the bereaved than ever before; that people can die without pain and with more medical care. He added that there is more understanding of the bereavement process, with, for example, greater assurance now available about the normality of the emotional turmoil experienced by the bereaved.

Nevertheless, despite this greater accessibility of the subject of death, people's awareness and experience of death tends to remain at an intellectual level, unless they have been personally bereaved and are able to mourn. Many people reach middle age without a personal experience of death. As Dora Black says:

> I was taking a seminar for medical students the other day, on death and dying, and we were doing a role play. I was trying to get them talking to the parents of a child with cancer. They found it extremely difficult to get into. They were very brusque and quite hurtful, and unable to get any sympathetic feeling into it. It seems they have to dehumanize themselves, in order to distance themselves. Very few have had any actual experience of bereavement nowadays. Probably the first time they come across death is in the hospital. (personal communication)

And, as Kübler-Ross (1975) writes, 'our medical schools prepared them [medical students] almost exclusively in the *science* of medicine and give them little help in its *art*'.

Indeed, doctors may have a particular need to deny the fact of death – they may themselves have fears of illness and death which are then denied and mastered by becoming doctors (Keniston, 1967; Liston, 1975; Black *et al.*, 1989).

Dr Richard Lansdown (Chief Psychologist, Hospital for Sick Children, Great Ormond Street) feels that there has been a considerable lessening of the taboo on talking about death in the hospital and the leukaemic unit, where he works, but:

> In society I don't think there has been any change – not that I can discern, and not from what parents say about the response they get from other people. Parents of children who have died, or who are dying, still have a sense of isolation, partly because they have cut themselves off – I think one must recognize that – and partly because society doesn't really know how to cope. (personal communication)

Black reminds us of the remoteness and rarity of child death today, compared with the days of her grandmother, who had ten children but only raised two of them. It is these not untypical salutary statistics that so greatly contrast with our present-day success in fighting death, and at least partly explain the alienation of death as a concept and as a reality. (The infant mortality figures in England and Wales, per thousand live births, were 117.1 between 1906 and 1910, whereas in 1984 they were down to 9.4. In 1985 they were again 9.4 per thousand births. The Figure for 1986 shows the first increase in sixteen years: 9.6 per thousand – Registrar General's *Statistical Review*.)

It is still commonplace for us to employ euphemisms. We talk about people 'passing away' or 'passing on', about 'losing' someone, about people 'pegging out', 'copping it', 'pushing up the daisies', 'kicking the bucket', 'giving up the ghost', 'ending one's days', and about pets being 'put to sleep'. We talk about funeral 'parlours', call coffins 'caskets', and undertakers' offices 'chapels'. All these sayings have an understandable logic and meaning, but nevertheless illustrate a propensity to deny an ordinary straightforward description of death. (Further on in this chapter I will explore everyday ways in which death *is* experienced, but not acknowledged, ways in which its existence is relegated to largely unconscious parts of the mind.)

A few other factors contribute to people's difficulty in negotiating death emotionally and integrating it into their lives, despite the intellectual accessibility of death as a topic. One important one is that nowadays more people (in fact, two-thirds) die in hospital and nursing homes away from their homes. This can be a distressing and isolating experience, possibly made more strange by the use of life-sustaining technology and notwith-standing the importance of effective pain control.

Another development is the expectation that the 'experts' will help with illness, death, and bereavement. In a sense, therefore, people can feel de-skilled from finding their own instinctual and probably appropriate ways of negotiating death. Just as the natural childbirth movement attempts to redress the 'high-tech' approach to childbirth, so some aspects of the death **awareness** 'movement' aim to restore the dignity of patients, to avoid technology which is seen as alienating, and to break down the barriers to discussing death (Kastenbaum, 1982).

Within the framework of medicine's success in saving people's lives, and against the background of no world war for over forty years, we need to question when to allow people to die, if keeping them alive threatens their autonomy and dignity (see Chapter 10). Perhaps we should remember the story of Asclepius, who was so skilled in the use of drugs and in surgery that he became known to the ancient Greeks as the founder of medicine. However, so successful did he become at raising people from the dead that he was killed by Zeus for hubris.

Without death, after all, life would have no meaning. The flowers of the spring have an appeal that is largely related to their impermanence. Similarly, if life were eternal, perhaps we would not bother to get up in the morning. The individual's impetus, zest, and appreciation are largely bound up with a span of limited duration.

The writer James Baldwin expresses a similar view thus:

> Perhaps the whole root of our trouble, the human trouble, is that we will sacrifice all the beauty of our lives, will imprison ourselves in totems, taboos... in order to deny the fact of death, which is the only fact we have. It seems to me that one ought to rejoice in the *fact* of death – ought to decide, indeed, to *earn* one's death by confronting with passion the conundrum of life. (Baldwin, 1963, p. 79)

An analogy with painting also comes to mind. Although this requires a leap of imaginative conjecture on the reader's part to consider the subject of 'wholeness' from a visual angle, it may remind us that not only poets and philosophers have grappled with ideas of life and death, but, more symbolically, so have painters. The resultant aesthetic experience of taking on board the darks and lights, the foreground and the depths, object and ground, the mysterious or abstract areas of a canvas as much as the more explicit details parallels our struggle to see death as part of life.

The art historian Wölfflin summarizes this process:

> If a nude in Rembrandt stands out on a dark ground, the light of the body seems as it were to emanate from the darkness of the picture space: *it is as if*

> *it were of the same stuff.* The distinctness of the object in this case is not necessarily impaired. While the form remains perfectly clear, that peculiar union between the modelling lights and darks can have acquired a life of its own ... figure and space, corporeal and incorporeal, can unite in the impression of an independent tonal movement. (Wölfflin, 1932, pp. 19–20, my italics)

The difficulty in 'seeing' death as part of life is rather like the mind's inability to 'read' both subject and background simultaneously in those black and white illustrations of faces in profile or of vases, where the viewer has to make a considerable effort to shift his vertex.

Linking this discourse with the psychoanalytic one to which I shall return, I find the words of a drawing teacher I once had – 'The spaces between objects are as important as the objects themselves' – remarkably similar to Winnicott's (1988) broad sweeps of understanding, that the 'life of an individual is an interval between two states of unaliveness'. And death, even before its arrival, is an 'absent presence', to quote Feifel (1962). With resignation and acceptance, Francis Bacon wrote in the seventeenth century: 'It is as natural to die as to be born.'

Yet this complementarity of life and death has not easily been embraced in an appreciative way by modern western man, for an acknowledgement of mortality and impotence in the face of death leads to uncomfortable feelings of helplessness. Hence, one might understand the need for religious beliefs in an after-life and for the Christian notion of resurrection. For, as Freud (1915a) observed, the body of a dead person can be seen to disintegrate, while memories of the person can live on, thus creating a very understandable division of the individual into body and soul.

While exploring man's fear of death, we need to acknowledge the other side of the same coin: his capacity to long for death, often seen as an escape route to peace. Freud saw protective concern as frequently harbouring murderous feelings (1900, p. 145n.). Therefore, implicit in the more usual fear of death, or the life instinct holding supremacy over the death instinct, lies its counterpart or repressed side: death's attraction or appeal for man. This may be consciously or unconsciously expressed as murderous or suicidal fantasies (Freud, 1920a, p. 162).

The wish for death as a way of escaping from life's troubles, but then a fear of the mystery of the unknown that death might hold, is powerfully conveyed, as is well known, by Hamlet:

> To die, to sleep;
> To sleep; perchance to dream: ay, there's the rub;
> For in that sleep of death what dreams may come

When we have shuffled off this mortal coil,
Must give us pause.

After dwelling on the many 'slings and arrows of outrageous fortune' in everyday life which could be ended by suicide, he continues to hesitate at this solution, with:

... the dread of something after death,
The undiscover'd country from whose bourn
No traveller returns, puzzles the will,
And makes us rather bear those ills we have
Than fly to others that we know not of?

Dramatists, poets, philosophers, and theologians have grappled with ideas around death through the ages, but, strangely, there have been few psychological and psychoanalytic investigations into the meaning of death. But Freud (1915a, p. 293) did pithily summarize philosophers' response to death: 'Philosophers have declared that the intellectual enigma presented to primaeval man by the picture of death forced him to reflection, and thus became the starting-point of all speculation.' However, he questions whether primaeval man was puzzled by death, suggesting instead that the *conflict of ambivalent feelings* towards the dead person (who was both loved and hated) was the stimulus for the spirit of enquiry in man. Freud speculates that it 'was beside the dead body of someone he loved that he invented spirits', for man would need to imagine other forms of existence beyond death, rather than accept the possibility of his own eventual total annihilation. He points out that it was only later that religions succeeded in depicting an after-life that was more desirable than our present life. He concludes in the light of the First World War that, as phantasies of killing are as much in the unconscious minds of modern man as they were in primitive man and colour our behaviour, we should 'give death the place in reality and in our thought which is its due', thus taking 'the truth more into account'.

Adults tend to use a wide range of defences against looking at the finality of death, employing (as well as the religious beliefs mentioned earlier) magical thinking; the externalization of the death instinct by splitting, denial, projection, and projective identification; and delusions. The use of the euphemisms described earlier is, of course, part of the denial. Yet, common though this denial is, it is psychologically costly, for the efforts made in keeping thoughts and fears of death at bay require energy that could be used for living with an awareness of our wholeness as well as our vulnerability. (It needs to be added, of course, that some denial is developmentally normal, and protects the personality from excessive anxiety. It enables people to take everyday risks, such as crossing roads and driving cars, even allowing oneself to fall into unguarded sleep.)

In order to understand further the origins of the denial of death, we need to go back to looking at the immature ego of the infant. As Freud described it (1938), the newborn baby is exposed, from birth and perhaps before, to the extreme conflict between the life instinct and the death instinct, or between Eros and destructiveness. Freud's writings on the death instinct are, at times, at variance with each other. On the one hand, he writes about the body's tendency to return to its original, inorganic state, and on the other hand, he writes about the instinct to destroy oneself or others. The 'nirvana principle' and the destructive drive are, as Fromm (1974) points out, two 'disparate entities' that cannot be brought together under the general heading of the death instinct. I therefore find Klein (1946) more helpful for the purpose of understanding the infant's early experiences.

According to Klein, the infant is exposed to both anxiety-producing experiences, like birth, hunger, pain, as well as life-giving experiences, such as physical closeness to its mother and feeding. When faced with the anxiety produced by the death instinct, or by negative or traumatic experiences, the infant's immature ego deflects it. In Klein's view this process is partly a projection, 'partly a conversion of the death instinct into aggression' (Segal, 1973). This primitive splitting and projection of that 'deadly' part of itself into the main external object, the breast, gives rise to feelings of persecution. Thus, the original fear of death is changed into fear of a killing presence, which, I would add, still carries undertones of death.

In parallel with this way of expelling the death instinct, the infant is establishing a relationship to an ideal object or, in Kleinian terms, 'breast'. This comes about through the fulfilling and gratifying experiences of being loved and cared for emotionally, and fed, which are also then projected in order to create a good object which will satisfy the ego's striving for the preservation of life. Thus, from the first weeks of life, the infant relates to two polarized objects: the breast is split into a gratifying ideal object and a persecutory bad one. This ongoing splitting keeps the good object separate and safe from the bad one. 'The infant's aim is to acquire, to keep inside and to identify with the ideal object, seen as life-giving and protective, and to keep out the bad object and those parts of the self which contain the death instinct,' Segal writes (1973). Klein calls this stage the paranoid-schizoid position.

As the infant develops and natural integration occurs, an attempt to mend this massive split begins: the infant begins to recognize and appreciate that these two separate objects are indeed parts of a whole, of a mother imbued with love and hate, life and death, who comes and goes, and who can be damaged in phantasy by the ravages of the infant. At the same time as the object becomes whole or relatively whole, the infant's ego becomes integrated through introjection. Thus, feelings of concern, of guilt that his destructiveness has caused the loss or the damage, recognition of dependency, emerge in this crucial process. But, as Segal writes, this, the 'depressive position, is never fully worked through. The anxieties pertaining to ambivalence and guilt, as well as situations of loss, which reawaken depressive experiences, are always with us' (1973). Later good experiences, embodying the early primary relationship, still carry the fear of loss.

One way of thinking about this could be that until the recent partial lifting of the taboo, our society was caught up in a collective splitting process, and the individuals within it reflected this. This whole notion of death, fundamental as it is to our definition of life, was split off to the extent that it was, and to some extent still is, banished even from our vocabulary, but perhaps projected on to 'bad' forces in a global or political sense. This paranoid-schizoid method of keeping life and death separate leads to an unreal life, of idealization and omnipotence, and possibly a powerful projection of violence and then to a feeling of persecution. An illustration of this can be found in the amassing of nuclear weapons by certain nations. Although the use of nuclear weapons would obliterate life over large areas of the planet, possession of the bomb is presented as a benign, peace-keeping stance. 'We' have no intention of using the bomb, except to defend ourselves; 'they', on the other hand, can only be restrained from a malevolent use of nuclear weapons by our own capacity to retaliate.

Thus, in attempting to bring life and death into the depressive position, we need not feel persecuted by death (or by anything else on to which death becomes displaced) nor omnipotently deny its place. We can use our creative and reparative talents to attempt to restore our good and loved internal and external objects which are always under the threat of loss. These attempts to repair – both actual losses as well as the anxiety of potential loss – fuel our creative drives: an anxiety of loss or at the prospect of loss leads to the wish to restore, through sublimation and the use of substitutes or symbols or directly through creative acts.

To summarize, then: in attempting to integrate death with life, we have to be able to stay with the pain of loss with which death is equated. The avoidance of this pain of absolute loss is at the root of our denial of the place of death in everyday life. An actual bereavement requires considerable emotional work to both decathect (Freud's term, meaning to extricate the energy invested in that person) and reintegrate the lost person, through the process of mourning (Freud, 1915b).

Throughout the life cycle there is growth that brings loss as well as gain. The baby loses the intra-uterine state in order to begin his own separate existence. The infant loses the breast in weaning in order to find his own identity and separateness. The toddler loses the security of the parental lap or arms, and risks falling and being hurt, in order to test out his own legs and the independence thus gained. Throughout all the changes in life there is loss and renewal. Even the finality of death can be 'the final stage of growth' (Kübler-Ross, 1975). Kübler-Ross believes death to be as much a part of human existence, growth, and development as being born, and suggests that this time limit urges us to use the time we have to live more fully. And for the survivor, involved in the death of someone close, when the mourning process is completed, the new phase of life can be welcomed as a fresh challenge to psychic growth, possibly strengthened by surviving the pain of loss.

If our lives can be seen to consist of recurrent tasks along the path from immaturity to maturity, transitions or transformations from one state of being to another, all experienced as struggles against inevitable difficulties, then the final stage, of death, can be seen as the last separation, as a letting-go of life with acceptance, and as the completion of a pattern. But just as an insecure child clings to his mother (because he feels he has not internalized enough of a secure 'holding' experience), so many adults cling to life and are unable to face death with equanimity.

Fairy stories and myths give us a useful analogy to the process that I have tried to describe. As we frequently find in fairy tales, a person is dead one moment and comes to life the next, or falls into a deep sleep and is reborn. This is not simply meant to represent wish-fulfilment and an avoidance of reality, but, rather, each rebirth or reawakening symbolizes the repeated reaching of a greater degree of maturity in the face of difficulty, as well as exemplifying the link between death and rebirth, as part of the life cycle. Death is not only bound up with the experience of loss, but is symbolized in many different ways that are commonplace and ordinary. Death is an aspect of decay, disease, damage, and the passing of the seasons.

At the same time, Anna Witham (1985) has written about the way in which some ideals of the contemporary death-awareness movement point to death becoming an exalted, idealized, perhaps transcendental experience. Similarly, a note of sentimentality or drama, which belies feelings of pain or suffering, often creeps into descriptions of death and dying by those who work with the terminally ill. Witham argues, quoting Menzies Lyth (1959), that this is an unconscious defensive process, in which individuals can get caught, as part of a collective system, in order to avoid overwhelming anxiety. In choosing to work with the dying, we are attempting to heal splits in ourselves, to restore and to repair. If we idealize the experience of death and dying, Witham suggests, we are using a manic defence against the anxieties of the depressive position as described earlier in this chapter (that is, feelings of sadness, fear of loss of important people, concern, guilt, and a realization of one's own dependency) which inevitably arise when caring for the dying. The extreme pressure and demands on the psyche in that situation lead us to avoid some of the anxieties. Thus, negative feelings about the dying person, or about that which they conjure up or reflect in our own inner world – feelings of helplessness, damage, anger – are completely denied by seeing all good in the dying person, in our role as worker, and in ourselves.

It is important, then, to differentiate between, on the one hand, reverence and respect for death, as a major event which has inevitably throughout the history of mankind stimulated fantasies and will continue to do so, and, on the other hand, idealization and therefore denial of the reality. The former emotions contain feelings of awe, perhaps of fear, of humility, of curiosity, which idealization lacks. Kübler-Ross's writings about death as a transcendental experience may therefore be useful to some people, for whom it may bring renewed psychic growth, but if our frustrations, disappointments, sense of vulnerability, strivings, can all be pushed to one side and replaced by a view of dying as something exalted and above everyday experience, then there is a tendency to expect more than the health-care teams can offer. Kastenbaum points out the basic dilemma, in an analysis of what he describes as the 'healthy dying' movement. 'Perhaps we should start to examine our underlying fantasies about what we expect. The dying-death situation is still not intimately known to many people. It is, therefore, a tempting screen on which to project aspirations and fantasies that have no other place to be displayed' (1982).

It appears, then, that for some the pendulum has swung far in the opposite direction, away from the fear and avoidance of death, to, possibly, its exaltation; it has become, for some, not only an achievement to die comfortably and with dignity, but there is the added expectation that it can be a 'beautiful' and spiritual experience (Levine, 1986).

This development towards a spiritual approach over recent years seems then to be not only a reaction to the taboo on death, and to the technological approach to health care and death, but, ironically, has similarities to the denial of death. Some recent writers revere a Zen approach to death, where the 'physical death is honoured and respected as a wonderful opportunity in the passing from the body to recognize the relativity of everything we imagine to be solid' (Levine, p. 252). Within this approach, this attempt to transcend mortality, there is an avoidance of the actual loss and separation that is death, and of the usually far from pleasurable experience. One has to acknowledge that certain kinds of death, such as cancer of the stomach, which lead to death by starvation, cannot be idealized. Dora Black (personal communication) believes that that experience can only be extremely grim for both the sufferer and the family, often leading to a difficult mourning for the survivors who have witnessed so much suffering. On the other hand she feels some people *are* ennobled by death, even a difficult death, the victims more than the families; and some children seem to mature more quickly when faced with life-threatening illness.

Kübler-Ross used the imagery of a cocoon and a butterfly: the child's ill body is like a cocoon, or chrysalis, and soon he will leave it behind, becoming the butterfly he always was, and go on. I will explore children's attitudes more fully in the following two chapters.

Chapter Two

Children's attitudes
to death

Every parting gives a foretaste of death...
Schopenhauer (1788-1860)

Healthy children are rather better at death
than healthy adults.
D. W. Winnicott, (1963, p. 62)

Freud (1915a) wrote 'that death was the necessary outcome of life, that everyone owes nature a death... in short, that death was natural, undeniable, and unavoidable'. He continues, though, to state that in practice it is otherwise – that in men there is:

> an unmistakable tendency to put death on one side, to eliminate it from life... the civilized man will carefully avoid speaking of such a possibility in the hearing of the person under sentence. *Children alone disregard this restriction; they unashamedly threaten one another with the possibility of dying....*
> (Freud, 1915a, p. 289, my italics)

The denial of death may be more generally understood through Freud's explanation that negation may be a stage in the process towards allowing a painful idea to be consciously accepted.

As with other concepts like birth and sex, death is an aspect of the child's world about which he has many conscious and unconscious fantasies and anxieties. These fantasies and anxieties tend to go more 'underground' as the child grows older and is more exposed to his society's mores and inhibitions, and as the child's emotionally charged early years often settle into a more taciturn relationship with his parents. Thus, a dialogue about death is probably more difficult for the adult than the young child.

This is not to say that a young child has an uncomplicated acceptance of the concept of death which only becomes inhibited through exposure to adults' anxieties. While it seems that generally children's understanding of death is not helped by adults' fears and inhibitions, the young child has many difficulties in his own right in understanding death. However, children feel themselves to be immortal in some respects: in the ways they take physical risks and need adults to restrain them, and in the difficulty that young children have, for example, in negotiating the concept of the irrevocability of death (see p. 19).

If we try to follow the development of the child's negotiation of death, we can begin by finding much evidence in psychoanalytic studies, in infant observations, and in the uncovering of infantile layers of the personality in adults in psychoanalysis, that the young infant registers the possibility of death through a sense of the danger of death. It is a common observation that newborn babies cry if hungry or cold, or if they feel unsafe, as a way of signalling for help and avoiding death. Death, to the infant, might be an inchoate 'nameless dread' (Bion, 1984, p. 116); a primitive fear of disintegrating, of falling for ever (Winnicott, 1962, p. 58). Earlier, Rank (1929) wrote about separation anxiety as being the primal human problem, equating it with a fear of death. Therefore one could say that in the infant there is a primitive awareness of death as part of a survival pattern, and that fear of separation and loss is, in origin, a fear of being totally abandoned and hence of being left to die. 'In every parting there is an image of death' (George Eliot, 1857, *Scenes of Clerical Life*).

Theories as to whether fear of death is a secondary phenomenon, arising from an environmental situation, or whether it is innate are expounded in a variety of ways, making it difficult to 'take sides'. On the one hand, Winnicott (1962) describes the infant as being 'all the time on the brink of unthinkable anxiety' (p. 57), as a result of the immature ego experiencing a less-than-perfect environment. He writes, 'Death, for an infant at the beginning, means something quite definite, namely loss of being on account of prolonged reaction to environmental impingement (failure of good enough adaptation)' (1954, p. 134).

Bowlby (1960) has written extensively on older infants' and young children's reactions to the unavailability - beyond a tolerable length of time - of the mother or mother figure. He calls this reaction - from six months onwards - 'grief and mourning', and describes, drawing upon Robertson (1952), states of fear, despair, and distress in young children. He concludes that this response to separation is as a result of the young child's inability to distinguish between temporary absence and a permanent loss. Therefore the infant feels that mother is lost, or dead.

In contrast to these environmentalist views of an awareness of death as a secondary phenomenon, Klein explains the fear of death as arising out of the infant's paranoid fear of being killed by his own projected aggression. Segal, writing about Klein's theories, states 'The immature ego of the infant is exposed from birth to the anxiety stirred up by the *inborn polarity* of the instincts - the immediate conflict between the life and the death instinct' (1973, p. 25, my italics). This polarity between the two forces or instincts leads to a dynamic interaction which Klein implies is as much a part of adults' mental processes as that of infants (1949, p. 211).

In both views, however, it seems that the baby is forced to come up against the feeling that no *good* experience can last for ever, and that this then leads to a need to negotiate a fear of something else – whether we call it a sense of fear of death, or annihilation, or disintegration, or a state of 'not-being', or, simply, of not feeling safe.

Yet, Freud, in the quotation at the beginning of this chapter, states that children have little fear of death. Although children do seem more obviously able to talk about the subject than adults, and to deal with it in their play, it does not seem correct to deduce that they lack fear. There may not be an *apparent* fear of death, but fear of separation and loss is a commonplace part of childhood as a survival mechanism, as well as the use of omnipotence as a denial of vulnerability.

If a child is confronted by an actual death, or an impending death, at close range – the death of an important family member, a loved family pet, or their own terminal illness – their understanding of death is, in a sense, enhanced considerably. They are forced into a premature grappling with the subject. This is borne out by research by Reilly, Hasazi, and Bond (1983). Therefore, in understanding children's concepts of death, there appear to be two rather different developmental time scales: the child with actual experience usually having a more developed-for-their-age understanding or a more developed defensive system than peers who have not been exposed in this way. This seems especially true in children over the age of six years (Kane, 1979).

In first considering the child's non-catastrophic encounters with the idea of death, there appears to be a lack of published research on the reactions of under-three-year-olds. This lack may be as a result of very young children being less verbally fluent and therefore less able to be interviewed on the subject. Another explanation is that few young children enter into psychotherapeutic treatment and therefore less has been discovered in this way; or, as I have suggested earlier, adults try to protect particularly young children from thinking about death because of their own anxieties.

Much of the research has delineated a recognizable first stage, in children of approximately three to five years of age, wherein the most striking feature is the denial of death as being irrevocable and universal (Anthony, 1973; Furman, 1974; Nagy, 1959; Orbach *et al.*, 1985). Kane (1979) gives a very clear and useful summary of children's concepts of death. She found that the previous literature regarding the effects of experience of death on the child was contradictory and specifically disagreed with the findings of Nagy who argued that the concept of death was inevitably understood by children by the age of nine. Kane, on the other hand, found that an awareness of death was frequently seen in children aged six or more. A minimum requirement for a child to be included in Kane's study was an awareness of death. This awareness was ascertained by all the children being shown nine specially produced pictures of rabbits. (The children were aged between three and twelve years.) One rabbit was dead and one sleeping. If the child did not choose the dead or sleeping rabbit, he was not included in the study. Perhaps this is both a strength and a limitation of the research: it is clearly a way of focusing on only those children with a conscious intellectual grasp of the primary concept, but it rules out those children who have an emotional block of 'knowing' about death. Therefore, Kane's findings of the universality of death awareness by specific ages is not necessarily truly widespread as it is only about children without that emotional inhibition. Moreover, she herself acknowledges that some of her findings may be influenced by the sample in the study being limited to a specific slice of the population: white and middle class. I feel that this is indeed a very significant limitation to the research.

Ten components (later reduced to nine) or aspects of death were ascertained by Kane in the children's responses, including irrevocability, dysfunctionality, separation, immobility, appearance, etc. Kane's conclusions are of basic stages. Young children aged three to five all have a basic *realization* of death, of the implicit *separation*, as well as of the *immobility* of the dead, although the immobility may be seen as partial. They tend to see 'dead' as being in a particular position: if you got into the position, you die; you could also make someone die by magical thinking or by the behaviour or wishes of others. The dysfunctionality of death is expressed as lying down immobile, with closed eyes.

Children a little older move from stage-one to stage-two thinking, where they add function to a structural description of death. Now they see death as an explanation for dysfunction: death induces dysfunction. This stage is marked by reality and the beginnings of logical thought: with further development of *realization, separation, immobility,* and the inclusion of the six remaining components: *irrevocability, causality, dysfunctionality, universality, insensitivity,* and *appearance.* However, they do not always realize that the components are inter-related: initially they believe that death is externally caused, later that it could be internally caused. They realize only the most obvious dysfunctions: those of not being able to eat or speak; as they grow older, they realize that the dead cannot drink or hear. Then, as they grow older still, they evolve from realizing that dead people cannot feel cold or smell flowers to the more subtle dysfunction of not being able to dream or know they are dead.

Once they can inter-relate the components they could be judged to have moved to stage three (at about the age of seven onwards) when they are able to think of death in the abstract. Although their thinking is logical and recognizes reality, they can speculate rather freely. Some can consider the existential issues of life and death. This stage indicates that they conceive of death as a state of internally caused dysfunctionality; death is a definition, of which *dysfunctionality*, *inactivity*, and *insensitivity* are the conditions, i.e., responsiveness is not just a characteristic of life, but a requirement of life. The alteration in the *appearance* of the dead is the last and most difficult concept for them to grasp; it is only by the age of twelve that they have a consistent notion of altered appearance: that the dead person cannot, or does not, look as though he were alive, or, on the contrary, that he may look the same.

Kane concludes by stating that her findings relate to the Piagetian three stages, 'pre-operational', 'concrete operations', and 'formal operations'. Her children first showed pre-operational thinking: they were tied to that which they could perceive, and could consider only one aspect of the situation at a time. Then they moved on to stage two, where they indicated 'concrete operations' thinking: could consider two aspects of the situation as existing at the same time and possibly influencing each other. Then, in stage three, the children showed 'formal operations' thinking: they could conjecture, think abstractly, be logical, and consider three different aspects of the situation.

Her findings differed from Nagy's in ways other than the age at which children consistently see death as an inevitable life event. She found that the children in her study did not reify death – that is, convert the person into something material. The younger children, however, may have visualized death in some form, and she speculates that perhaps the magical thinking of younger children could have inhibited them, for to name 'death' could bring it or create it.

Most of the published research on children's ideas about death and dying is based on interviews. The limitations of this technique have been pointed out by Wenestam (1982): children may say things that are undigested quotations from adults. Therefore Wenestam quotes Weininger (1979) who studied the way sixty children played with dolls which were supposed to be seriously ill or dead. His findings confirmed some of the more obvious earlier research findings: that the accuracy of the way children understood concepts of death and dying increased with age. However, an important new finding was that there were inconsistencies between the way children expressed themselves verbally and the content of their play. The play sometimes indicated a more developed understanding than was found in their answers. It is not until the age of approximately nine years that the content of the play and the verbally expressed concepts are more compatible.

The research carried out by Wenestam, on the depiction of death in children's drawings, concludes that the socio-cultural environment (children's books, television, comics, plus the ways in which parents and teachers talk to children about death or, more usually, avoid the subject) influences children's thinking, especially up to about the age of nine. The violence frequently depicted as a cause of death leads to a negative and fearful association, he asserts. Then children in his middle age range sample (average twelve and three-quarters) show a belief in a spiritual life. By this age they have been exposed to five or six years of socio-cultural expectations, assertions, beliefs, and values. Wenestam suggests that while adults may tolerate divergent thinking in young children, a child over twelve years may well be subject to criticism and correction when stating his view of the world. Thus there are 'rules' as to how the child should think, and these become more convergent as the child grows up.

Of course this then leads to a new generation of adults whose views of life and death have been largely determined by socio-cultural expectations, and who will in turn find it difficult to talk to children about death in a way which is open to the child's feelings.

A conclusion drawn by Orbach *et al.* (1985) is that while in some children distortions of the concept of death reflect a lack of knowledge and cognition, in others they reflect a defensive process – usually a high level of anxiety. Therefore children's progressive understanding of the meaning of death is not simply linear or accumulative, but relates to experiential and emotional factors. The authors suggest that children's understanding of the death of humans is generally more advanced than their understanding of the death of animals. This is either because they have experienced the death of a pet and not of a close adult, and they may then erect more defences against death in animals because they can relate emotionally and identify with animals more readily than people, or because their cognitive development is as yet unable to apply what they understand specifically to a broader conceptual framework.

My own daughter, when aged just over three years, asked, 'Does coffee die when it spills on the floor?' She was clearly grappling with the concept of that which undergoes a drastic physical change, can no longer be useful in its intended way, and eventually is lost, and was questioning whether inanimate objects too can die.

A four-year-old child (who was not physically ill) said to me in a psychotherapy session:

> 'If I put sellotape over your mouth and your nose, would you die?' She became rather anxious, and continued, 'I saw a bird that was dead. My cat had chopped its neck. Mummy put it in the rubbish bin.' She paused, then continued reflectively, 'When creatures die, they go away and never come back. My cat died. But then it went to hospital to be maked better. I did not want it to die. It's still away. It hasn't come back yet.'

This child is struggling with the concept of the irrevocability of death: dead creatures 'never come back', she says, yet, a few seconds later, she hopes that her dead cat will be made better in hospital, and maybe return. It appears that as she has a *relationship* with the cat it is clearly more painful to acknowledge the full implications of its loss, while the dead bird, with whom she presumably did not have a particular relationship, she can logically assign to death and the rubbish bin. She also recognizes the bird's altered appearance as being connected with its death.

This same child often returned to the theme of death, perhaps as a result of many traumatic losses she had sustained. These are some of her musings: 'When you die, you don't get better... You get buried... What is the colour of this "buried"?' On another occasion, she initiated a game wherein she was 'buried'. I asked her how she got buried. She replied 'Under leaves, of course!' This would be a familiar and ordinary explanation for her, unlike the strange world of coffins and graves.

Later she told me, 'When you get buried you go in one of those red round things that are poisonous and which can kill you if you eat them.' She was clearly confused between 'berry' and 'bury'. Her reasons for this confusion were not simply a cognitive problem, but were linked with her actual loss of her mother and foster mother. This rich material certainly provided the opportunity for further detailed analysis of her many confusions and fantasies about death, including the causative factors, and the part her own oral aggression played in these fantasies. She is both inside the dreaded poisonous berry while having it inside her in this fantasy, leading one to speculate about the pervasively persecuting nature of her fantasy world.

A five-year-old summarized his view of death to me, thus: 'If you die, you never see your mum again.'

The writer, John Berger (1988, pp. 36-7) reflects on a child's view of death: 'From the age of five or six I was worried about the death of my parents. The inevitability of death was one of the first things I learnt about the world on my own. Nobody ever spoke of it yet the signs were so clear.'

His understanding of his fear of death conveys a deep-seated, almost archetypal fear:

Every time I went to bed – and in this I am sure I was like millions of other children – the fear that one or both my parents might die in the night touched the nape of my neck with its finger. Such a fear has, I believe, little to do with a particular psychological climate and a great deal to do with nightfall.

He continues to describe his seeking reassurance through the invention of a euphemism, 'See you in the morning', instead of asking the real question. It seems that fundamental to his fear of his parents' death was the fear of his own death for, if the parents die, the infant feels he would be left to die.

When asked simply what he thought about death, a bright eight-and-a-half-year old boy said, 'It's saddest if somebody that you know well in your family died – then it would be sad, because you knew them the best. They wouldn't have had much of their life and it wouldn't be fair on them. If an older person dies, it's not so bad, because they're none the wiser – but they're still missing out on things.' When asked what happens after they die, he replied very seriously, 'They get buried. Some people get burnt and sprinkled on flowers. And they dissolve and their bones rot and they fall to bits and they help flowers to grow.'

This particular child's only direct personal encounter with bereavement had been the death of a grandfather four years previously and the recent death of a friend's baby brother. It seems that he is able to embrace many aspects of death in this spontaneous statement, including its irrevocability; the sense of loss for both the bereaved and the person who dies, as well as loss being related to attachment – that is, to whom you 'knew the best'; the difference between the death of a child and that of an older person; the truly dead state of the person who dies and therefore cannot feel that he is missing out on life; and, last but not least, a grasp of the life cycle.

Piaget's (1951) research adds an interesting dimension, when he states that the child is, early on in his intellectual development, looking for causes or motives behind every event, including death. The lack of adequate explanations from the adults in the child's life then leads the child to the conception of physical causation, such as 'killed' or 'murdered', unless the child is given theological explanations. This view is compatible, in a sense, with Klein's formulation of the working of the death instinct within the infant: 'from the beginning of post-natal life... destructive impulses against the object stir up fear of retaliation' (1952, p. 48), and in 1937 she wrote: 'A most important feature of these destructive fantasies, which are tantamount to death-wishes, is that the baby... feels that he *has really destroyed* the object of his destructive impulses...' (p. 308). Using Klein's psychoanalytic insight into infants, one might add to Piaget's ideas above: that the child feels or fears that his own aggression has killed or murdered the dead person (or caused an absent person to cease to exist). The capacity of the child to feel guilt and concern would play a part in the outcome of these processes.

It would seem that there is in fact a contradiction between, on the one hand, the research which firmly states that children of under five years of age do not view death as irreversible and final, and therefore have no real concept of death, and, on the other hand, the psychoanalytic findings of Freud, Klein, and Winnicott (on the role of the death instinct from birth or its inception soon afterwards) and those of Bowlby (on the child's devastation at the separation from and loss of his primary caretaker).

The available research is largely based on empirically testable data, equating the child's ability to 'understand death' with the ability to explain its meaning, and showing that in the absence of this concept there cannot be a fear of death (for example, Richmond and Waisman, 1955). This unfortunately does not always do justice to the complex topic of death, where accompanying feelings of sadness, anxiety, and a sense of loss cannot easily be measured. The language of science, describing observable data, is inadequate to describe the psychic development of the child, whether in the sphere of normal emotional development or specifically in relation to the subject of responses to death. Therefore the mystery of the inner world and some of the child's inchoate responses can only be *partly* explored through questionnaires, psychological tests, and interviews. The scientist attempts to be objective, while a psychoanalytic view of infants (including their responses to death) would include some reliance on a particular kind of subjectivity. This attempt on the part of the psychoanalytic psychotherapist or researcher to look inward as well as outward is based primarily on training in infant observation, where much that appears unintelligible may, in time, come to form some pattern in the mind: where there is an attempt not to form preconceptions. As Klein often states, the infant, from the start, is involved in an intense personal relationship both with the outside world and with his inner world. Therefore, we, as researchers, observers, or authors, have to be aware of our subtle interaction with the subject, with our countertransference, even if at a relative distance.

We need to follow the *child's* concepts in conjunction with those of their environment. Therein we can see that the young infant's reaction to loss, separation, and death is 'lost and gone for ever', and that a more sophisticated construct then develops which says that it is lost but perhaps not gone for ever. Although there is a corollary here in adults' use of denial, this development in relation to separation and death arises mainly out of the non-deprived child's developing capacity to *internalize the absent object*, and thus, by holding on to it mentally and emotionally, the then internal object, or archaic imago, is sustained in a lively way with the promise of its return. (A severely deprived child may have experienced more loss, trauma, fear, and impotence than can enable him to sustain hopefulness and a 'good enough' internal mother.)

In conclusion, therefore, the child's capacity to sustain temporary separation and loss leads to its capacity to conjure up similar hopefulness in the face of the impending or actual death of a loved one, or in experiencing traumatic separation (i.e., longer than the child's optimism can sustain). Of course the child's optimism can be truly tested and may be devastated by an encounter with an actual loss. The child may then have to begin the complex process of mourning, as well as the painful work on a re-kindling of the hope that may have been dashed by an early bereavement.

Intimately bound up with the child's capacity to hold on to the absent object in a way which is hopeful and creative is a complex defensive structure, which uses mechanisms of denial. The task then seems to be for the developing child to integrate the fact of death, as a natural biological event in the outside world, with his own internal constructs, including his denial – which is often fuelled by parental messages, perhaps unspoken, that talking about death is not part of the social repertoire.

Denial is a useful way of avoiding the accompanying deeply disturbing effects of being confronted by the cessation of function – for this is an aspect of death of which a young child is aware. Young children are able to grasp the difference between animate and inanimate. A four-year-old child told me that she knew a bird was dead because it was not flying or moving its beak. Therefore it is hardly surprising that defences quickly emerge in the form of fantasies of the possible return to life of the loved object, and so on. Although the form and substance of these fantasies are largely fed by adults' interventions, the child himself, quick to equate the death of another with his own possible death, needs to employ a range of defences. This could include avoidance; denial; displacement of anxiety on to some other area; obsessional ritualized behaviour as a way of attempting to ward-off a recurrence or to placate; phobias; as well as the use of cultural and religious 'stories' to explain the disappearance. This unspoken dread may be manifest in, for example, nightmares; dreams; night fears; fears of certain objects or people, bodily products, sounds, shapes, certain foods, or certain animals. The inevitable persecution that the child suffers at the hands of the 'bad objects' can be understood as a fear of retaliation for his projected aggression and anxiety.

Children and adults pay a heavy price in their deep repression of thoughts about death – for, as I have explained, it then becomes extensively symbolized. Although adults and children alike can live daily with a generally not unrealistic view that their own death is not imminent, the concept of 'not-being' is nevertheless as much a part of everyday life as 'being' or living. It is in this area that our children may be helped by adults' awareness of this duality.

I would agree with Janssen's findings (1983), which tie in with those of Wenestam, when she hypothesizes that the children categorized as having a defensive organization in their knowledge of death may have passed through a phase of discovery of death, with the difficult feelings that accompany it. Then, as their fantasies develop, there is a need for a more rigid stance in relation to death, partly as a result of adults' inhibitions. This seems much like a child's sexual development – as expressed in play and fantasies – which is turbulent, manifest, and florid in the early years, but then goes 'underground' during latency; much the same often happens with a child's creative output, as expressed in drawings. Thus one can deduce that a child's sometimes more withdrawn stance in relation to death during latency arises from the general quietening down of his emotional life through a greater use of defence mechanisms.

Tests carried out by Alexander and Alderstein (1958) bear this out. They assessed children's GSR (galvanic skin response)* as they listened to words about death. They discovered that the youngest group (aged five to eight) and the oldest (aged thirteen to sixteen) gave the most emotional response, while the middle group (aged nine to twelve) responded with practically no anxiety. This probably reflects the emotional turbulence of the early and late stages of childhood, while the middle age group uses defences which lead to greater calm in the face of death.

Rochlin (1959, 1967) has carried out interesting studies of the emotional forces which influence children's attitudes to death. He clearly believes that children know about death as the extinction of all life from a very early age, but that they then utilize a range of defences in order to avoid the full implications of this awareness. As their cognitive development is not yet mature, they can more easily not only deny the meanings of death, but oscillate towards and away from a proper understanding almost from moment to moment. Thus, as Orbach (1988) summarizes, they 'reflect the duality of knowing and denying the existence of death'. This shifting understanding is often a part of adults' behaviour, too, depending on their circumstances, situation, and emotional state, as I tried to explain in Chapter 1.

Therefore, if we come full circle, to Freud's view – quoted at the beginning of this chapter – that children, unlike adults, are in touch with the implications of death, but use defences of omnipotence, denial, and magical thinking, we can see that some of the more recent research, half a century later, is basically compatible with his findings. I would only add that the child's increased independence and ability to feel that there is a helping network beyond his prime caretaker contributes to the lessening of a primitive fear of death. In fact, the child's means of survival widens, as he physically and emotionally masters his environment – walking, talking, etc. – and in that sense he is realistically further from death.

---

*A change in the electrical resistance of the skin, related to sweating. It can be produced by a tiny electrical current and is useful as an indicator of an unconditional, autonomic response to emotion or anxiety.

Chapter Three

The dying child's awareness of death

The wonderful thing about children is that
they tend to want to get better however ill
they are.
Professor Lewis Spitz, 1988

Bearing in mind the non-dying child's awareness of death, I shall now survey the literature on the reactions of a child with a life-threatening illness, facing his own impending death.

Early studies (i.e., pre-1962) acknowledged that only children over six years of age revealed anxiety or apprehension relating to their impending death (Natterson and Knudson, 1960). They concluded that the child under six is most concerned about separation, while the child from six to ten is more fearful of physical injury and mutilation. Most studies were based on overt expressions concerning impending death. The problem when analysing these findings is that they reveal the same anxieties found in hospitalized children generally. Therefore they fail to distinguish the specific effects of fatal illness on a child.

More recent research (Debuskey, 1970; Howell, 1967; Sigler, 1970; Spinetta, 1974; Yudkin, 1967) does manage to take into account the psychological reactions of children specifically related to the fact of having a fatal illness. Their findings conclude that the older child with a fatal prognosis can be aware of, and apprehensive about, his impending death. The authors agree with earlier research in that they state that for the fatally ill under-five-year-old, a fear of separation is the main symptom. However, in the middle age group (six to ten years) the writers tend to base their observations on parents' and professionals' observations, rather than on direct data from the child. They feel that if the adult does not discuss the issue of the potentially fatal illness with the child, the child does not experience anxiety. Once again, one can see the mechanisms of denial operating in the researchers, as well as in the reported observations of parents and staff.

However, a number of researchers do conclude that, if not aware at a conceptual level, children are at least aware that something serious is happening to their bodies. Perhaps the most useful approach can be found in a book edited by Anthony and Koupernick (1973). In this volume, Vernick states that 'blows cannot always be softened' and exposes the lack of progress in this field of communicating meaningfully with the fatally ill child. Natterson (in the same volume) further defines the subtle approach needed, when he states that 'the psychotherapist trades in life, not death', and concludes that 'working with fatally ill patients and their intimates is not helping them accept death but groping with them to find a way to live with meaning in the shadow of death.'

When discussing the final stage of a child's life, before death, Vernick observes that the patient is often very weak, sometimes devoid of feelings, and oblivious. Natterson and Vernick erroneously interpret Kübler-Ross as defining this state as 'acceptance' and therefore a potentially happy phase. Indeed, Kübler-Ross specifically states: 'Acceptance should not be mistaken for a happy stage. It is almost void of feelings' (1970, p. 100). And yet there is another problem: a seeming contradiction of terminology. 'Acceptance' here is defined as a rather numb state, whereas I would have thought that in this context 'acceptance' would mean some ability to feel a sense of loss, to grieve, and perhaps to let go. It would seem, then, that there is a difficulty in interpreting a child's weakened state, as the child is often uncommunicative. This could be a defence *against* a full awareness. The child would thus be particularly susceptible to the projections of those people who are involved with him, including researchers.

However, alongside a recognition of the reality of an impending death, there is a need to keep in touch with hope and hopefulness. Kübler-Ross expresses this aspect thus: 'It is this glimpse of hope which maintains them through days, weeks or months of suffering... In a sense it is a rationalization for their suffering at times; for others it remains a form of temporary but needed denial' (1970, p. 123). It is exactly this duality that is extremely difficult to sustain, and links with my comments in Chapter 1 about the difficulty in keeping an awareness of life and death concurrently. As with Escher's (1961) graphic images of optical illusions: how hard it is to 'read' both interpretations of his dual-meaning stairways that can also be convoluted ceilings. In fact, the psychological impossibility of 'seeing' both simultaneously is an analogy for the oscillation between hope and acceptance, or hope and despair; they cannot really be felt simultaneously.

Following the rather complex path of researchers into children's awareness of death is rather like following Freud's theories of infantile sexuality. Not only did Freud have to be open enough to what he could observe in his consulting room, but society at large had to be able to receive his findings. Similarly, with the trauma of a child facing his own death, the subjects' families, carers, researchers, as well as society at large, unwittingly limit their capacity to care and understand through their own inhibitions.

Their main preconception seems to be that they don't want to frighten children, especially young children, and put ideas into their heads, by talking about death, or, indeed by really listening to *their* ideas about death.

It was not until Waechter (1968, 1971) that studies emerged which showed the probability of fatally ill children aged six to ten years being able to express an awareness of their condition directly. In a study by Spinetta *et al.* (1973), the authors conclude that

> fatally ill children show significantly greater awareness of their hospital experience than chronically ill children. The leukaemic children... showed more preoccupation with threat to and intrusion into their bodies and interference with their body functioning than did the chronically ill children... The children with fatal illness also expressed more hospital-related and non-hospital-related anxiety than did the chronically ill children. (pp. 841–5)

This significant difference between the level of anxiety, present from the first admission to hospital, between the fatally ill and chronically ill, tells us that despite the parents of the leukaemic children maintaining that their child did not know that his illness was fatal, the fatally ill child's level of anxiety is markedly higher. The chronically ill child in this research study generally received the same number and duration of hospital treatments. Therefore, despite attempts to protect the fatally ill child from his prognosis, he nevertheless picks up a sense of the seriousness of his illness.

This research was able to discern the more subtle expressions of a death anxiety in the six- to ten-year-olds, even though they were not always overt. Just as research into the physically well child's concept of death did not take adequate account of the inevitable denial and defences in many children, so the pre-1968 research into this area of the fatally ill child has relied too heavily on that which is easily observed and recorded or talked about in adult terms, and therefore has not necessarily tapped the actual anxieties and concerns.

A slightly later study (Spinetta, 1975) shows that awareness of their illness seems to persist with fatally ill children, even when they are not in hospital. As with the fatally ill hospitalized children in previous studies, this 1975 study indicates that the fatally ill out-patient children conveyed significantly more preoccupation with the threat to their body integrity and functioning than did a control group of children with chronic illness. Not only did they express greater anxiety, but the leukaemic children exhibited a lack of adaptability to the necessity of clinic visits, becoming increasingly anxious about the clinic both as visits became more frequent and as their illness became more protracted.

One of the means of testing which the researchers used was a projective test of a three-dimensional replica of a hospital room, as an analysis of interpersonal distancing. The authors found that the fatally ill hospitalized children repeatedly placed the four little dolls (of a nurse, doctor, father and mother) at significantly greater distances from each other than did the children in the matched control group of chronically ill children (Spinetta *et al.*, 1974). This distance increased with further hospitalizations. The authors inferred that this physical positioning and distancing of the figures by the fatally ill children reflected a growing sense of psychological separation and isolation of the dying child from the hospital and from the significant adults in his life.

In order to extract, then, how much of this distancing was hospital-related, further tests were carried out, and the authors concluded that the fatally ill hospitalized children showed a greater sense of isolation than leukaemic children in remission. They also discovered that as the leukaemic child becomes older, his anxiety towards the clinic or hospital increases. Frequency of visits in the chronically ill led to a lessening of anxiety, while the opposite was true for the leukaemic children. Similarly, with the chronically ill, as the illness's duration increased, so their anxiety lessened, while with the leukaemic children the longer the duration, the higher the anxiety. The child is therefore aware that this is no ordinary illness. Even in remission, the leukaemic child is not able to live a normal life, free from concerns about the illness. An important aspect to this anxiety would be that the child is picking up parental anxiety. I have been told about a four-year-old with cystic fibrosis, who apparently conveyed a remarkable grasp of her own impending death. Just before she died she was given a gas balloon, and her questions about this clearly conveyed her wondering about her death: 'What will happen to my balloon when there's no more air in it? Can you buy a new one?'

In considering the hospitalized dying child's awareness of death, an important matter which appears to focus the child's awareness more sharply is, not surprisingly, the death of another child on the ward. If the child who has died has the same illness, of course the link between that event and the dying child's imminent death is made more immediate. Fortunately nowadays there is a more open and truthful attitude on children's wards in most hospitals, where the event is often discussed openly in response to parents' questions, and sometimes with children, depending on the ethos of the unit. This is not always the case, however. Some hospitals have not altered much since this account by a consultant paediatrician, Yudkin, of the approach to a death of a child on the ward, a little over twenty years ago:

Our present method of dealing with the solemn situation that arises when a child dies in a children's ward is both ugly and obscene. There is a whispering and a scuffling behind the screens, a furtive moving of white-covered trolleys in and out of the ward, usually during the night. Nurses and doctors are preoccupied and don't answer questions and are unduly irritable. Above all, there is a stupid pretence that nothing at all unusual is happening... But do we really think that the 'secret' is not known to every child on the ward? (1967, p. 40)

Yudkin writes that this furtive behaviour was an affront to children's intelligence and instead of helping them to regard death as a 'very sad but solemn and dignified event', characterized death as something fearful and secretive. It deprived the child of the opportunity to talk about his fears.

Richard Lansdown (1987) of the Hospital for Sick Children, London, has summarized the stages of understanding his own death that a dying child goes through:

I am very sick
I have an illness that can kill people
I have an illness that can kill children
I may not get better
I am dying

However, the child's age, anxiety level, cognitive development, and environment would of course influence the course of that understanding. For a child under three years of age the 'I am dying' concept would probably not embody a real understanding of dying, with its irreversibility, but may be a feeling of not understanding what is happening to his body and an anxiety about this unpleasant state of being unwell separating him from his parents.

If an underlying anxiety of dying exists in these seriously ill children, there are many more conscious anxieties which surround the ill child. In order to complete the picture of what the child may mean by 'dying' we need to understand further what is happening 'on the surface' as it were, to the body, and the attendant fantasies in order to fully understand the causes of the fear of dying. In other words, we need to excavate the more accessible layers of the psyche before we can reach and comprehend the sub-strata.

As I explain more fully in the following chapter, the child with leukaemia feels unwell and fragile, picks up adults' anxieties and hears medical terminology more usually associated with aggressive warfare (such as 'kill', 'attack', 'wipe out', 'invade') in relation to his illness. The phantasies in the unconscious must surely abound with extreme feelings of persecution from some unseen omnipresent source, attacking the very marrow of his bones and the vitality of his blood. After all, 'The blood is the life' is stated in the Bible (Deuteronomy 12: 23). In psychological terms, no illness can be more central to one's being than leukaemia, except, perhaps, heart or brain disease. An aspect of the treatment of bone marrow transplants involves processing and freezing some of the patient's bone marrow – for possible future use – and carries echoes of Shakespeare's description of utter horror: 'Would harrow up thy soul; freeze thy young blood' (*Hamlet*).

The inevitable blood tests at different stages of the illness, as well as the insertion of the central venous catheter (Hickman line, see p. 80), penetrate the skin surface. Psychologically, the skin gives the body an essential sense of intactness, of being held together (Bick, 1967), as well as being our first line of defence, psychically as well as physically, against injury and infection. The skin acts as a boundary between the me and the not-me in favourable circumstances (Winnicott, 1962). It is of course also able to receive pleasurable sensations from the touch of others and of ourselves. Yet it is repeatedly violated by the treatment, as well as perceived as having failed in being part of an effective immune system to keep out germs/poison/bad things, depending on the fantasy. Other aspects of the *meaning* of illness to the child are described at the beginning of Chapter 5.

Moreover, the adults in the child's life appear to the child to have failed in their protective function. Just as their own bodies (the skin, the blood, the marrow) are failing, so are the parents, in the sense that they are allowing and facilitating the treatment. This dichotomy for parents, between supporting the child's emotional state and pursuing medical treatment, exists in many illnesses. However, when there is indeed a life and death struggle, the parents may become more adamant, determined and rigid, and more detached from the child's feelings, in order to allow unpleasant treatments to be carried out. Some parents purposely absent themselves when the child is undergoing very unpleasant procedures, in order to be able to be perceived afresh by the child as a comforter and not a perpetrator. (Of course much depends on the child's age and maturity in understanding the necessity for treatment.) In a way, though, it is a dilemma whatever course of action is chosen, for the parent who thoughtfully absents him- or herself or does not help to hold down a protesting child has still 'failed' the child in the child's eyes in the sense of not preventing the 'assault' or simply not being there.

I have found that young children usefully use 'splitting' in these situations: the selfsame mother can be perceived as a 'witch' mother when she is part of the treatment team and a good mother at other times. This mechanism helps the child to feel that there is a protective, helpful mother (or father) who is not contaminated by the other 'bad' one. The older child has, in a way, the more emotionally challenging and painful task of integrating the two aspects of the one parent, but may still usefully use splitting or projection in other ways: for example, by perceiving a particular doctor or some other person as all bad, thus again finding a receptacle for much of his anger and aggression.

Six suns and a slide drawn by a six-year-old with a
life-threatening illness

The fundamental anxiety, then, underlying the foregoing phantasies and
ways of coping with them, is a fear of being annihilated and therefore of
dying. A five-year-old boy who was about to undergo a tonsillectomy
declared unhesitatingly that 'of course they cut your head off to get at the
tonsils'. He then briefly muttered, 'And then you die', before adamantly
changing the subject. This dramatic fantasy around surgical intervention is
not all that unusual: the child can very easily feel in danger of being killed.
Of course in this example the child's condition or treatment is almost certainly not life-threatening. Nevertheless it arouses similar anxieties to those
which are and, as we see from the research quoted above, the persistence,
degree, and progress of the anxieties differ in children who are actually faced
by a life-threatening condition.

A six-year-old boy with a life-threatening illness did the drawing
reproduced above in a psychotherapy session. Although he was not yet ready
to talk about his anxieties about dying, this drawing, which he said was of a
slide, comes to a dramatic stop under the row of six suns. After talking to him
about the drawing, I felt that he seemed to convey here the feeling that he
was on a fast-moving downward course, which suddenly stops, possibly
leading to a feeling of falling (if we notice how the bottom of the slide is well
above the ground level). Again, this confirms that the abrupt ending was
ahead of him.

The sun in a picture often denotes a parental presence, or, in drawings of
bereaved children, it is often placed over the dying or dead family member

(Mary Sue Moore, personal communication). The ordinary or usual depiction of the sun in a six-year-old's picture would be in a corner. This unusual display of suns here seems to carry a rich range of meanings: the six suns refer to his six years, which stop at the point where the slide stops; they hang over the picture oppressively, conveying both an over-attentive parent as well as, possibly, marking out the *whole* slide: he was leaving no doubt that this symbol of the person who is dying truly 'covers' the area. Interestingly, this child had never really thrived: he had experienced severe eating difficulties all his life. This background seems to tie in with the oppressive suns which go back to the 'beginning', in the past – the left of the picture (Bach, 1969).

This drawing opened up the possibility of talking about his fears, and, indeed, his awarness that he was dying, but my comments on the drawing are not meant to be prescriptions or recipes for interpreting other drawings: any understanding of a drawing is arrived at in conjunction with the child's comments, the situation in which the drawing is made, and possibly the overall knowledge of the child. Wide experience of the normal developmental stages through which children's drawings evolve is also important, as a yardstick for any unusual or striking features.

Chapter Four

Should we talk to children about death?

> Look, the dying, –
> surely they must suspect how full of pretext
> is all that we accomplish here, where nothing
> is what it really is.
> Rilke, 'Fourth Duino Elegy'

Recent research has challenged the 'protective' approach in relation to whether to tell the child of his or her impending death. As conveyed in the previous chapter, children sense that their illness is serious, even if they are not explicitly told this. It seems from the weight of evidence that children need to be given the opportunity to speak 'about their concerns so that they can receive support in their struggles' (Spinetta, 1982).

The withdrawn or passive child may be a product of an environment that does not facilitate open communication. In an important study, Bluebond-Langner (1978) found that terminally ill leukaemic children often failed to communicate with people close to them about their concerns. They felt despair and became withdrawn in a silent or angry way, in an attempt to 'protect' the adults around them. Thus both the adults and the child become caught up in a mutually protective falsehood. Other studies show that where families managed open communication throughout the illness, there was a high level of self-regard in the patient and a greater degree of closeness to other family members than in those families who did not use open communication (Spinetta and Moloney, 1978). Glaser and Strauss (1963), too, criticize the 'mutual pretence' communication patterns which surround the dying patient and his family. In these each one acts as though the other does not know the truth.

In considering the responses of family, friends, and health-care professionals to the child with cancer, research shows that although their reactions to the patient's diagnosis and illness are primarily negative, they believe that they have to remain cheerful, positive, and optimistic in their relationship with the patient (Dunkel-Schetter and Wortman, 1982). (This research partly concerns adults with cancer, but I am selecting aspects which are applicable to children as well.) Meanwhile the patient himself is likely to be extremely anxious and uncertain, and so have a greater than usual need for emotional support, as he is facing many fears, including fear of separation, altered body image, pain, physical deterioration, increased dependency, isolation, and death (Davies, Quinlan, *et al.*, 1973).

This need to pretend, to act 'normal', often becomes greater as the child deteriorates and approaches death because there are fewer reasons to feel genuinely hopeful. In families and with professionals where there are considerable constraints on what is considered to be a safe topic, and where there is avoidance of the subject of death and of unpalatable evidence before their eyes, the possible conversations and points of real emotional contact become fewer and fewer. When family and workers assume that they have to make a concerted effort to control their feelings and conceal their anxiety and distress, there is an increased danger of their breaking down and betraying their feelings to the patient (Parkes, 1979). This anxiety about saying the 'wrong thing' makes encounters with the patient increasingly awkward and tense. In the story of Robert which follows in Part Two, I think he increasingly withdrew in the final stages in an avoidance of that which was all around him and inside him, but about which his parents could not talk.

As an example of this kind of avoidance, a sixteen-year-old girl, Ruby, with a rare degenerative illness, in the last months of her life, comes to mind. I saw her for psychotherapy in a special school in which I worked. Her physical condition was markedly deteriorating, and in her first meeting with me the clearest 'message' she gave me, although she had great difficulty in talking as her breathing was laboured, was that she wondered why she did not do computer work any more at school, when it was something she used to enjoy. This gave me an opportunity to begin to talk with her about the many things that she used to enjoy, and her need to address the question as to why she could no longer do them. During the next session she laboriously drew an apple. She began by painstakingly drawing the two little (leaf?) shapes on the right of the picture, and then, after 'screening' them behind a line, drew, with an enormous effort, a circle. She rotated the paper bit by bit to complete it. And then added a stalk and a leaf. She did not say what it was, but seemed pleased when I recognized it as an apple.

The drawing opposite seems to show some sense of something fragmented and weak to the right of the picture, that is, possibly, in the future (Bach, 1969). I am reminded of hearing of diabetic children conveying an unconscious sense of dying when they frequently draw decaying trees with dead falling leaves (personal communication, Mary Sue Moore). The light touch with which this drawing is executed conveys a feeling of being decathected from the external world. The choice of pencil, in preference to colours, also often conveys diminished energy.

After further work with Ruby, and basing my interpretation on the

An apple drawn by sixteen-year-old Ruby

accumulated impressions, I suggested that the big solid apple – something good, that grows – represented the 'good breast' or alive Mrs Judd who feeds her 'talking food', with whom she feels in touch in the session, and yet cut off from. I suggested that perhaps there was a sense that she could leave an alive part of herself with me, perhaps after her death (and I pointed to the fragments on the right). After my interpretation she relaxed, her eyes became unfocused, and she slumped forward, ball-like in her wheelchair, seemingly feeling relief at being understood.

Another young person with a deteriorating degenerative condition, fifteen-year-old James, was able to refer symbolically to his sense of deterioration and fear of death by telling me about an anxiety that the ceiling of his bedroom was going to fall in on him, and that if he had another operation he would ensure that a nurse woke him up soon afterwards in order to watch a favourite television programme. This distancing from the actual reality is an understandable defence. However, James appreciated my efforts to translate his associations into the deeper level of anxiety that they represented, for later he grinningly told me that he slept better since coming to see me, 'because it was like putting some of it on someone else's shoulders'.

An account by a worker with patients with malignant diseases summarizes this problem:

The ordeals through which these people moved always contained elements of profound tragedy. However, the worst phase of all was one in which patients, families, wives and husbands did not talk or tell what they knew about the disease in order to 'protect' each other. The result was the isolation of both parties and this was the most devastating experience of all ... Of course they did not 'escape' but only suffered greater turmoil in their isolation. (Hageboeck, 1962)

Another way in which a child may sense that he is being left alone, perhaps to die, is well documented in the research into the way in which dying children receive less attention, including nursing attention, than other ill children (Rothenberg, 1974; Vernick and Karon, 1965). They therefore - quite appropriately - deduce that that which they have is unbearable to others and they are left with a sense of isolation, loneliness, and worthlessness.

If children are aware of the serious nature of their illness and this is then hidden under a veil of secrecy or even hypocrisy, their curiosity can become inhibited, they distrust their own senses, and tend to find everything unreal. All this can lead to a chronic distrust of others. This is described by Bowlby ('On knowing what you are not supposed to know and feeling what you are not supposed to feel', 1979) in a different scenario: that of children who witness some aspect of a parent's suicide and are then pressurized by the surviving parent to deny or discredit their own observations. The less acceptable and painful feelings are shut off, in both the situation described by Bowlby and that of children who are under pressure not to communicate openly in certain other important situations of conflict.

In considering the extent to which a child with cancer picks up the implications of the illness, it is important to bear in mind the metaphors commonly used in descriptions of cancer, as Sontag (1978) points out. The patient's body is considered under attack, or 'invaded' by leukaemia. The language is therefore one of warfare and of military terminology. 'Cancer cells do not simply multiply; they are "invasive"', she writes. We talk about the body's 'defences' in its attempt to obliterate, wipe out, or fight the cancer. The treatment, too, uses military terminology: the patients are 'bombarded' with radiotherapy; chemotherapy is chemical warfare using toxins. Treatment, of course, aims to 'kill' the cancer, and in the process, damages and destroys healthy cells.

Bearing this in mind, it would not be difficult for the child to receive messages of a dramatic and deadly war being waged within his own body. This may be exacerbated by the institution of barrier-nursing: for the child in isolation, who has to be handled by people with gloves and masks, may feel that he is truly *contaminating* as well as - the more conscious message - *open to contamination*.

Where the problem arises of an ill child's awareness of his impending death running counter to his parents' denial, a child thus emotionally isolated may benefit from the help of a child psychotherapist, paediatric social worker, and/or other professionals to reintegrate the family, and to provide clear explanations of what is happening. Without such help, a child's fantasies can become even more frightening than the reality.

Research findings on the psychosocial reactions of children with cancer include a prevalence of regressive behaviour patterns, disturbances in body image, severe depression, lack of co-operation in treatment programmes, and a high level of anxiety. As some of these symptoms are part of the adaptation process, they are not entirely negative. Indeed, they may be adaptive mechanisms for negotiating loss and other unpleasant aspects of their illness. Some refuge in denial may be a way of buffering the child against the slow acceptance of what is likely to be the outcome, as I explain more fully in Chapter 5. Therefore to talk about all aspects of the illness and its prognosis is far from a general prescription.

I interviewed Dr Richard Lansdown, who has worked with dying children for the past seventeen years, about his views on children's attitudes to death. He says:

I think it's quite important to get some idea of children's understanding of illness, so that their understanding of death is in context. The example I give is of a boy I saw many years ago. I first talked to him when he was five. He had Stage IV neuroblastoma and I asked him when he was going to die. He said he was going to die in an aeroplane crash. On a little more probing I learned that he was going to join the RAF when he was grown up, and he thought that he would be killed in battle. He knew that he had a serious illness, but he was not equating his illness with death. It didn't then seem appropriate to encourage his parents to talk to him or to foster a discussion with him about death, because he wasn't seeing 'one equals one'. A year later I saw him, and he talked about having a second and third tumour. He produced a marvellous phrase, 'One tumour enough, two tumours too many', which was about right. He had radiation to get rid of the tumours, and I asked what would happen if he hadn't had the radiation. He said, 'If I hadn't had the radiation, I might have died.' That was a very different story from the one the year before. It seemed much more appropriate then to get him in some sort of communication pattern [about death and illness].

This is something I think is often misunderstood in the literature and by the public. People either say you shouldn't talk about dying to anybody, or you should always talk about dying to children with cancer, because there's such a taboo on the subject. Well, I think you've got to be more sophisticated than either of those views, and take your cue from the children's understanding. What really counts is when the child sees another child dying. It is crucial when the child knows of another child who has died of the same condition. We certainly get this on the ward. Children may be told that they may die. Their parents may say to children, 'If you don't take your medicine, you will die', but children also hear mum saying, 'If you don't tidy your bedroom, I'll kill you', and she doesn't really mean that. And granny talks about, 'I'm dying for a cup of tea', but she doesn't really mean that either. But when Elizabeth in the next bed dies of leukaemia, and she's got leukaemia like I have, then that really does hit me in the guts. That is a crucial time, a turning point in children's development and understanding of mortality.

Lansdown summarized this by saying that having that experience does not necessarily speed up the cognitive process of understanding the concept of death, but that it certainly brings it home to children, by a shift of focus about their own future and by making their attention more precise.

I then asked him to clarify the distinction between children with a life-threatening illness who may not die soon and dying children's awareness of death. In other words, whether for example, all children with leukaemia have some sense of the seriousness of their illness? He replied,

I'm not sure that they do. The literature says that they do, but I've recently been talking to a number of children in their teens. They do not necessarily remember what they felt when they were younger. How much *unconscious* fear there is is a very different matter. A lot of them very possibly do have unconscious fears of dying, which they would deny if you talked to them when they were seven or eight.

A good example of this is a girl that I saw years ago, when she was eight. She had been told that she had cancer, but that it was not a serious illness. That is what her father told her. She told me of an old man who died in the street, aged seventy-five. She said 'It couldn't have been cancer – I don't know what he died of, it couldn't have been cancer because that's not a serious illness.' She also had the most horrendous dreams of being put in a dark hole, and her parents looking down over her, and all sorts of very clear death anxieties. I saw her recently – she's now seventeen and she denied completely that she'd ever been worried about dying or death during that time. Consciously it may be so. Therefore I think one is into many problems in saying whether or not a child is 'worried' or 'anxious' about death or not. What also makes a difference, as I said earlier, is whether a child has been an in-patient or not, and whether the child has come across other children who have died.

Another child who died when she was sixteen had been ill since she was about ten. She had hardly been an in-patient, and hadn't come across other children who had died. It was only in the very last stages of her illness, when she was told that she was going to die, that she said that she knew she had a *serious* illness, but she didn't realise it was *fatal.* I believe that, I believe what she said. I'm very wary indeed of the Bluebond-Langner (1978) type of generalizations that 'all children know this, all children believe that.'

Lansdown talked about the different category of very young children:

How do you communicate to a three-year-old, or a four-year-old, anything about death, particularly the death of a sibling or the death of a parent? I do find that immensely hard. I still don't really have an answer to it – before all those Kane (1979) concepts have really developed. Aged five or six is a different matter; they've often got a very good idea of what death is about. But a three- or a four-year-old – it is very difficult. Like George Sand, who had been told that her father had died in a riding accident. The next day she said, 'Is Papa still dead today?' It's that kind of difficulty that children have.

He then addressed the different problems facing the approach to the older child, aged approximately eleven to thirteen years, who is 'post-concrete' in his thinking, and who is beginning to grapple with the notion that maybe there is not an after-life. Lansdown continued:

The child from this group says 'I don't think there is a heaven, but I don't know.' I find this group quite hard to help. Of course it's difficult when parents don't have religious beliefs, and the child then says, 'I'm going to heaven, aren't I?' But that's not as hard as the other problems I've just mentioned, because parents can suspend disbelief in the interests of the child.

He clarified the problem of what to say to a dying child, and the issues that frequently arise:

We've never said to a child 'You are going to die.' I don't think we have a right to say this, ethically or scientifically. But we sometimes say to a child 'You may die soon.' Then we're looking at the developmental stage of the child, to see where anxieties, if any, may arise. Always there is anxiety about separation – 'I shall miss you and Daddy.' There isn't always anxiety about the transition to death, but sometimes there are questions like 'How will I get to heaven?' as a four-year-old asked. Her older sister said 'By aeroplane'. The other area of anxiety is, 'What is heaven going to be like?' Some children are worried about being lonely in heaven, and this again comes back to separation anxiety.

In an account of his own experiences with cancer, a six-year-old boy (Jason Gaes, 1987) writes, referring to heaven: 'Once we get there we won't want to come back here. We'r just scared about going to heaven because we never been there.' (*sic*)

I asked Lansdown if in his opinion separation anxiety is age-related, and he replied,

> No, I think it goes all the way to teenagers. I don't know when it stops, if it stops at all. Like the teenage girl who was dying, and who had a sense of loss about the future, saying 'I haven't achieved anything, I haven't even done my "O" levels yet', who was in touch with the loss of a life. She really felt that she had missed out on everything. She and I then planned her last few months, so that she could make the most of them. She made various goals as to how she was going to spend her remaining time.

Lansdown added that physical contact is also very important, partly in relation to separation anxiety, and partly as a means of communication. 'If people have been open with a child about the possibility of their dying, then non-verbal communication is going to be so much more important and meaningful for children and parents.'

I explored with him some of the difficulties around the transition from therapeutic care to palliative care (see also Chapter 10). I asked him how clearly defined was this transition for all the members of the team?

> It *is* clearly made, but I think it is a difficult decision, and what is particularly difficult is, to what extent you involve the child in that decision. I mean, do you, for example, say to a fourteen-year-old, 'There is very little more we can do with conventional treatment. There is an experimental drug we might try. It will give you a very poor quality of life, and we don't know if it will work anyway. Would you want us to try that, or for us to give you care, comfort, as much comfort as possible?' We would certainly say that to an adult. Do we say that to a fourteen-year-old? Do we say that to a ten-year-old? To an eight-year-old, a six-year-old? And if we don't decide to do it by age, then what are the criteria? We certainly recently had two eight-year-olds who said they didn't want any more treatment.

I asked if these children were asked directly. He replied:

> One was asked, and one volunteered the information. I'm just speaking of the ones I know. We must have had many cases, many others that I don't know personally, because we have a great many children here – something like 120 cases of leukaemia and solid tumours a year. The general pattern seems to be that the more that children are asked, the

more they opt for no treatment, but just to be made comfortable. Of course, the parents are very involved in all this, in all the decision making.

I asked Lansdown whether, in his experience, the doctors are always the last to give up therapeutic treatment. His view was:

> Not always; I think it's men who are the last to give up, and women who are more likely to just opt for care, as opposed to treatment that is available. Mothers more generally opt for palliative care, and tend to want the child to be allowed to die peacefully, at home. This tendency for doctors to want to try treatment to the bitter end may still be there in young and junior medical staff, but not in senior medical staff. They've been around too long to think that. They know that one's got to look after the last few months of a child's life, and that to subject them to a barrage of drugs in the hope that you might have a one percent chance of a cure is not in the child's best interest.

I wondered whether research has to play a part in this decision making, especially on the part of doctors? He replied that he thought there was an element of that, but that there is plenty of research being done on children with a reasonable prognosis. He went on to emphasize the place for truth:

> The ethos on the unit is always to tell the truth to everybody. Junior medical staff at first sometimes find it hard to fit in with that, but after a while they pick it up, and realize that it is in the interests of everybody. Sometimes the parents won't allow us, but that's a very different matter. Mutual pretence. If the parents flatly refuse to allow us to give any information to the children, then we abide by that; we don't contravene what the parents ask. We may try to persuade the parents otherwise, but in the last analysis we go along with it. Sometimes children find their own way of asking, for example through a project they're doing with a teacher on the ward. One way of approaching this problem is for us to suggest to the parents that someone can work individually with their child, and then the pretence stays there, but the parents, by agreeing to somebody seeing the child, by implication are allowing the child to work in their own way on the issues.

Giving an over-view of the changes in nursing ill children over the past twenty years, Lansdown emphasizes that

> There's much more a sense of bringing children into decision making, not only in the leukaemic unit, but also on the other ward I work on, which is plastic surgery. Also I think I've detected a loosening of relationships between children and staff: far more first name terms, for example, and there's virtually an absence of white coats now. Oh yes, and of course,

visiting hours! When I first came here some wards had visiting hours. That has completely and utterly gone.

Chapter Five

The stages of emotional reactions to terminal illness

> .... I wanted to know. There is no
> protection, unless it is in knowing. I wanted
> death pinned down and isolated behind a
> wall of particular facts and circumstances,
> not floating around loose, ignored but
> powerful, waiting to get in anywhere.
> Alice Munro, *Lives of Girls and Women*

In attempting to describe children's reactions to something as over-whelming as a life-threatening illness, I find myself faced with inchoate terms about psychic development, leading me back to the infant's reactions to the death instinct (as described on pp. 13–15). This beginning – if it is a beginning, for there may indeed be some experiences of a threat of annihilation *in utero* – needs to be borne in mind as a *sine qua non* when we try to think about the infant's and the older child's reaction to any actual life-threatening illness. Not only does duality of life/death have to be carried in the reader's mind, but also the dyad of mother and baby or mother and child, or parents and child, for the child cannot be considered in isolation. Similarly, the duality of the internal and external world of the child is an important constant axis within the metapsychology of the child.

Therefore, if we talk about the child's *reactions* to the illness, we need to bear in mind the parameters of emotional growth: whether the illness is felt to be located entirely inside him; whether it comes from outside; whether it is 'caused' by mother or anyone else, or by bad behaviour; the extent to which mother is felt to be separate and 'out there' or a part of the child; as well as the child's level of understanding of his illness and of death. These com-plexities need to be borne in mind for the rest of this chapter in order to avoid a simplistic view of the child's reactions. Just as there is no 'baby' without a 'mother' (Winnicott), so there is no illness without a patient, no child without care-givers, and no intellectual concepts and reactions to illness without corresponding or conflicting internal phantasies.

Psychological effects of facing a life-threatening illness depend on many factors, including the child's age at time of onset, maturity, duration and degree of treatment, the severity of the malaise, the degree to which the body image is impaired, and separations from the child's main care-giver(s) (Kahana, 1972). In charting this pattern it is important to realize that it is certainly not a blueprint: *there are considerable differences from situation to situation.* Nevertheless, a common pattern is often discernible, indicating that a distinct psychological process takes place. And, within this discernible oft-repeated overall pattern there is much similarity with the stages of bereavement (Parkes, 1972). This is hardly surprising. With both an impending death, and the aftermath of a death, there are similar physiological and psychological reactions to this crisis involving loss, fear, a state of alarm, and the human responses to dealing with it. I am basing this summary partly upon my own observations, and partly upon some of the literature (Geist, 1979; Kendrick, Culling, *et al.*, 1986), for Geist clearly describes the stages that children facing chronic illness go through, and many of these findings would also apply to children with leukaemia in the light of its course being delayed if not cured. Corr and McNeil (1986) address many of the concerns around death and the adolescent.

One point is worth stressing. Adolescence, particularly with its inherent struggle for identity and independence, strikes us as being totally at odds with death: it is against the grain for adolescents to accept death. Their new-found sexual capacities; independence; physical, intellectual, and emotional growth; need for privacy and control: all are jeopardized by a terminal illness. It is difficult to evaluate and quantify the different responses to death in the various stages of childhood and adolescence, but, briefly, it seems that adolescents perhaps have the most difficult time, for they have usually emancipated themselves from a close relationship with their parents and yet are not adult themselves.

As many hospitals nowadays do appreciate the value of a full explanation of the diagnosis and the proposed treatment for children and their parents, I am also giving this summary of the stages on the basis of generally open communication.

UPON DIAGNOSIS: NUMBNESS

An initial reaction of numbness can be common to both the child and parents, and links with observations of reactions to bereavement (Parkes, 1972). This numbness, or 'blunting', is an understandable protection against the shock. A feeling of disbelief and a sense of unreality can be part of this stage. Some realization of the serious implications of the diagnosis often breaks through the numbness in bursts. Gradually a more complete awareness of the diagnosis emerges.

However, it is difficult to generalize about the impact of a diagnosis, as much depends upon the way in which the disease is explained to the parents, on their preconceptions, and of course on the way that the child is (or is not) then told. For many children who have felt unwell for a while before diagnosis, there may be little surprise when they hear or intuit that it is 'something serious'. There may even be some relief for the child that his malaise is being taken seriously.

DENIAL

Part of the numbness described above may be a more generalized denial, especially on the part of the parents, as a result of a direct or indirect awareness of the possibility of death. This denial can take the form of suppression (i.e., a conscious attempt to forget or deny and to avoid thinking about it) or repression (i.e., an unconscious process whereby the unaccepted and painful thoughts or feelings are prevented from coming to consciousness). Denial, accompanying feelings of numbness, is frequently part of the initial reaction. However, it can continue to operate, especially if the child's symptoms exacerbate.

The usefulness of denial is that it allows the patient and his family gradually to accept a change in life expectations and the possibility that death may occur. If it is an initial diagnosis and not a relapse, denial and minimization is more possible (Slaby and Glicksman, 1985). Denial of the severity of the illness or its implications is not necessarily maladaptive. It can be a useful way of dealing with loss until there is a readiness for other more realistic responses. For some, perhaps particularly for adolescents, a degree of denial is necessary in order to continue to cope with their remaining life and to go on living (Corr and McNeil, 1986; Detwiler, 1981). For example, Charles, aged fourteen, had been diagnosed as having a malignant abdominal tumour. He acknowledged that he had cancer, but denied that the disease could be fatal. When another child on the ward died, and Charles heard that it was from cancer, he became extremely upset because he realized that he too could die. Thus he was only gradually allowing reality to register.

If defences enable the child and his parents to carry on living without unbearable degrees of anxiety, then they are effective and useful (Chodoff *et al.*, 1964). However, if the defences lead to family members being locked in a 'web of silence', unable to talk to each other for fear of breakdown, this adds to the stress and anxiety of each individual (Turk, 1964). They may continue to function without breakdown, but at considerable psychological cost.

Solnit and Green (1963) also point out that the child's lessening energy and possible eventual stupor in the last stages of a terminal illness is an incidental protection from a full awareness of the situation. It is often hard to define how fully sensate a child is at this stage, and I faced this dilemma with

Robert (see Part Two). I wonder if some denial of the child's awareness takes place on the part of the adults involved. For example, at times with Robert I tended to want to feel that he was 'on the edge of life' rather than fully in it, in order to protect him. He then proved me wrong on a few occasions by rallying rather dramatically and displaying liveliness.

Some researchers have found that resistance is greater in older children, who may regard their illness as 'an inequitable breach of contract and its unacceptance is far more taxing' (Debuskey, 1970). Meanwhile, the younger child, being less aware of alternative forms of illness, may find it easier to accept the restrictions imposed on him.

THE FIRST MONTH AFTER DIAGNOSIS: ASSIMILATION

Children (and their families) are, after diagnosis, particularly receptive to learning about their illness from many sources. Children appear to be particularly alert to assimilating relevant information from other children, doctors, nurses, teachers, parents, domestic staff, books, and television. They quickly learn the meaning of key words which relate to their illness.

Similarly, they soon learn about hospital procedures. As with their quick assimilation of the facts around the illness, this knowledge of procedures is a way of attempting to master a strange, and in some ways frightening, new environment. Part of this new understanding includes an appreciation of the necessity for treatment. Even children as young as two years of age are reported to adjust to submitting to painful or unpleasant treatment when they sense the urgency and insistence on the part of the adults around them.

This considerable understanding of their illness, and of the procedures, often exceeds the child's cognitive development and usual capacity, and links with the more mature concepts of death grasped by children who are facing a life-threatening illness (as has been explored in Chapter 3). This seems to be in the service of adaptation – an attempt to organize and control the experience – while *not* understanding or knowing leads to a higher level of anxiety.

However, there can often be an *intellectual* grasp of what is entailed, without much emotional acceptance. For example, a nine-year-old child with a chronic renal condition had a knowledge of the working of the renal system which almost rivalled that of some doctors, while still objecting to some of the treatments, protesting at the pain, and at times refusing to comply with the necessary intake of fluids. This child's cognitive grasp did not mitigate his sense of outrage at what was happening to his body.

There is research evidence to show that preparing children for bone marrow transplants reduces anxiety during the procedures themselves (McCue, 1980). My own observations of children with serious illnesses show that there is frequently a hunger for factual information. Children usually devour whatever familiarizing books, photographs, films, or information are offered to them. This opportunity to go over the procedures is as useful retrospectively as prospectively: the child needs to work through what can feel like an invasion of his body or an aggressive attack on it by doctors or equipment. A facilitator – an adult who can explain the familiarization project and listen to the child's questions, whether it be parent, nurse, play leader, psychotherapist, or doctor – is as important as the familiarizing material itself.

REGRESSION

Alongside this adaptation, regression can usually be found. Quite often the child adapts to the main part of the treatment, but will find a more minor aspect over which to be resistant. This, again, is the child's way of feeling he has *some* control and mastery of the situation.

Regression can take the form of simply reverting to behaviour that was more appropriate at an earlier stage of development, such as increased dependency, and a need for greater physical care and contact. However, regression can also take the form of the child making unreasonable demands, having temper tantrums, and being excessively irritable.

For example, a six-year-old boy, Mark, with leukaemia, in isolation in hospital, was engrossed with a set of little hospital figures and play equipment which I provided for him. In the play he identified with the doctors giving injections. He turned their aprons round so that they became Superman, flying above all the medicines, operations, and illnesses. When I had to tell him I had to go in ten minutes, but would be back next week, he called for his mother in a complete panic. When she arrived he threw the toys at her angrily. Mark had clearly been denying that he was the patient, and had used a manic defence against all the feelings of helplessness and anxiety about his illness. My impending departure seemed to remind him of his lack of control over the many comings and goings around him, as well as over the illness itself. This same boy was adept at helping the doctors with their regular checks on his catheter and their taking of blood by turning the taps on the tubing and pressing the phials with the dexterity of a theatre sister.

There are many vicissitudes, from child to child, and within each child, between passive acceptance on the one hand and angry resistance or denial on the other. Stephen, aged fourteen, would sometimes retort to me, 'I'm not going to be a rag doll and just sit there!' Yet, at other times, he begged to be allowed to use a wheelchair, although he could walk. When he heard about another child from his school dying, he asked directly, 'Am I going to die?'

Lorraine, aged seventeen, never mentioned her illness or its implications, but displaced her anxiety on to worrying about her stepfather's bad leg, or whether she had upset her mother over something apparently trivial. Her massive denial did not really seem to help her to feel less anxious, for she became extremely upset about these other situations and people.

Children who choose the path of regression with its implicit request for more mothering often seem to be those who appear not to have had, or made use of, a 'good enough' experience of being allowed to be appropriately dependent infants before their illness and who were therefore forced into pseudo-maturity. Jane, aged three, is an example of this. Her mother proudly announced to the hospital staff that Jane had been 'clean and dry' by the age of eleven months. It was not surprising that Jane very soon used the hospital experience to regress to a stage through which she had not been allowed to go at a more appropriate pace. Indeed, she made this quite clear to everyone by smearing her faeces in her cot if left unattended.

There are mothers who, when faced with an ill child, become over-protective and over-anxious. In the light of a life-threatening illness, however, this can be a very understandable reaction. Indeed, few parents do not alter their attitude to an *ill* child. But if there has been a history of a child knowing he can procure his mother's *special* attention when he is ill, being ill may well lead to a rapid submission in order to gain the desired attention: the child might feel that being more infantile than his state of health necessitates will bring extra rewards.

Besides the infantile 'gains', passive submission can also be part of a giving-up of a life instinct or life force. This may be as a result of a feeling of despair, that the infant has lost in the struggle against annihilating forces. These children often become mute and further lose the desire to eat. Although in some ways this makes the nursing role easier, it augurs less well for the emotional (and therefore, in the long run, physical) state of the child. It seems that the child is then giving in to dying. A little boy with leukaemia, Tommy, went through a phase of 'giving up the fight' to the extent that he would lie completely still on the bed, yet not asleep. Once his therapist momentarily thought he had died. (Tommy, as it turned out, was not after all in the terminal stage of his illness, for he responded well to the bone marrow transplant and is in remission at the time of writing.)

Another type of submission and seeming acceptance on the part of the patient is prompted by the use of masochistic defences as an attempt to master the situation. So, although it may appear that there is passive submission, the child's fantasies may be more about a perverse *control* of the situation through the adoption of a masochistic defence, *viz.*, 'I am allowing them to do this to me. I even like it, and want them to do it to me all the more.' Yet another passive response is a withdrawal into a type of mindlessness which can be a useful defence against an awful reality.

The welcoming of a re-experiencing of dependency, whether through masochism or a need to renegotiate early stages, is very different from the more widespread negative reaction of resentment found in children. Having to be looked after like a baby is an indignity to most children from approximately three years onwards. For it is not only the fact of relinquishing control over certain bodily functions that pains the child, but the concomitant ego development. The various developmental landmarks signify a detachment from the mother, and the beginning, at least, of owning his own body.

Having to relinquish these physical and psychological advances leads, in those children who are strongly defended against passivity, to very difficult behaviour while they forcefully oppose the enforced regression. Others – such as those described above who have not had a secure or sufficiently lengthy experience of dependence – fall back into a state of helplessness without much apparent resistance. These children may lose their perhaps precariously acquired bowel or bladder control or the wish to feed themselves.

Clearly, an adolescent suffers a different range of feelings when faced with a loss of bodily, and therefore psychological, independence. An adolescent, however, like a young child, is making considerable bids for independence and autonomy and can find enforced regression particularly humiliating. Inevitably, sensitive nursing and parenting is of paramount importance, with a respect for as much privacy as is possible.

Adolescents often view their illness – perhaps at an unconscious level – as a retaliation against their strivings for independence. Parents often report that ill adolescents who need help with toileting, washing, and eating are very difficult to please. It is hard for the parents to strike the correct balance between over-doing the care and leaving it too much to the young adult. One mother related how she was snapped at by her daughter for 'hurting her' when she washed her too thoroughly, yet told off if she did it too gently.

Increased masturbation, as a form of reassurance, is often a reaction to the anxiety and restrictions imposed by the situation (Geist, 1979), as well as possibly a wish to find pleasurable experiences in the face of so much displeasure.

ANGER

Aggression, too, can be a way for the adolescent to express anger about the restrictions, as well as being an expression of anger towards the illness itself. Thoughts of 'why me?' and of it being unfair are common with the concomitant feelings of guilt (Geist, 1979). Adolescents are particularly sensitive to distortions of their body image: alterations to their appearance caused by drugs, and specifically hair-loss, produce a considerable sense of worthlessness and interfere with their capacity to function. They not only have to cope with their inner turmoil about the distortions, but with the reactions of society, which can be insensitive and rejecting. Anger often emerges when earlier denial and numbness fade (Kübler-Ross, 1970). This, too, links with the stages of bereavement.

Anger and aggression in younger children are often more directly expressed, especially as a reaction to fantasies of being attacked from some unknown internal or external persecutor. As Anna Freud writes, quoting Klein, the young child is often unclear as to the actual origin or cause of the pain, operation, illness, or restrictions. 'If... the child's fantasies are concerned with his aggression against the mother projected onto her person, the operation is experienced as a retaliatory attack made by the mother on the inside of the child's body (Melanie Klein)... or the operation is experienced as mutilation' (1952, p. 74).

Anger is often suppressed, perhaps unconsciously, by hospital staff and parents, in their attempts to make the environment as jolly as possible. The young person may then feel, 'How can I be angry with them when they are doing so much to cheer me up?' This dilemma appears in the detailed account of Robert which follows in Part Two. An example of this attempt to cheer up the children, perhaps taken to extremes, is the Clown Care Scheme in the United States, where clowns dress up as doctors in order to make the children in hospital laugh (as reported by Jonathan Charles on 11 May 1988 on Radio 4). There may indeed be a useful role here in familiarizing children with unpleasant procedures, and perhaps in breaking down the medical hierarchy, but perhaps there is also scant attention to children's needs and rights to *be* depressed or angry.

If the child's mixed feelings of anger and dependency towards those adults who seem to impose their will on him during treatment are expressed, it can make the roles of the carers more difficult. In the case of Robert (see Part Two), the doctors were usually kept 'good', while the nurses could be mocked or resisted. His mother was generally felt to be his lifeline, while his father went through a phase of being seen as all bad. This split was psychologically expedient for Robert, but made caring for him more difficult for some.

As an example of the anger that a parent can feel, I am reminded of one child with leukaemia, who had had a bone marrow transplant. She had relapsed and was untreatable. She was in considerable pain and was on massive doses of pethidine. The mother had not slept for many days. The student nurses were horrified by this mother saying, 'The little cow won't even die for me, she just keeps me hanging on.' It is interesting that the mother felt that she was 'hanging on' as much as the child.

DEPRESSION

Depression is a widespread reaction in children facing a life-threatening illness and seems specifically to be concomitant with loss of autonomy, loss of control, and helplessness. The term 'depression' is often loosely used, and has both a popular and professional psychiatric meaning. The popular use describes a frequent occurrence, is a part of normal existence, and is not an illness. The psychiatric term may have features of an illness, depending on its severity. Winnicott summarizes the phenomenon thus:

> Depression belongs to psychopathology. It can be severe and crippling and may last a lifetime, and it is commonly a passing mood in relatively healthy individuals. At the normal end, depression, which is a common, almost universal, phenomenon, relates to mourning, to the capacity to feel guilt, and to the maturational process. (1963, p. 79)

Therefore, in the way Winnicott describes as relating to mourning, depression appears to be a 'part of normal existence' in response to the abnormal situation of being confronted by a life-threatening illness.

Depression may be interpreted by the carers of a dying child as a giving in or a giving up, yet dying people generally fluctuate in and out of their depression. 'Sadness tends to be an intermittent, and in most situations complete clinical depression is not that common' (Feifel, 1962, p. 90).

The ability of the care-givers and parents to bear the child's depression and sadness links with their own capacity to mourn the loss of the healthy child. The parents may feel guilt and depression and withdraw emotionally or even physically, thus conveying to the child that his situation is unbearable. If the child's depression is more of a depressive nature (see pp. 12–13: 'depressive position', Klein), they may feel concerned that they have exhausted their parents' tolerance or love, and this will evoke earlier feelings of having emptied out and damaged the 'breast'. Furthermore, there may be various fantasies about what the parent or parents are doing when they absent themselves from the child, leading to futher feelings of envy or jealousy which may contribute to anger or further withdrawal.

If, on the other hand, the child's depression is of a more persecutory nature, he will feel that he is being punished by his illness or by his parents' negative response. Again he may feel that his illness, or that he himself, is unbearable.

An attempt to jolly the child up (as mentioned earlier under 'Anger'), to lift him out of his depression, can lead to despair on the part of the child – despair that no one can bear the pain of the loss of the healthy self and the possible loss of life. The child then is not being helped to work through the loss and the feelings of sadness as a foundation for yearning and keeping alive memories of the good missing person/mother/healthy self. Of course if the life span of the terminally ill child is crucially shortened, there will not always be time for a working-through of these feelings, although there appears to be a telescoping or condensing of the psychological phases which parallels the physical condition.

BARGAINING

Kübler-Ross delineates this phase as one of the stages of grief. 'The bargaining is really an attempt to postpone: it has to include a prize offered "for good behaviour", it also sets a self-imposed "deadline" ... and it includes an implicit promise that the patient will not ask for more if this one postponement is granted' (1970, p. 73). This form of bargaining would no doubt be much in evidence in the prayers of anyone of religious convictions, and seems more a part of the parents' reactions than that of the child. However, a child might well use superstition and ritualized or obsessional behaviour in an attempt to 'bring luck' or ward off further illness.

ACCEPTANCE

When considering the possible acceptance of the death of a child, the feelings of outrage, of a life not yet run, emerge, and make this stage far more complicated and difficult for the dying child and, inevitably, for his family – 'Rage, rage against the dying of the light', as Dylan Thomas (1966) writes.

However, without at least some acceptance, at some levels, it is not possible to maximize the remaining time before death. The length of illness plays a significant part in whether this stage can operate at all, with a long illness leading to a *relatively* easier acceptance of death. However, this is by no means necessarily the case, for having battled and 'won', perhaps several times, it can be felt to be worth continuing the battle – or, 'If we've gone through so much and carried on so long, we're not going to give up now.' With some acceptance there can be a shift from active medical intervention and treatment to palliative care, thereby possibly making the patient more comfortable physically. This shift, if it does occur, on the part of the professionals involved and the family does not necessarily imply completely relinquishing hope. The hopefulness can be either for some 'miracle' to occur or, at a more ordinary level, for the patient and family to be able to make the most of the remaining time together. The child may need this time to speak of matters which are important to him; parents and siblings may wish to express their love for the child, to the child. The dying child, or the family left behind, may wish to express gratitude – gratitude for the times they *have* shared. This is a chance to say goodbye, directly and indirectly. Where the course of the illness makes the final stage very sudden parents often feel robbed of the opportunity to say goodbye.

Although anticipatory mourning is often carried out at any of the preceding stages of an illness – on the part of both child and family – this final stage appears to be a valuable time for specifically this particular process to take root, possibly then making it easier for the actual mourning to be set in motion.

From the point of view of the dying child, he can feel a sense of relief at being allowed to 'be', whether that is interpreted as being comfortable in his body or allowed to be dying. Otherwise, the child who is being carried relentlessly towards death by a clearly deteriorating physical condition can feel more tortured by parents pulling him in the opposite direction or beseeching 'Don't go, don't go, we need you' – reassuring though that may be at one level.

It is often reported in the appropriate literature (Elliot, 1981; Norton, 1963) that when a child is dying, they know it. 'Every one of those kids knows what's happening to them inside, because you can feel it' (Elliot, 1981, p. 138). The writer continues, 'when the body is close to death, a signal goes out to let the person know.'

The child who is talked to honestly about the progress of his illness has the opportunity to build up trust, at a time when he needs a foundation of trust above all. This can be trust that those upon whom the child is dependent will tell the truth and trust that the parents are there to help the child with the last stages of their life to the best of their ability. Yet there is a strange irony in a situation where, from birth, the parents have helped to sustain the child's life, and they now find themselves having to talk honestly to the child about the child's possible death. This 'unnatural' shift in the laws of parenting may, however, be a great relief for both parents and child, once it can be grasped and talked about. It is a bitter truth that a parent may be able to help his or her child to die. This is beautifully conveyed in *A Way to Die* (Zorza, 1980).

A boy with whom I worked who had a chronic renal condition and a failed transplant expressed this need for honesty thus: 'Underneath the clown Ronald MacDonald there's a man, pretending.' He had turned to his father to tell him the truth about the proposed treatment, yet remained suspicious of the subtly differing messages he received from his father and from the medical team. There is a need to give even bad news, but to give it tenderly and sensitively, at a level at which the child seems able to grasp. Rather than cutting across or through defences which the child might need, there is the approach of asking the child if he has any questions, or anything he wishes to tell you, and responding honestly. This allows the parent or professional to find the appropriate level, which is, of course, the level at which the child is.

I will now come full-circle back to the 'Kleinian' picture of the infant, with his use of splitting and projection, as the foundation for understanding much of the foregoing. Klein believed that the infant develops through forming good internal objects. At the beginning of life, pain (in the form, for example, of tummy ache, hunger, thirst, fear, not being held) is experienced as persecution. The infant then attempts to get rid of this pain by expelling or evacuating it, probably into that which the infant feels has caused it, that is, the mother or the part of her with which he has an active relationship, i.e., the breast. This unconscious activity is an attempt on the part of the infant to preserve the 'good breast' – that which nourishes, comforts, and protects – by expelling persecutory anxiety into the 'bad breast'. Thus the 'bad breast' incorporates those unbearable unwanted feelings of the infant. Therefore, in illness, especially extreme illness, the young child would attempt to rid himself of the pain by projecting it on to aspects of his outside world.

This splitting-off can, of course, be very useful to survival and psychic comfort. Whether the young child continues to use this primitive form of splitting and projection, or will feel that the mother, or some internal resource, is available as a remedy, depends on the child's psychological development, as well as on the capacities of the mother. However, in a young child who has had to undergo lengthy and traumatic experiences in hospital, it is very difficult for the child to sustain the notion of a good protective mother who can ameliorate the bad experiences. She has to be effectively split into a 'witch' mother who feeds him 'poison' (medicine), on the one hand, and, on the other, a good mother. If this split is not adequate, she may be felt to be totally bad and persecuting (Judd, 1988). It takes some maturity for the young child to be aware that it is one and the same mother.

The extreme situation suffered by a child undergoing torturous treatment links with Bettelheim's description of concentration camp victims. He describes how some victims of the camps would find ways of preserving a sense of autonomy, and managed not to respond with schizophrenic or suicidal reactions, even if it was a small private gesture or a way of making life a little more bearable.

> Those . . . who remained convinced they could act in their own behalf and who did act, remained free . . . of the severest pathology . . . Sometimes it was an extra morsel of food, a piece of paper to wrap around the body for extra warmth, a task successfully avoided . . . It did not matter as long as one could rightly feel that by taking action one had ever so little improved one's estate. (1967, p. 65)

These mechanisms enabled the prisoners, who were so fundamentally restricted and brutalized, to retain some sense of control over their fate. Similarly, many of the foregoing stages and responses to a life-threatening illnesss and the often extreme accompanying treatment can be understood as the child's attempts to retain some degree of autonomy. It may even be worth considering the possibility that in certain ways some *young* children undergoing horrendous treatment and isolation are in a worse situation than a concentration camp victim, *because the parents are necessarily obliged to be part of the system which imposes the treatment.* Thus, potentially, the child's love and trust for his parents is severely jeopardized. The 'protective shield' breaks down. The child then resorts to the primitive mechanisms of splitting, projection, and denial.

Chapter Six

Support available

CHILD PSYCHOTHERAPY

As Part Two of this book is written from my own perspective – that of a child psychotherapist – it is important for there to be an understanding of this role. This is an expanding service, one which is fairly widely available as part of the Health Service in the London area but is sorely lacking in other parts of Britain.

Child psychotherapists have often had a first career in another profession, such as teaching, social work, or nursing. The child psychotherapy training is specialized and extensive, taking a minimum of four years, after, in some trainings, two years of a pre-clinical course, as well as previous experience with children. The teaching throughout is linked to ongoing professional work with children. An important aspect of the training is the weekly observation, and discussion in a seminar, of a baby in his own home for the first two years of the baby's life. The training in psychoanalytic psychotherapy involves treating three children – a young child, a latency child, and an adolescent – three or more times per week, under supervision, as well as a number of less intensive cases. The study of psychoanalytic theory is another component. Each student has to undergo a personal psychoanalysis in order, partly, to experience more fully the infant and the child in himself. Thus, he may be more able to recognize and address the patient's problems.

Perhaps I should clarify what a child psychotherapist basically does in the more usual non-hospital setting, in order to explain the particular psychotherapy input possible in a hospital. In essence, the psychotherapist pays attention to the child, and the understanding of the child's behaviour thus gained, is then, in time, fed back. Mood, play, and speech, as aspects of behaviour, are experienced by the therapist. Both child and therapist then have an opportunity to share and explore aspects of the child which previously were not accessible to his conscious mind. Through this process, some integration of the less acceptable aspects of the child may, hopefully, take place. Anxieties, often originating in earlier, infantile experiences, which may interfere with the child's development, can perhaps be tolerated by therapist and child. This process is specialized and detailed, and requires a considerable time commitment – often years – in order for fundamental changes to the personality to be brought about. Researchers have found that psychotherapy for paediatric patients with cancer markedly decreases the frequency and severity of their emotional problems (Watson,1983).

The transference phenomenon is one of the central forces at work in any therapeutic relationship (Freud, 1905; Klein, 1952). Therein, strong feelings and impulses, usually left over from earlier childhood relationships, are transferred on to, or directed towards, the therapist or analyst. The feelings are then transferred to the present therapeutic relationship. This tendency for earlier relationships to re-surface (which is present in all relationships, not only in therapeutic relationships) is encouraged and facilitated by the setting. The transference and its interpretation becomes one of the main tools in bringing about change. In working with a dying child, the repetition of transference feelings may be kept in mind by the therapist, as part of an overall understanding. The therapist might use the transference to interpret maladaptive behaviour, if this behaviour was leading to greater unhappiness on the part of the child.

For example, Tommy, a five-year-old dying boy, became extremely clinging towards his mother. This anxiety was re-experienced when the therapist left the room. The therapist then said, 'You don't want me to go, because it reminds you of when Mummy leaves the room.' The therapist had often talked to Tommy about his 'baby part' and 'baby feelings', so she was able to say, 'The baby Tommy is frightened that I, or Mummy, won't come back. It's because you need a lot of looking after now, and have worries about being so ill, that you don't want to be alone with all the worries and illness.'

Through Tommy's baby needs and anxieties being understood, and 'held' in the therapist's mind, his level of anxiety and stress may be reduced.

The setting in which the therapeutic relationship takes place is normally an important consideration. Just as the therapist tries not to clutter the relationship with his or her own problems and anxieties, so an uncluttered and constant room and simple play equipment can make it easier to see what the child is expressing or bringing emotionally at any particular moment. Constancy of day and time and length of session are similarly important.

However, in a hospital in-patient setting, many of these considerations have to be put aside. It is obvious that factors such as unpredictability of a child's illness necessitate that the therapist adapts to the ebb and flow of the situation. The child may be too ill, or asleep, or discharged, on the day of the appointed session. Thus the hospital setting automatically imposes limits and conditions on the hospital therapist. One of the main limits is also that contact is usually restricted to the child's stay in hospital, regardless of emotional need (depending of course on where the child's home is, and on practical considerations such as out-patient follow-ups). Recommendations for future therapy may be made, but the therapist's task is primarily short-term intervention, focusing mainly on the child's reaction to his or her illness. In a more usual setting (say, in a child-guidance clinic), child psychotherapy aims at restoring normal emotional development. However, in a hospital setting the main focus would be on allowing the child to work through the traumatic situation that causes the child to be in hospital and the child's response to the trauma.

It is also important, in the hospital setting, for the child psychotherapist to be in communication with the child's parents, either directly or through a co-worker. The parents' state of mind is clearly crucial to the child, so the child-within-the-family is, of necessity, the overall perspective for the workers involved.

Similarly, the child psychotherapist's understanding of a particular child can usefully be shared with the nursing and medical staff, particularly where the medical person's role precludes close emotional contact with the patient. It is here that the psychotherapist can be an important link and, in a way, an interpreter, between the child and the doctor. The therapist, understandably, can learn from the medical staff's observations and experience of the child.

I will illustrate the unique contribution which a hospital child psychotherapist can make with the following example. A four-year old boy with leukaemia, undergoing arduous chemotherapy, became extremely unco-operative about his treatment and threatened to pull his Hickman catheter out (for an example of 'Hickman' see p. 80).

The nursing staff felt extremely anxious about the child and stressed by the demands he made upon them. The intervention of a child psychotherapist, providing regular sessions, enabled this child to express some of his anger and frustration at his restricted and unnatural existence. He expressed this anger through aggressively throwing things at her, as well as symbolically in play. Some of these negative feelings could then be contained by the therapist verbalizing and interpreting the child's feelings and tolerating his rage. Containing the child's rage led to a lessening of his aggression towards the nurses and towards his already overwhelmed mother.

FAMILY THERAPY
Family therapy can be offered alongside, or instead of, individual psychotherapy. Indeed, family therapy is more widely available than individual child psychotherapy, and is a very suitable therapy of choice in

many instances. Dr Dora Black, in talking about a family approach where there is a child with a fatal illness, said:

> One of the things that my work with families has taught me is that one can't actually look at an individual in isolation. For example, in all the families with which we're involved, where there is life-threatening illness, we're concerned about the effect on other siblings of an ill child. The whole family dynamic is very severely and constantly stressed and that diminishes the amount of flexibility that parents have. This leads to lack of spontaneity, of relaxation, and of the joys of family life. There's this kind of chronic cloud that hangs over that makes it so stressful. (personal communication)

Black went on to point out that the family probably has to cope with the actual absence of the mother, as she is usually the one who has to care for the ill child, and the hospital may be many miles from home: 'With the rarer childhood illnesses you usually have to go to a centre of excellence and that may be very far from home.'

Black stated that this leads to the other parent, if there is another parent, or grandparents, or neighbours, all sharing in the care of the child or children remaining at home: 'In my experience people are good at rallying round. But I think that the siblings then feel the strain. They have to be on their best behaviour.'

She continued to talk about the often considerable financial strain, despite the National Health Service paying for the actual treatment. Extra financial problems arise out of the mother having to give up her job, father forgoing promotion, extra travel incurred, extras to keep the children happy.

I asked her about her views on the father's problem in having a role, when the mother is usually the main caretaker. She replied:

> Yes, I think that's often a problem. Walker (1983) writes about this. Mother and the nursing staff often form a unit, or system, from which father is excluded. This is certainly true. Fathers are not anyway as happy in hospitals as mothers, and I think that the reason for this is that all mothers have experienced hospitals through giving birth and/or ante-natal visits, whereas many fathers have never been in-patients. My experience is that a lot of men are actually very uncomfortable there. It's partly because it's a very female institution, and young nurses are not necessarily very good at talking to fathers – but then also because fathers are not involved in the day-to-day care of children.

When looking at the stress that having a fatally ill child puts on the parents' marriage, Black said that statistical research evidence shows that marital breakdown is not any higher than average, because, although the increased stress does lead to some, perhaps already discordant, marriages breaking down, this is counter-balanced by others where the illness actually brings parents together (Lansby, Cairns *et al.*, 1978).

GROUP THERAPY FOR PARENTS OF CHILDREN WITH CANCER

Studies have shown that other parents with leukaemic children 'were regarded by most mothers as the most important source of emotional support' (Bozeman, Orbach *et al.*, 1955, p. 15).

However, one study (Hoffman and Futterman, 1971) shows that in fact mothers of children with leukaemia interact very little with one another in hospital waiting rooms. The exchanges are likely to be superficial. This type of exposure to others could be detrimental, since it could lead to parents feeling that their anxieties and doubts are unusual or abnormal. Thus, resorting to trivial subjects may be partly the result of cancer generally being a stigmatizing disease; or of a fear of upsetting others by being open about feelings.

As a way of addressing this need for a safe and structured setting in which parents of children with cancer can share their anxieties, some hospitals run support groups for parents of children who are seriously ill. I will describe in some detail a group which was run for many years at the Hospital for Sick Children, Great Ormond Street, by Margaret Atkin (principal social worker) and Richard Lansdown.

The group was structured to run for eight meetings on alternate Saturdays. Each meeting lasted for one and a half hours. The parents were self-selected. The only criterion was that they have a child with leukaemia, and this could be at any stage of the illness. Later the group also included parents of children with solid tumours. The meetings were task-orientated. Ten to fifteen people frequently attended, but at times there were fewer. A comfortable room was chosen in a part of the hospital away from the wards and the treatment rooms. A crèche was provided. Parents were reimbursed for travel without question, if they asked; some parents, who lived far away, travelled for several hours to reach the group.

When the group was first set up, less effective medical treatment was available for the illness, and the improvement in treatment over the years led to a different emphasis or atmosphere within the group. In other words, there was a shift from an almost inevitably fatal illness to one with a much better prognosis, so that the parents' task generally became to live with uncertainty, rather than inevitably facing death.

The parents' stress and anxiety were the main themes. A search for meaning, a turning to religious beliefs, and a grappling with the concept of suffering were some of the recurrent topics. The vast majority had recourse to spiritual or philosophic beliefs as a way of coping beyond their own resources. They came from all walks of life, but, as they all had the common factor of a child with cancer, they had similar anxieties.

Margaret Atkin (personal communication) recalls that at the beginning of the series of meetings the atmosphere was extremely tense; the coffee and biscuits would quickly disappear and the room would be filled with cigarette smoke. However, as the weeks went by the meetings became calmer, and sadder, and the coffee and biscuits disappeared less quickly.

There were often indications in the anecdotes parents brought that they were unable to cope with the day-to-day ups and downs: sometimes they were jocular, but ended up in tears. Frequent problems that surfaced were about disciplining their other children, about over-indulging the sick child, and about their sexual relationship. One father spoke about the loss of family freedom and about resenting the intrusion of the illness into family life.

'Why me? Why us?' was a frequent refrain. Atkin says that most parents feel that their child is 'special'. One mother announced that 'Our Timmy is cradled in the arms of the church'. This made it difficult for other parents who did not hold such clear religious convictions.

Some parents found that taking long walks helped them. Many turned to writing poetry, or to making things. On one occasion a father felt unable to talk about how he felt but, instead, read a poignant poem about his child. The group then fell silent.

Atkin reports that there was always a 'doctor bashing' meeting when parents felt that doctors were too brusque, insensitive, or clumsy. This often included their feelings about how they heard the diagnosis. This learning of the news nearly always seemed to remain a watershed in the parents' minds, between the way of life before and the way of life after. It is not surprising to learn that parents of a child with a life-threatening illness remember vividly the way in which the diagnosis was imparted. Approximately half the parents interviewed were satisfied with the way in which they had been told (Stein, Wooley, *et al.*, 1988). In this recent study parents reported that they coped better with the imparting of the diagnosis of life-threatening illness if this was divulged early, in an open snd sensitive way. This was best done in privacy with both parents present. The news needed several repetitions over a period of time for it to 'sink in'.

Considerable marital strife was manifest in the group. As it was often very difficult for parents to agree, it was therefore difficult for the ill child to be in a safe structure. Some parents were very outspoken. Marital tensions are not surprising at a time like this, when one understands a probably unconscious process of projecting blame on to one's partner. Just as the infant uses splitting and projection of dangerous feelings as a way of preserving and keeping separate that which is felt to be good, so adults, especially at times of stress, may fall back into this more primitive way of functioning. Thus, a wife may undermine her husband's efforts to deal with the ill child, as a way of locating separately from herself and her child that which she feels is worthless and helpless. This is an attempt to avoid feelings of guilt, powerlessness, and persecution. Anger, too, may well be directed towards a partner – displaced from the disease itself or even from the child for 'causing' so much upset. However, Atkin states that there was also considerable marital support within the group – where the illness seemed to bring the parents closer together.

The group could 'bring home' to parents the fact that their child had cancer. In other words, some parents had not fully digested this fact until the group met, and were then 'moved on' from their disbelief.

Some meetings focused on how they would feel if their child *did* die. Sometimes a child who had died was talked about. (If there had been a death on the ward, the nursing sister would usually have told the other parents.)

By the end of each series of meetings, an atmosphere of great bonhomie had developed, with parents finding it difficult to leave at the end of the hour and a half. Parents could decide to attend a second series of meetings if they wished.

Unfortunately these groups are not being run there at the time of writing. Instead, there are more informal *ad hoc* meetings, as well as meetings on the ward.

SYMPTOM CARE TEAM

Another important approach in the care of the last few months of a child's life is in the example of the Symptom Care Team attached to the Hospital for Sick Children, Great Ormond Street. This team was set up about three years ago. It is a team of three people, a paediatrician and two senior nurses, whose job is to look after children and attend to their symptoms in the last stages of their lives. They are peripatetic and cover the whole of the area in and around London. They do home visiting, they liaise with GPs and with schools, and work with siblings as well. They can administer drugs and keep children comfortable and relatively pain-free. They also provide a great deal of psychological support. This facility means that many more children die at home than before, with full medical attention. That, incidentally, is a private provision – not part of the National Health Service. In fact, a large part of this leukaemic unit is not NHS funded. There is no charge for the service – it is NHS in the sense that it is free – but it is not funded from central funds, as it is on 'soft money' (that is, money that can be revoked, such as research grants). This also applies to many of the medical staff's salaries.

HOSPICES

A major development in the care of the dying has been the emergence of the hospice movement, although it is based on long traditions. The word 'hospice' arises out of the twelfth-century Knights Hospitallers of the Order of St John of Jerusalem ordaining that ill or weary journeying pilgrims should be put to bed, carefully tended, fed, and given spiritual support. These original hospices, which became fairly widespread, did not have the distinctive function of terminal care, though many of them must have provided it. It was often the religious orders who cared for the dying, particularly the victims of leprosy and plague – diseases which inspired such fear or disgust the sufferers were shunned by their families. During the centuries when few illnesses could be cured, monks and nuns offered shelter to the terminally ill in a way which anticipates the work of the hospice today.

The first modern hospice to be opened in England was St Christopher's in Sydenham, in 1967. The first hospice for children was Helen House in Oxford, which was founded in 1982. As with St Christopher's, and many other hospices which have opened all over the world, there is a religious orientation. This Anglican hospice's multi-disciplinary team is led by Mother Frances Dominica, who founded the hospice, but it makes no discrimination in serving people from all religious denominations, as well as the agnostic and atheist. (There is now one other children's hospice in England: Martin House, in Yorkshire, which opened in 1987.)

The main groups of children whose condition may cause them to die slowly are those with progressive neurodegenerative disease, those with major congenital malformations, and those with malignant disease or major organ failure for whom treatment is not possible. It is these children and their families who may need support over a prolonged period.

There has been criticism of the special provision for dying patients in hospices from those who believe that the existing hospital system is adequate (as elaborated by Kastenbaum, 1982). Anxieties are also expressed about the quality of medical care available in hospices. At another level the public is often anxious about many dying people being put together to die, and whether this becomes too macabre or gloomy for the workers, the patients, and the neighbourhood (Lamerton, 1973).

These questions, and others, were answered for me by meeting Mother Frances in July 1988. Not only were some of the hospice myths dispelled, but many fresh insights were gained. Her face was alert, readily opening into a broad smile, her body tall and graceful in long blue robes. Her voice sounded vigorous, matching her energetic manner and mind.

Helen House was purpose-built, in the grounds of a convent. Most of the rooms open on to beautiful gardens, where I watched a dog trot, doves nest, and fountains play. Two children rushed joyously behind the shrubbery. Despite their odd gait, it was hard to believe that they must have a terminal or degenerative illness.

Mother Frances showed me the rooms. Immaculate pastel-coloured walls, clean carpets, sturdy attractive modern furniture – yet all with the children's needs in mind. Cots, mobiles, pictures, appliqués on the walls, gates to keep the children safe. Signs on doors designating their use, decoratively adorned with hand-painted pictures in a way that evoked a home rather than an institution. I heard a piano playing 'This is the way we . . . on a cold and frosty morning.' Rooms for parents and children; rooms for parents; rooms for siblings; laundry room, sluice room – all the rooms a large family home or children's home would have, plus a room for drugs, dressings, and equipment and a small room that can be made very cold so that children who have died can be laid there until the funeral, and parents can be free to be with the body, if they wish.

I asked Mother Frances whether Helen House was not necessarily for dying children, but primarily provides respite care for children (and their families) with chronic illness. She replied:

> That's right. We provide for children which chronic life-threatening disease – but they do have to have degenerative illnesses. Otherwise the floodgates would open, and if you decide to specialize in something, you've actually got to stick to the criteria, otherwise you're just going to offer false hope to people. In the early days, when we weren't anything like fully booked, it was tempting to say 'yes' to all sorts of families when they had a severely handicapped child, but whose handicap was not life-threatening. Then we recognized that as we became better known, and were providing a useful service, probably more children with a progressive disease would come, and we would then disappoint the others by having to give the children with progressive illness the priority.

So, I asked, you have many, many families on your books, and they call upon you when they want to?

> That's right. At any time there are probably about 120 families on the books with their child still living, and there's room for eight at a time. And it just about works out. There are peak times, like summer holidays, when we have to limit the length of stay, and sometimes we have to juggle dates a bit, but we haven't acutally had to turn anybody away, ever. That figure doesn't take account of the bereaved families we have in continuing contact. We do keep in touch with all our bereaved families for as long as they want.

I wondered whether the whole bereaved family still came to stay sometimes.

This again is difficult because we don't have elastic walls, but quite often the bereaved families will come and spend a day or part of a day with us, and occasionally they come overnight, and we do a fair amount of home visiting as well. We don't have a defined catchment area, so we travel widely. We feel it's very important. To go to the family's own home alters the relationship completely, because you're then accepting their hospitality, and I feel it's good to do that. I always feel much better when I've been to a family's own home, even if all they've had is the opportunity to offer me a cup of tea or something, but still you've gone to *their* place and seen them in their environment, and accepted their hospitality, and that alters the relationship.

I asked Mother Frances whether fund-raising was a constant worry, as they receive no state funding.

No, it isn't, and in fact we spend very little time on it now. Obviously at the beginning a lot of time and energy was spent on it, but we were in the extremely fortunate position of never having to initiate any fund-raising. People heard about the plans, and very quickly word spread, and all we did was produce a little leaflet and then try desperately to keep up with answering invitations to go and talk to groups. Obviously we have to be careful financially, and not be irresponsible in any sense – it is other people's money after all. We've been very fortunate. I hardly ever go to talk to a group just because they want to fund-raise for us. I confine my speaking now almost exclusively to professional groups, because I feel we've got a lot to share: groups in hospitals, or sometimes clergy groups.

I then asked her about the criticism levied at hospices, especially hospices for children, as being inappropriate from the medical care point-of-view, as well as taking children out of the familiarity of home or even a hospital which they may have grown to know well.

Until people understand why we're here, then we are a target for criticism. Initially when we were trying to set it up, we encountered a lot of adverse criticism, particularly from paediatricians saying 'How dare you!' and 'This is all wrong thinking'. You see they were thinking that these children who would come here would almost exclusively have cancer or leukaemia, and in fact very few of our children have malignant disease. I think it's 17 percent of all the children who've been here, and I think that's because a child who is going to die of malignant disease is probably – and this is generalizing – but is probably going to be cared for, able to be cared for, at home, because the tendency is to treat right to the last, and so probably the time of palliative care is going to be relatively short. In our experience people will rally round in a crisis, and you can get all sorts of support and help at home, and if that's what the family chooses then I think that's what should be possible and available to them. An alternative is, of course, for the family who doesn't feel safe or secure at home to go back to the hospital where they've received treatment while they were still hoping for a cure.

But there are a few children, for example, with slowly growing inoperable brain tumours, where it's not going to be a question of days or weeks – it's going to be months or probably years, and therefore we can offer the kind of respite care that we offer to the other children with slowly progressive diseases. I think it's important to recognize that the number of families needing this type of respite care, where the child has a degenerative disease, is small, thank God. Most of the children who come to us have rare diseases so the numbers are quite small in the UK, and even of those families, not all of them will need this type of respite care. Some of them will have built-in support systems anyway, whether it's extended family, or good neighbours, or friends. Or they may have negotiated some sort of private foster scheme, whereby their child might go for two nights a week to another family, or they may be in the fortunate position of being given adequate support in their own home.

It's important to remember that the public usually define 'hospice' as a place where you go to die. We prefer to define it as a place where hospitality is offered to those on a journey. We still think we can justify calling ourselves a hospice, but it needs to be explained.

However, there is a national controversy over the place of hospices for children. At a symposium in 1987, sponsored by the Help the Hospices charity with the assistance of the Royal College of Physicians of London and the British Paediatric Association, the question of ways in which the needs of dying children and their families might best be met was discussed. The conclusion was that the widespread development of hospices for children was unnecessary, as the number of such children is small – estimated at approximately six a year in each health district. An article in the *British Medical Journal* (Chambers, 1987) points out the need for health districts to review their services for dying children, whereby 'provision would be made within the child's home or as close to it as possible'. The author argues that if a family prefers hospital care, the existing wards may not cater for the 'more measured pace' required by the dying child. He concludes that institutional arrangements are second-best, and that professionals should be offering more domiciliary support. He emphasizes the importance of domiciliary night nursing, as 'sleeplessness is most destructive of paternal morale'.

The book *A Way to Die*, by Rosemary and Victor Zorza (1980), gives a very moving account of the authors' daughter's illness and death. It is particularly illuminating on the type of care a hospice can offer, with its skill in managing physical pain. Once the physical care of the patient was eased by the experienced hospice workers, the parents and the patient herself could relax and even enjoy the remaining time. Where chronic pain cannot be eased by hospital doctors, it seems that the highly experienced hospice doctors and nurses can often succeed.

Part Two

Robert, aged seven and a half

Chapter Seven

Diary of my work with Robert over three months

No need to be so scared of words, doctor.
This is called dying.
Luigi Pirandello on his death-bed (1936)

To live a half life half dead, a living death
Milton, *Samson Agonistes*

BACKGROUND

This is an account of my work with a seven and a half-year-old boy whom I shall call Robert. He was diagnosed as having acute myeloblastic leukaemia about two and a half years before I met him.

I introduced him briefly in the Preface. His large eyes, with their enquiring look, conveyed more vigour than the rest of his thin body. Perhaps the size of his eyes was emphasized by his lack of hair. His scalp was bald and smooth, covered by a very fine down, reminiscent of a young baby. The beautifully curved dome of his head seemed to invite gentle stroking.

Before proceeding with his story, and how I came to know him, I will convey some necessary background. Inevitably, many of the details which follow are bound to be painful for the reader. Perhaps this is unavoidable in an attempt to gain some understanding of the situation surrounding one particular child and others like him, as well as raising important issues over the ways that we approach illness, death, and, more specifically, the death of a child.

The causes of leukaemia are generally unknown. However, there appears to be increasing evidence that some leukaemias are caused by living in close proximity to nuclear power stations. A report published in June 1988 by Comare (the Committee on Medical Aspects of Radiation in the Environment) has concluded that the 'raised incidence of leukaemia near Dounreay, taken in conjunction with that relating to the area around Sellafield, tends to support the hypothesis that ... nuclear plants ... lead to an increased risk of leukaemia in young people living in the vicinity (*Guardian* 21 July 1988). Another recent report has uncovered a raised incidence of childhood leukaemia in the area around Hinkley Point, an Electricity Generating Board nuclear site (Milne, 1988). There is also a hypothesis linking living in the shadow of high voltage electrical power lines with above-average rates of leukaemia (Sadgrove, 1988). Robert's mother showed me a photograph of the pleasant rural surroundings in which they live, commenting on the many large electrical pylons spoiling the landscape. Even though I realize how many different risk-factors play a part in every leukaemia and in Robert's illness, I could not help wondering about the possible connection between that and Robert's leukaemia.

In order to confirm some of the factual medical details which follow, I had to contact one or two overworked hospital doctors in order to show them my rough notes. One of them caught sight of my description – on another page of my writing – of the hospital as 'encapsulating' and its atmosphere as alien for these parents. He became very disapproving of my seemingly emotive language on that page. This reaction demonstrated the distance between many of the doctors and myself, as a child psychotherapist, and, as I observed, between the doctors and the rest of the team. The considerable load of work which the doctors face can only partly explain this. The extreme pressure provides them with an inbuilt 'escape clause' – 'there's not enough time to get involved' – as a way of avoiding some of the emotional implications of their work. This phenomenon is similar to that described by Menzies Lyth (1959) in her research into the ways in which the hospital system colludes with nurses' denial of painful feelings (see Appendix 3). These difficulties are part of a much wider debate, but the problem has relevance to the various situations which I shall describe later.

As I mentioned in Chapter 1, referring to the training of medical students concerning issues around death and dying, there are fundamental residual obstacles preventing some doctors from embracing a psychodynamic understanding. I see this partly as a result of the intensely hierarchical system within the hospitals, which, at least in some respects, may arise from the methods of selection of medical students and from their training. I suppose it was partly this 'divide' that perhaps explains many doctors' unavailability for discussion of issues arising from this book, as well as what I perceived as their impatience with a 'mere' child psychotherapist. However, there were one or two exceptions.

The facts and figures which follow are gleaned from many different publications; from my researching into bone marrow transplants for a hospital familiarization project for children; as well as from some very helpful communications from Professor Judith Chessells, of the Hospital for Sick Children, Great Ormond Street, London.

Leukaemia is commonly known as cancer of the blood. The word describes a group of malignant disorders that arise in the blood-forming cells. One of this group is acute myeloblastic or myeloid leukaemia (AML). As with all types of leukaemia, it involves the production of abnormal, immature white cells in the bone marrow, which results in the excessive accumulation of the cells both in the bone marrow and in the blood stream. It is therefore really a bone marrow disease which appears as a blood disorder.

This type of leukaemia, AML, accounts for approximately 35 percent of all diagnosed leukaemia cases in western countries but is not common in children. It accounts for about 20 percent of childhood leukaemias. Twenty years ago the outlook for AML was so grim that it was questionable whether patients should be treated at all. Treatment of children by bone marrow transplantation (BMT) has only been carried out in Britain since the early 1970s. Considerable advances in treatment over the last decade have led to remission being possible in approximately 80–85 percent of children with myeloid leukaemia. Despite this initial remission, most patients eventually relapse. Prolonged survival now seems to be possible for up to 30–40 percent of those treated.

BMT is offered to some patients who do not respond to chemotherapy, who have relapsed, or who are at high risk of relapse. It has been discovered tht BMT is more likely to succeed in patients who are in complete remission, rather than in those who are in partial remission or relapse. Therefore, it is usually recommended that AML patients receive transplants during the first remission. The perfect situation would be one where a sibling with a perfect tissue-type match can donate bone marrow.

To convey the background, Dorothy Jordan, a paediatric sister in a large teaching hospital described the set-up for the leukaemic children:

Most of our deaths are from the children with leukaemia. These children are sometimes in hospital from three to four months. We also get to know them quite well because they come back again. Because medicine, and the treatment of leukaemia, have improved so much, parents now have to deal not only with the statement that 'your child has got leukaemia', and therefore their whole life is turned upside down, but with the drugs and the regime that we use. For some it is relapse, remission, relapse. So for the parents, you can imagine the strain that they are under. As a paediatric nurse I would stress that when you're treating a child it's the whole family unit as well, and obviously support for parents is needed. I think we could do better here than we do. Many times, when off-duty, we take parents out to get them off the ward, take them for a cup of coffee, and sit and talk. We tried to form a support group for the parents, but it's never materialized. A helpful factor is that parents of children with leukaemia do support each other. Because of the way the ward is – that we don't just have children with leukaemia, and there are many other demands on your time – we don't have time to give more. In an ideal situation, I'd like to give them much more support than I do.

However, many units would try to ensure that children with leukaemia, who have reached the stage of care and not cure, die at home whenever possible. The crucial issue, of the approaches to this final stage, I will explore more fully further on. Certainly social work support should generally be available for families, thereby relieving the nursing staff of this responsibility. Many of the designated social workers are funded by the Malcolm Sargent Fund for Childhood Cancer.

Robert received chemotherapy after the diagnosis, and had been in remission for about two years when he relapsed. He then received further chemotherapy, leading to another period of remission when he had no physical complaints. About six months after this relapse, and during this second complete remission, he was admitted to a large hospital in the North of England for BMT. This is a potentially life-threatening and highly sophisticated procedure. It was to be a mismatch (that is, of a different tissue type) allogeneic transplant. 'Allogeneic' means that the donor's marrow is genetically different from the recipient's. His father was to be the donor. Donors are usually siblings, since the chance of finding an acceptable tissue type match is one in four for siblings and much lower for anyone else. However, Robert's father's bone marrow was found to be the most suitable.

Under these circumstances, Robert's chances of a successful outcome were probably around 5 percent. There was some doubt in the care team over whether the doctors had in fact told the parents that his chances of success were around 10 percent. Parental consent was of course received, but it is debatable as to how *informed* this consent was. This ambiguity indicates either the doctors' own difficulties in really facing some of the implications or the parents' need to believe in a more optimistic prognosis. The confusion itself reflects the lack of a cohesive care team. The divisions, at times, in the care team reflected the division between the parents themselves, and their oscillations between approaching the reality and withdrawing from it.

It is important to point out that this type of transplant, which could be called an experimental one, is very unusual, and would probably not be considered by most paediatric bone marrow transplant centres. It therefore does not serve to illustrate the more typical pattern of BMT treatments in paediatric oncology. Nevertheless, it raises significant issues as to the moral and ethical implications of whether this type of treatment or research should be carried out at all (see Chapter 10). It probably accounts for approximately 10 percent of paediatric BMTs. Is that 10 percent too many? It also highlights dilemmas common to all terminally ill children and their families: can the quality of the remaining life be the main priority and focus, rather than an attempt to cure that which is probably incurable, through treatment which is particularly aggressive and invasive?

I knew Robert for the last two and a half months of his life, from his admission at the end of September to this death in mid-December. He had visited the hospital a few weeks earlier for tests. He arrived with his parents, Mr and Mrs Campbell, from their home in the Highlands of Scotland, for the transplant at the end of September. He spent the first day in a hotel, going to the hospital, going for a walk in the park with his parents, and visiting a toy shop. These were the last acts of freedom and health – although no one was to know that they would be the last. Mr and Mrs Campbell had resolutely wanted everything medically possible to be tried for Robert even if the chances of survival were slim. Without a bone marrow transplant the chances of survival would be even less. So, although the consultants did not hold out great hopes for the success of this treatment, the parents wanted this attempt to be made. When Robert was admitted, his medical notes stated that he was well, had no specific complaints, and had a good appetite. He was taking no drugs.

Robert had an eleven-year-old sister, Julie, who was staying with an aunt back home in Scotland. The family came from a rural part of the country, and were involved with farming. They had rarely visited big cities, and had never before stayed in this part of England. In time I gathered that not only did they feel totally out of their usual environment and away from their support systems and extended family, but the encapsulating air-conditioning of the modern hospital with its hermetically sealed windows exacerbated their feeling of landing on a threatening, and at times alien, planet.

On the day after Robert's admission, some of his own bone marrow was harvested. In this procedure, under general anaesthetic, some bone marrow was removed from the pelvic bones, using special needles. The marrow obtained in this way was then processed and frozen. In the event of the bone marrow graft from his father failing, this could then be used instead, for an autologous, or 'self' transplant. At the same time he had a lumbar puncture, in order to see if there were leukaemic cells or infection in the spinal fluid, and to inject a drug to prevent the recurrence of leukaemia. A programme of intravenous cytotoxic chemotherapy was commenced, in order to obliterate the existing bone marrow which would contain many leukaemic cells. He also received total body irradiation to compound the effect of the chemotherapy, as well as to get rid of his own immune system and thereby reduce the likelihood of rejecting his father's bone marrow. Total body radiation is frightening for many young patients, as it requires an hour of immobilization alone in a shielded room. Both the chemotherapy and the total body irradiation induced nausea and vomiting as predictable side-effects. (Total hair loss is another inevitable side-effect of this treatment, but this is temporary; permanent sterility, as a result of radiation treatment, is yet another.) These treatments alone would be lethal without the transplant, which would eventually repopulate Robert's bone marrow, and then his blood, with healthy cells.

The transplant itself, which then followed, was quite a simple procedure. This central event is, paradoxically, brief and uncomplicated. The bone marrow was harvested from Robert's father in exactly the same way as the back-up bone marrow was taken from Robert. This was then processed so that only cells necessary to repopulate the bone marrow remained in a very small volume, and were then given to Robert directly into the Hickman line, like a blood transfusion.

The Hickman line is a central venous catheter via a skin tunnel from the chest into the superior vena cava of the heart, to give ease of access for the blood, blood products, antibiotics, intravenous feeding, etc., and for blood sampling for laboratory tests.

The transplanted, or transfused, cells would then find their own way back into Robert's bone marrow spaces, where they would multiply, mature, and engraft. In two or three weeks the then mature cells from the marrow would spread into the blood stream. Until then, Robert would have no cells of his own to protect him from bleeding, bruising, and infection. Once these cells have spread into the circulation, these risks would decline.

The risk, once the new marrow begins to 'take', or grow, is of graft-versus-host disease developing. This is a phenomenon whereby the implanted cells attack those of the recipient, and is potentially fatal.

The detailed consecutive diary, forming the rest of this section, conveys the way in which notes, made after the meetings, are used as an *aide-memoire* and as a way of thinking about the situation. Theoretical understandings often emerge later, with the help of notes. Minute detail gives the reader the opportunity to get close to the actual events, and to evaluate and apply the foregoing chapters. It is also, admittedly, a way of putting the reader through one part of the ordeal, thus experiencing, albeit at a distance, one family's tragedy. For it is salutary to remember that if this diary is, at times, almost unbearable to many readers, it reflects only two, and occasionally three, meetings per week with this child. This is little compared with the almost constant deep involvement of the parents over this period, plus the preceding build-up of two and a half years of illness – let alone the experience for the child himself. However, the parents and the patient can and do use necessary defences, while the therapist, and perhaps the reader, can 'afford' this intense pain because the contact is not constant. The mother of another child (who had a brain tumour and was hospitalized for a year of treatment) said to me: 'I feel that he was put through Auschwitz and then they did experiments on him.'

In the account which follows, the reader will see the many occasions when my own courage failed, when I avoided what perhaps I should have said, when the team of professionals was divided, as well as when family members were at odds with each other. But perhaps through reading this, others facing similar situations, personally or professionally, will find some useful guidelines, warnings of possible pitfalls, rather than hard and fast prescriptions.

FIRST CONTACT

30 September (Thursday) 3 p.m. I am taken by Dr Simmons, a child psychiatrist, to meet Robert for the first time. I see an attractive child with a bald head lying on the bed. He looks at me with large eyes. I feel slightly shocked by the baldness. I naïvely had not anticipated it. It is the result of previous chemotherapy. To those unfamiliar with leukaemic children who have lost their hair, this baldness seems to give them a 'sameness' of appearance, making it more difficult to discern their age, sex, and even their individual facial characteristics.

I am introduced to his mother, Mrs Campbell, and to Robert. Mr and Mrs Campbell have already agreed to my seeing their son regularly. My role as child psychotherapist has been briefly explained to them (see Chapter 6 for a description of a child psychotherapist's role). Robert was referred to me for psychotherapy because of the isolation of this family from their normal environment as well as the grim prognosis. It was anticipated therefore that they would experience extreme stresses. Peter, the paediatric social worker, was to keep in touch with the parents regularly, and liaise with me. Robert was also to receive frequent visits from the play leader, and from a particular teacher from the hospital school assigned to him. Unfortunately, owing to limited resources, only a few children in hospital have the opportunity to receive psychotherapy.

I decided to plan to see Robert regularly twice weekly. This seemed to be the maximum time I had available, and, I felt, was the minimum requirement of a child in his situation where continuity was important, and where inevitable physical fluctuations, such as being too unwell or asleep during therapy session times, necessitate frequent contact. Moreover, to a child in hospital, unable to escape from bed, and being nursed in isolation – as I explain further – even one day can seem like a very long time.

Mrs Campbell sits between Robert and us. She is a pretty, delicate-looking woman, slim and bright-eyed. By answering for Robert, mother seems to be acting sensitively as a buffer between her son and the outside world. She seems thus to be percolating the myriad strange experiences that her son is having to face. I notice a worn-out little yellow teddy bear on Robert's pillow, and ask him about it. Robert tells me its name is Sunshine.

I leave, telling Robert that I will have my first proper meeting with him next Tuesday, and then on Thursday, and so on, each week.

4 p.m. I see Mrs Campbell and Robert going down in the lift. Robert is being carried by his mother, his large head again so reminiscent of a baby's. Mrs Campbell's lips seem to brush the downy surface. Robert looks bright and happy.

A few days after I met Robert I began writing a diary of my visits to him.

SECOND MEETING

2 October (Tuesday) 11 a.m. The blinds are drawn on Robert's door. Unsure if it's the right room, I knock and enter, recognizing his bright red dressing-gown hanging up before I see him.

He is in bed, slightly curled up, his father sitting on his bed, showing him cards he has just received in the post from his school friends back home. I introduce myself to Mr Campbell, who is a large man with a gentle manner, and remind Robert who I am. Robert just looks at me. I talk about all the different people they must be meeting, and how muddling it must be. Mr Campbell agrees, but smiles and says, 'It's not too bad. I'm getting it all sorted out.' He invites me to sit on the bed as he moves to a chair.

I explain to Robert that I'm not a doctor or a nurse. Mr Campbell quickly interjects, 'So she doesn't have to do any horrible things to you . . . but you're not afraid of doctors or nurses, are you, lad?'

I explain that I'm really here for Robert to talk to if he wants to, and that I'll be bringing some play things which will be specially for when I'm with him. Mr Campbell quickly and attentively says, 'That will be nice, won't it, son?' Robert seems to half shake his head, looking at me. I say to him that it must be difficult, all these strange people, and a strange hospital, and not knowing me.

Mr Campbell then talks about the strangeness of it all. We exchange comments about the hospital being a world of its own. He talks about a need for him and his wife to get out sometimes – to take it in turns.' (Weeks later I realize that this is *his* strong need – to escape from the claustrophobia of the hospital – and not, at least overtly, his wife's.) Mr Campbell asks if I've met his wife, who is out at the moment. He conspiratorially mimes something about what his wife was doing, that looks like ironing. He talks rather breathlessly as if he is overwhelmed by it all, and somewhat shocked. His eyes are full of feeling, his face flushed, yet I feel that he is holding back in Robert's presence. He talks about a lovely walk the three of them had in a park a few days ago.

He shows me a card made by several of Robert's school friends, quickly explaining that of course Robert hasn't been in school much for the past two years, but his friends still remember him, 'Don't they lad?' I read out some of the names on the card. When his father and I cannot decipher one name, Robert calls out in a loud, definite voice.

Meanwhile, he is fiddling with a card depicting a picture of Jesus. I ask him if he'd like me to fetch the toys now. He shakes his head. Mr Campbell volunteers that he's not feeling too bad today as he didn't have to have a treatment today (radiotherapy). He adds that tomorrow would be the last one. Robert shakes his head. Mr Campbell repeats, 'You have your last treatment tomorrow, Friday, Bobby.' He seems to hit out at his father with his hand. I say, 'You don't want to talk about some things? I'm wondering, Robert, if it's your Dad saying that it's the last treatment you disagree with?' He seems to nod.

I say that I know that he would be having the transplant next week. Mr Campbell says, 'Yes... on Monday. He has more radiotherapy, and then the bone marrow transplant.' He adds that he has to 'go in' on Sunday evening as the donor, and has to 'starve' himself before the anaesthetic. Robert looks round and fixes his eyes on father for the first time.

I say something to both of them about this being one of the things a Mum or Dad does for their children. Mr Campbell nods in agreement.

I say that today I am really introducing myself, and that I wanted also to say that sometimes boys and girls find it easier to talk to someone who isn't their Mum or Dad about any worries they might have, because sometimes they don't want to upset Mum or Dad. I say that I am saying this in front of Dad so he would understand too about Robert having me as someone who won't tell Mum and Dad everything. 'It's because Mum and Dad are such important people in your life that sometimes it's useful to have someone else who's separate from them.'

Robert is still bending the card of Jesus. Mr Campbell asks him to stop. He continues. Father says, 'It's a special card; Agnes gave it to you at the airport.' He takes it from Robert, straightens it, and puts it on the ledge with other cards.

As if to cheer Robert up he says, 'I telephoned Julie [Robert's sister], didn't I, Bobby? She's glad to know you're OK, and you're glad to know she's OK.' He then tells me that Julie is staying with her aunt, and continues, 'I was saying to Robert that when we get him on his feet again, he could trot along and give her a ring.' He gives me a big wink. 'That would be nice, wouldn't it, Bobby?' Robert is fiddling with his ears, twisting them, and now bends them over, as if to block off any sound. When Father talks about Robert getting on his feet, I feel he is inviting me to join him in his denial of the possibility that Robert will not be 'on his feet'. I feel trapped between his wishes and Robert's needs. Robert seems to be feeling not only doubt about whether that was the last radiotherapy treatment, but also anger when he seems to hit out at him and then attack the religious card. But I do not at this point feel able to say much more to both of them. I need to wait until I have built up more of a relationship with Robert on his own.

As I leave, saying, 'See you Tuesday', Mr Campbell says, 'Don't work too hard!' (I wonder if this is a covert expression of his resentment at my going off for four days, leaving them with the distress of the next few days.)

6 October (Monday) Robert is given the transplant. During the preceding radiation treatment he was apparently extremely silent and some of the medical staff express concern about his emotional state. They notice that he is withdrawn, and sense that he may be depressed. As they know he is being given psychotherapy, they appropriately pass these worries over to me.

THE PSYCHOTHERAPY BEGINS

7 October (Tuesday) He is now being barrier-nursed, in isolation, so anyone entering the room has to don mask, gloves, and plastic apron in order to reduce the dangers of infection. If I feel very cut off behind the mask, what must it be like for Robert to see only the eyes of everyone, I wonder.

10.30 a.m. I go in and find him very perky and smiling. He is sitting up, wearing smart striped pyjamas. He shows playful aggression towards the nurses, openly criticizing the big nose of one of them. This spirited rapport between Robert and the nurses seems a denial of anything serious. Mrs Campbell seems tired. I ask about Mr Campbell – he, apparently, is 'sore', recovering from being a donor, and is on another ward. Robert tells me he thought Daddy would be recovering with him, and not in another part of the hospital. Both Mrs Campbell and Robert refer frequently to Julie as a missed member of the family.

I introduce the box of play equipment, which includes a miniature hospital set. Robert examines the tiny figures and objects. He calls the little television in this set an X-ray machine. (Another hospital patient had thought this same little television was 'an ambulance kit' – instances of the unusual distortion of the lives of children who have lengthy exposure to hospitals.) He attempts to get the tiny vase of plastic flowers to stand up. Its repeated toppling, and his repeated attempts to right it, convey to me something of his precarious state, and his wish for greater stability.

As Mrs Campbell is there, I feel that it is not a 'proper' psychotherapy session – as I am unsure about some possible interpretations in Mother's presence.

As I leave, Robert says to Mrs Campbell that he is 'starving for a cheese sandwich'. His Scottish accent makes his speech particularly attractive.

Later, I hear one of the sisters describing Robert as a 'really cheeky delightful child'.

9 October (Thursday) 11.30 a.m. I arrive on the ward with Robert's box of play things. All the senior nursing staff seem very busy, so it's not the right time for me to explore with them the possibility of making the sessions a little more 'private' – there are innumerable medical check-ups each time I am with Robert and I wonder if non-essential ones could wait for half an hour or so. He is bed-bound, tied to his Hickman catheter. Because of the catheter, there is no possibility of my taking him into another room. I look for someone to tell me more about bone marrow transplants. But it can wait.

I ask Dr Fish (Robert's senior house officer) in passing if he has done his ward round yet (hoping to time my session around this) but he says amicably, 'No... but never mind... I'll just pop in.' In time, I learn that I have to try to work around and with the environment.

Through the blind on Robert's door I can see Mrs Campbell. I don the mask, gloves, apron, spray the toys and the box with sterilizing fluid, and go in. Robert immediately tells his mother that he wants the bedpan. Mrs Campbell lifts him on to it. He seems so full of lines leading to the Hickman. Later a nurse calls it Spaghetti Junction. Although Robert seems not to mind my presence while he defecates, I look out of the window, but have noticed his thin white body. Mrs Campbell says something about Robert's trousers being dirty. She wipes him and then makes him comfortable under the sheets, and takes the bedpan out.

Robert then says something quietly to his mother, who then asks me about leaving the toys in the box here for Robert. I explain – with difficulty – that it is important for me to bring them each time as part of my sessions with Robert, so that they remain special, and Robert and I can try and understand each time what meaning they have for him. Robert replies to his mother, 'It was *you* who wondered about it!' Mrs Campbell says that she had thought that I took them away each time because I had to use them with other children. I said that I could see that it must be frustrating when I take them away each time – but no, they are only for Robert's use.

Mrs Campbell asks Robert if she should show me the letter from Julie received today. Robert is silent. I say, 'You're not sure.' Robert then nods to his mother, giving permission. Mrs Campbell shows me the letter, and we talk about their wish for Julie to be here, and how feasible this might be for a few days. Robert interjects, 'Not for a few days, for a *week*!' Robert shows me a card from a school friend. The name looks like hieroglyphics – and then I realize it is 'Stevie' backwards. Robert smiles brightly and says, 'Oh yes, he always used to write backwards!'

I've left the therapy box a little way from the bed, and am sitting on a chair by Robert's bed. Mrs Campbell says, 'You've got to take your medicine. Come on, Bobby.' He sullenly sits there. Mrs Campbell hands him a cup. He refuses. Mrs Campbell says, 'If you don't, maybe Mrs Judd will have a go.'

Robert still sits there. I say, 'Is it horrible?' He nods. Robert takes little sips of it. Mrs Campbell praises him, but tells him to finish what is left at the bottom. Robert refuses. I ask how often he has to take this? Twice daily. Mrs Campbell tells Robert kindly but insistently that the doctors say it's important. I feel tense, caught between the opposing pull of the mother (and the doctors) and Robert's assertion of some autonomy. She relents, with the retort, 'I'll put it down the sink and that won't do much good! And I'll have to tell the doctors!' as she tips it away.

A student nurse comes in, to take nose and throat swabs. Robert protests. Mrs Campbell appeals to him. The nurse suggests that Robert does it himself. No. The nurse then gently carries out the simple procedure, Robert acquiescing, but he seems to feel very invaded and upset. The nurse asks to have a look at his dressing (around the Hickman catheter). Robert sulks. The nurse gently lifts his pyjama top. He co-operates by removing the sticky strips himself, then looks down at the plastic tube entering his chest. (I wonder to myself what it must feel like to have a hole in your chest so near the heart.)

Mrs Campbell watches, close by. Robert says something to his mother and then mimes with his hand a pumping action, meaning he can feel his heart beating. The nurse wipes his skin with a swab. Robert flinches. I ask if it's cold, or does it sting? He tells me it's cold. When the area is wiped further, Robert squirms more than before. My questions indicate my need to become familiar with the *many* procedures he has to undergo, and to begin to sense what their impact is on Robert.

The nurse then has to dress the site – and as we all wear gloves, we cannot peel the sticky tape, so Robert volunteers, struggles, and succeeds; then helps to stick the strips down. He pulls off more tape, beckons the nurse towards him, and sticks some across the nurse's mask, half on the bridge of her nose. The nurse jokes about it and leaves. I think how sensitive some of the nurses are to Robert's need to attempt to control some of the procedures.

Mrs Campbell asks her son if she can go off for a while. He nods, adding, 'But only to the coffee lounge.' I say that I can be here until one o'clock, depending on how Robert feels. Mrs Campbell says, 'Oh, in that case, I'll go and get Dad to come and have lunch with me ... he's still quite sore', and leaves.

I take up with him the question of my taking the box away each time. He interjects conspiratorially, 'I often think that if you have a toy or something *all* the time, you get bored with it.' (I do not try to interpret his feelings about my coming and going. Perhaps my hesitancy arises out of the difficulties in working in an unsequestered setting, as well as the feeling that Robert's death may be imminent. This latter possibility partly explains *my* difficulty and reluctance to encourage a deepening of the transference through my own separation anxieties, and, with hindsight, he may have been helped more had I not felt this inhibition.)

I clear Robert's bed-table surface, and open the therapy box. He peers in, takes out a new box of plastic figures, opens it, and then skilfully constructs the family. As it is new he has to assemble many of the parts. He finds a little piece of foam rubber and exclaims, 'This must be the soft pillow.' He seems to enjoy the process of organizing, making, deciding for himself. When I voice this observation, adding, 'especially when you have to have so much done to you these days', he nods wisely.

He then tries to get the mother doll to push the little pram, but mother's hands are stiff, so he uses the father instead, adding, 'He's too little!' Interestingly, although he could make his feet touch the ground, he leaves him as seemingly too little, thereby conveying a weakened father. This clearly relates to his current perception of his father, now debilitated by the donation of bone marrow, and may have further-reaching implications of his feelings. But at this stage I do not interpret, as it is too early in the contact. These are simply some of my thoughts and understandings at the time.

He says that they are on an outing, '... to the *park*', the last word said with great enthusiasm. He takes out the box of animals, and asks me which ones would not be in a park. I comment on there being wild animals and farm animals. He leaves the two lion cubs (calling them puppies), takes a baby kangaroo, and says that Skippy must be in a park. He then enacts what he calls a hippo (but is really a rhinoceros) fighting with a tiger, the tiger hitting the 'hippo' and the 'hippo' then charging at the pram and knocking over the baby and the mum and dad. The mum then rides on the 'hippo' to take it, and order is restored.

I comment that at first he seemed to want to keep the wild animals separate from the peaceful scene in the park, but they soon attacked everything. I say that I wonder if Robert sometimes feels very angry, like the hippo - angry at having to be like the helpless baby in the pram. (I also wonder - to myself - if the hippo represents the disrupting invasion of the illness, upsetting the family triad. Although there is a fourth member of the family, it seems that Robert's focus is on those who are with him in hospital.)

By now he's placed two little lambs on the baby's pram. I ask what he feels about this. 'They're horrible,' he says expressively. I say that although they look gentle, they're frightening to the baby '... like the horrible things you have done to you... things that may look gentle as a lamb but are very upsetting'.

Now he gets the mum to push the dad, while the dad pushes the pram. I comment on this being like his family at the moment - 'you're like the baby, lying down a lot and having to be looked after. Dad helped you with the transplant, and so pushes you along, in a way, but he is now weak like this

Daddy – and Mum has to look after both of you.' He listens to this with interest.

And then he takes out the plasticine, looking at all the colours. He wonders aloud which one would be skin coloured, and chooses white, although there is some flesh-coloured plasticine. (This choice not only seems to reflect Robert's very pale skin, but may also reflect his having probably heard talk about the important part that white cells play in leukaemia.) He models a head, and adds two brown eyes. He wonders how to make hair. I ask him what ideas *he* has? He proceeds with the body. I say, 'You seem to be leaving it without hair, perhaps so that the little figure is like you?' (See photograph opposite)

He darts a look at me, and then nods. I say, 'You must miss your hair.' He nods emphatically. I say, 'What colour was your hair?' 'Reddish brown,' he says feelingly, with pride. Then he adds arms and ponders the problem of how to add legs.

Dr Fish comes in, and chirpily holds up one of the animals, asking, 'What's this?' Robert says, 'Hippo!' Dr Fish bursts forth: 'No, it's not! It's a rhinoceros! Javanese... or Sumatran... very rare... only about a dozen left in the world... that's its armour...' Robert just looks at him.

He asks Robert how he's feeling and looks in his mouth. Robert is ultra co-operative; then he listens to his chest. He asks if he hasn't eaten because he feels sick or because he's not hungry? Robert just shrugs. He asks where Mum is. I explain. He says, 'Dad's very sore, he's got lots of holes in his back – like a tea-bag.' Robert stares at him.

He goes. I feel, through a strong identification with Robert at that moment, as if the hippo (or rhino!) had charged over me. I say to Robert, 'It's difficult being interrupted when you're busy with something.' He nods. After further doubts about how to add legs to the figure, he succeeds and shows me how it can stand up.

I feel that his difficulty in executing the legs reflects his present bed-ridden existence, where his own legs are out of action and not much use. The upstretched arms convey helplessness and an appeal to be comforted or picked up. The exceptionally large eyes, and the exclusion of any other facial features, emphasize the need to look and to take in through the eyes. This seems to reflect Robert's own scrutiny of his environment, for literally vital information.

Later, when I look at this figure, I feel that it is like a little ghost. This is confirmed when, months later, I photograph it and then photocopy the photograph. The photocopy is both ghostlike and skeletal.

He then methodically packs up the plasticine. I say, 'You seem to have had enough.' He says, 'No – now I'm going to play with the hospital set', and sets it up. Again the tiny vase of flowers topples over. He is more resigned this

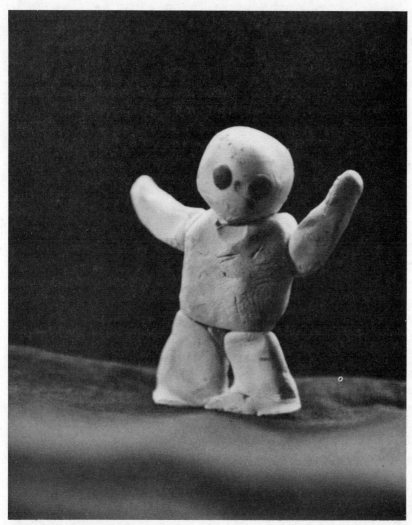

Robert's plasticine man

time. The same student nurse comes in, shows an interest in the toys, and asks Robert to remember to do a specimen of urine in a special container next time. Another nurse gaily comes in. A porter pulls faces at Robert from the door. He pulls faces back.

Suddenly, he says, 'I feel sick!' I quickly fetch a vomit bowl, and he is very violently and copiously sick into it, remaining stoical throughout. I find my role immediately has to change to a more maternal one.

When the vomiting is over, I talk to him about my now really seeing some of the awful side to being ill. He continues to play with the hospital set, making a little boy doll get out of bed, put on big slippers belonging to the mother doll, and then enacts him eating his dinner. He then makes the little boy go back to bed.

Most play sequences are very rich and complex in meaning, and the child psychotherapist often attempts to deal with only some aspects of that which is revealed at any particular moment. I will give a detailed analysis of the foregoing sequence as an example, to illustrate my understanding – some of it with hindsight – of this last passage of material, although I did not attempt to tell Robert much of what I understood. The therapist stores and processes the child's information and feelings. This is rather like the way a mother might hold a crying baby in her arms and feel responsive to, and think about the baby's mood, without actually crying with the baby, nor, necessarily, saying much to the baby.

If we look at this last sequence, it seems that Robert, using the little boy doll as a symbol for himself, shows this doll becoming, in a way, a coping mother: the child literally steps into the mother doll's large slippers. Perhaps Robert feels the mother doll is able to walk around and cope at this point because I became the coping mother helping him when he vomited, and also because of repeated experiences of his own coping mother. This little-boy-inside-the-mother can now take in good food in this sequence. Interpretations that I give him may indeed feel – to a more infantile part of Robert – like 'talking food' or 'food for thought'. He has literally evacuated the 'bad stuff' in his stomach, now feeling symbolically able to leave the sick-bed, sit at a table, and eat good food. With a child who is actually ill, and who actually vomits as a side-effect of some of the medicines he has been given, the situation cannot be understood simply at a symbolic or psychological level. However, although the cause of the vomiting may be predominantly or entirely *physical*, there are nevertheless accompanying psychological processes. It is the understanding of these processes that is my focus, while at the same time I acknowledge the purely physical aspect. Anna Freud adds to one's understanding: 'The child is unable to distinguish between feelings of suffering caused by the disease inside the body and suffering imposed on him from outside for the sake of curing the disease. He has to submit uncomprehendingly, helplessly and passively to both sets of experiences' (1952, p. 70).

So, to a child undergoing chemotherapy, as Robert is, the *repeated* experience of diarrhoea, nausea, and vomiting links with early infantile experiences of defecating, feeding, and being sick. Of course, in a healthy baby, as Robert seems to have been, good experiences hopefully outweighed the inevitable tummy pains, moments of feeling unheld, and infantile rage and distress. These earlier good experiences would help to mitigate some of the unpleasantness now encountered.

Therefore, if we try to understand how Robert feels, perhaps the vomit, or 'bad stuff', at a psychological level, feels rather like the anger at what is happening to his body or like poisonous medicine invading him. He cannot express this anger directly to the nurses, doctors, or parents; there seems to be a need, on the part of the staff, for him to be happy, even though there is much more for him to be angry than happy about.

As an illustration to this, at this point a doctor with a Scottish accent puts his head round the door and calls out, 'Come on, smile! I must teach you to speak Gaelic! Can you see what I'm doing under my mask?' Robert correctly deduces, 'Putting your tongue out!'

A nurse comes in again. I tell her that Robert has been sick. She says breezily, 'First time today!' I ask her about a bell for when I have to go. She places it near Robert and leaves the room.

I tell Robert that I will have to go soon, and that I'll be here again in a few days. I ask him if he remembers my days here? 'Yes, Tuesdays and Thursdays.' I confirm that I'll see him next Tuesday at two o'clock.

We pack up the box. I feel he is being bravely self-contained. I ask him if he wants me to pass him anything before I leave. He shakes his head.

I leave. He doesn't turn his head in my direction. A few minutes later I pass his door and glance through the glass panel. He's lying still, looking straight ahead.

After this session, I wonder for whose sake Robert has to be cheerful. And the doctor's emphasis on the damage to his father seems an unnecessary burden.

14 October (Tuesday) 2.00 p.m. I arrive to find Robert fast asleep, his mother sitting by him. Mrs Campbell tells me Robert has a high temperature. An electric fan is on by his side. Mother says he has been sleeping most of the day. He is wearing hospital pyjamas instead of his own smart ones. The hospital name is printed largely on the chest. It seems to indicate part of a general loss of individuality and autonomy. Loss of hair, loss of home, loss of freedom of movement...

After waiting a while, I write a brief note to Robert, telling him I visited and that he was asleep, and that I would see him on Thursday.

16 October (Thursday) 10.30 a.m. I look through the door and Mrs Campbell shakes her head at me. To warn me? To keep me away?

I had seen in the medical file that his condition had deteriorated considerably in the past twelve hours. The file mentions jaundice, haematemesis (vomiting up blood), pyrexia (fever), extreme bruising, liver dysfunction, oedema (swelling due to fluid retention), diarrhoea, poor platelets rise (poor response to platelet infusion), rash. Robert's rash, skin colour, jaundice, and general condition indicate that he has graft-versus-host disease. This occurs when the new, donated marrow reacts against the recipient's body. This disease may slow the growth of the new marrow and immune system and can in itself be fatal. Medication is given to fight this disease.

Mrs Campbell comes to see me at the door with tear-stained eyes. I say that I gather Robert is very poorly today. She tells me that he's much worse. I ask if I can still see him, and she agrees.

I am confronted by a shocking sight when I see Robert. There are reddish-blue patches around his eyes and mouth, his face is swollen, and the rest of his body is covered in a bizarre red rash. Even in the muted darkish room he appears in technicolour. Mrs Campbell understands intuitively that Robert wants to say something, approaching her son who then whispers in her ear. Robert wants Coca-Cola. Mrs Campbell says to me, 'Last night, do you know what he wanted to have with his medicine?! Tell us, Bobby!' Robert croaks, 'Vodka!' Mrs Campbell says, 'Next thing you'd be singing... and the doctors won't know what's going on when they come to take blood!' All this jollity seems bizarre in the face of Robert's appearance, but understandable as a defence.

Apparently Mr Campbell is giving platelets for Robert at this moment.

Robert very forcefully rejects medicine which Mrs Campbell tries to give him. Anna Freud explains this, referring to Klein:

> For some children the taking of medicine presents a major difficulty. Though the taste or smell of the drug is in the foreground so far as the child's conscious reasons are concerned, analytic investigation discloses invariably behind these rationalizations the existence of repressed ideas of being attacked by the mother through the symbol of the drug (Melanie Klein), of being poisoned... by her. (1952, p. 74)

He rejects other interventions. Mrs Campbell beseeches him. The nurse seems very sensitive to Robert's resistance. Robert still has a very high temperature. I feel that his very powerful rejection of medication is paradoxically a sign of his strength and his wish to live: he seems to be saying that he is not passively going to give in to all this paraphernalia, but is going to fight it in his own way. He is showing some autonomy when there is little enough of that now in his life.

Suddenly and unexpectedly he evacuates his bowels before he can ask for a bedpan. Mrs Campbell and I perform a major change of sheets, while Robert is very co-operative. His little body is so hot when I help to lift him. He peers to see his mother come and go through very puffy eyes. He doesn't want to wear pyjama trousers any longer.

A bed is then moved into the room for Mrs Campbell to sleep in at night, instead of the parents' shared room a little way away.

When Robert falls asleep, Mrs Campbell cries, saying to me, 'It's so sudden... he was so fine... did we do the right thing, bringing him here?' I try to acknowledge these doubts now that Robert seems worse, but add that if they hadn't tried this treatment they might have had regrets too.

Meanwhile Robert wakes and sleeps fitfully, biting his nails, shivering, and fiddling with his teeth when awake and shivering.

Then suddenly he is sick, very sick, vomiting in a projectile way. Momentarily Mrs Campbell recoils at the vomit all over her, and then quickly rallies and goes forward to help him. We both hold him. He vomits up a big clot of blood, and then says that now that 'the thing' at the back of his throat has gone, he feels better. Mrs Campbell tells me that she used to hate 'vomit and that sort of thing, but if it's your own child, it's different'. The Catholic priest puts his head round the door and asks how Robert is. Mrs Campbell says, 'Not too good, not too bad', and pops out to have a word with him in the corridor.

I say to Robert, 'This must be the worst you've felt so far...' He shakes his head. I ask what was worse? 'Radiotherapy,' he whispers. I say emphatically that that tells me how awful the radiotherapy must have been. (Yet radio-therapy is usually considered by patients to be less unpleasant than chemotherapy.)

When Mrs Campbell returns, I have to go. I feel that Thursday to Tuesday is such a long time when Robert's condition is so precarious, so I decide to come in again on Saturday. I say to Mrs Campbell (Robert is asleep), 'See you Saturday.' She shrugs, saying, 'Maybe, see how it goes...' She has tears in her eyes. She adds, 'You don't normally come in on Saturdays?' I say, 'No, but I will be this Saturday.' Mrs Campbell says, 'Thank you.' I feel that indirectly we have both acknowledged the gravity of the situation.

I speak to one of the ward sisters about Robert. She seems very understanding of Mrs Campbell's present situation. She talks of Mother's need for a place to cry and says that she tries to provide this, by talking to Mother alone. She says that Mr Campbell doesn't seem to know how seriously ill Robert is. I suggest that he cannot bear to acknowledge this; and with the exception of the support of the staff, Mrs Campbell is left alone with the realization of the severity of Robert's illness.

Sister seems very sensitive to Mrs Campbell as Robert's most important person. She is aware that Robert appropriately demands Mother as his nurse, but that Mother is becoming totally drained, as she is at Robert's beck and call practically all the time. Sister seems very supportive of my in-volvement, as indeed I am of hers.

Later, I think back to this session. I feel outrage at all this happening to a child. Then, on further reflection, I observe a regression in Robert from the baby that he seemed when I first met him, with his bald head, being cradled in his mother's arms, to this foetus-like state: his large head, his red colour (as if his skin is transparent), his curled-up posture, his dependence on sustenance from the 'umbilical' tubes entering his body. It is as if he is taking a path back into the womb, yet not towards life but towards death. 'In my beginning is my end' (Eliot, 1944).

Am I becoming over-involved? What do I mean by that? I find myself waking up in the middle of the night, confronted by the dreadful vision of Robert. I compare him with my own child of the same age: they have the same seven-year-old little shoulders, the same big new teeth, and yet set on such different paths. My child's robust physical health seems so precious, and makes Robert's state more poignant. Perhaps this pain I feel is a part of what is of value to him and to his mother: that I can, albeit peripherally, begin to comprehend and share some of their nightmare.

18 October (Saturday) 11.30 a.m. I feel faint as I leave the lift and walk towards the room. I tell myself that this is ridiculous. The hospital has enough to worry about without an over-involved child psychotherapist collapsing in the corridor. I feel worse. I tell myself that I can always leave, turn around and go home, tell people I have a cold and shouldn't see Robert. This 'escape clause' relieves the faint feeling.

Through the door, Robert looks even worse: more swollen and purple. Positioned outside the room, Mrs Campbell seems resistant to my going in to see him, saying something about not disturbing Robert. (Why? I quietly wonder if she feels fearful of my reactions to her son in this grotesque state? Or fearful that she would break down and cry if I gave her permission? Or anxious that I would talk to Robert about death?) I wait, walk off to see one of the other children on the ward, and then return, and look through the door. I see Mrs Campbell repeatedly stroking Robert's forehead, through her rubber gloves. It seems a pity that there is this barrier, as well as the mask and plastic apron, between mother and child.

Eventually, I enter the room when a nurse enters and disturbs the peace anyway. I stay for only a few minutes, when Mrs Campbell and I exchange a few words. I say to Mrs Campbell that the important aspect is that Robert has her with him. I think to myself about Mr Campbell hardly being around, so I ask Mrs Campbell about religion – does she find sustenance in that? She says she tries to pray but cannot.

After a few minutes, I say that I'll be back on Tuesday. She says, 'I hope we'll still be here...' and breaks down and cries. I put an arm around her.

21 October (Tuesday) 2.00 p.m. I gather at the haematology meeting that Robert has deteriorated further. There is a note in his file not to resuscitate him in the event of cardiac arrest. He has been bleeding rectally, and is on morphine to control the pain. The paediatric social worker and I wonder if we should talk to the senior house officer about whether barrier-nursing (especially masks and gloves) could be dispensed with now, in order to give Robert and his mother closer contact. (The effectiveness of barrier-nursing is scientifically debatable. For example, masks can only effectively keep germs at bay for a couple of minutes.) In the meeting, anxiety over Mr Campbell is expressed: he seems so 'out' of all this, possibly feeling guilty over his donations of bone marrow and platelets not helping. He goes to the chapel frequently, wanders around the hospital and goes to the pub, while Mrs Campbell is with Robert all the time. Yet Robert so clearly needs his mother, checking up on her presence all the time. Mr Campbell was going back home to fetch Julie but that is felt by the parents no longer to be appropriate while Robert looks so dreadful. Apparently, when Robert's appearance suddenly changed, Mr Campbell could not face him.

On my way to seeing Robert, I meet Mr Campbell. He says his son is somewhat better, and asks me how *I* am. *He's* just given another lot of platelets, and looks shell-shocked. He goes off to find his wife, as they are both due to meet with the paediatric social worker.

I don mask, gloves, and apron, and go in to see Robert. He is on his own, lying there, still, his eyes open. He looks grotesque. His head seems so large. I angrily retort to myself that I thought they said in the file that they had reduced the swelling! He is a deep purple colour. His eyes are now affected: they are bloodshot, the pupils look grey and clouded, and the puffy lids make it difficult for him to open them properly. He is lying on his side, awake, quietly poking his fingers into his nostrils. The pillowcase is smeared with streaks of blood. His fingers look so frail in contrast to his head. I say, 'Hello, Robert, Mrs Judd has come to see you.' After a while, I ask if Mum has gone to lunch? He nods. He coughs an awful rattling cough. He seems so approachable in spite of everything.

I lean over towards him and talk about remembering when he played with the toys I brought ... the little hospital scene, and I briefly recount some of the play he had enacted. He seems to listen intently. A nurse come and goes, checks the drip and gives Robert a drink.

I hear his mother's voice in the corridor. He seems to be listening too. I ask if he can hear Mum's voice. He nods. Mrs Campbell enters, saying to Robert immediately, 'You've been picking at your nose again! I wasn't too long, was I?' Robert points to his cup. 'Drink?' asks Mrs Campbell. 'I'll get you some fresh ...' 'No! That is fresh! I already had a drink!' Robert bursts out, loud and clear. I tell Mrs Campbell that the nurse gave him one a few minutes ago.

Then Robert says, 'I want to go!' and Mrs Campbell smiles and fetches the bedpan. She uncovers Robert whose abdomen is now plump and swollen, purple all over except for whiter-than-white speckled areas on his thin legs and hands. I wonder *what he feels* about the state of his body.

I offer to help but they have their own routine by now. Robert hangs around Mrs Campbell's neck and lifts himself onto the bedpan. He suddenly burps loudly, saying 'Pardon me!' Mrs Campbell says, 'Of course, my love.' Robert urinates and defecates copiously. His arms look strong as he leans back on them. Mrs Campbell wipes him, while Robert beseeches, 'Quickly!' As Robert lowers himself back onto the bed, he complains violently about the pain. Mrs Campbell acknowledges this pain 'in the tummy', as Robert settles down on his back now with relief. I say, 'It must feel better now you can tell when you need the bedpan, Bobby.'

He beckons to his mother, whispering in her ear. Mrs Campbell duly announced, 'You don't want to be called "Bobby", only "Robert".' I say, 'Of course... perhaps you feel "Bobby" is a little boy's name, and Robert is a big boy's name?' He nods. Mrs Campbell says, 'When you go home we'll have to tell Julie that... she'll have to stop calling you "Bobby"?' He nods.

The sister comes in to check Robert's drip and lines. Mrs Campbell says, 'Where would we be without it?' (She is referring to the almost constant infusion of medicine and food via the catheter.)

In a little while Mrs Campbell calls him 'Bobby' and then checks herself. I say, 'Perhaps only Mum can call you that... it's Mum's special name for you.' He nods.

He says his eyes are itchy, and Mrs Campbell wipes the lids with tissues. Robert begins to fiddle with what seems to be his genitals under the sheets and then demands, 'Cotton buds!' Mrs Campbell gives him one. Robert pokes repeatedly into each ear, examining closely the substance on the cotton-wool. Mrs Campbell remarks that Robert has always liked poking into his ears. I do not have to wonder long to myself about the significance of that – for Robert gives Mrs Campbell the cotton bud and demands another. She says reproachfully, 'What for?' Robert says, 'You know well enough what for!' Mrs Campbell resignedly gives him one. Robert pokes around under the sheets. She says, 'They're not for bottoms!' Robert replies, 'Well this one is!' I think to myself that for someone who is on morphine, he is remarkably alive. Or perhaps the morphine disinhibits him.

(Clifford Yorke [1985] writes about a seriously ill girl focusing on a stye on her eye to the exclusion of a recent amputation she has undergone. He writes, 'Does the displacement of her anxieties to the comparatively trivial matter of the stye have a defensive and, in the circumstances, adaptive function?')

Mrs Campbell looks exhausted. Robert continues to be very busy under the sheets.

I say to Mrs Campbell, but also to Robert, that perhaps it is important for Robert to get different, maybe pleasurable, sensations from his body at the moment, when there is so much *dis*comfort; perhaps this reassures him in the face of feeling so uncomfortable.

Mrs Campbell nods half-heartedly, as if it is the least of her worries what Robert might be up to. Robert then brandishes a soiled cotton-bud, which Mrs Campbell wraps in tissue and disposes of.

Greenacre has written about children who are hospitalized and kept immobile for long periods of time: 'prolonged early restraint, producing a condition in which stimulations to the body far exceeded possible motor discharges, also resulted in an increased general body erotization' (1980, p. 105).

I feel quite surprised and, in a sense, relieved by his liveliness and mischievousness. It is a delicate area, where he is engaged in an activity which should be allowed to be private, and yet he is carrying it out in front of his mother and me, albeit under the sheets. As he has scarcely any privacy, it may be erroneous to deduce that this is a direct communication to us.

However, upon reflection later, I realize that I am caught up in his denial, and am avoiding the underlying meanings of his activity and his mood. With hindsight, I ponder the possible accompanying masturbatory phantasies of passive and active identifications with either parent. He may have phantasies of getting inside his mother's body, in order to fuse with her. The sense of triumph he conveys suggests this, with its avoidance of any sense of loss or damage. It may carry a wider meaning of an omnipotent attempt to wipe away all his sickness.

These thoughts, along with many others, remain at the back of my mind. In this setting with the many interruptions and intrusions, I cannot really attempt to analyse much of the material with Robert to the level at which I might take it in long-term psychotherapy.

I say I have to go soon. Robert then pipes up, 'I'm bored!' I ask him and his mother what he does in the long hours of lying here? (There is a tape-recorder and a television in the room.) Storytapes? Music? Mrs Campbell says, 'Yes... and I read to him.' I mention that Lorraine, the teacher, is away this week, as it is half-term. Mrs Campbell said she had not realized that. (As Lorraine visits Robert several times a week, I feel it is important to spell out the holiday, in case Mrs Campbell feels that the teachers have given up on Robert.)

Mrs Campbell seems deflated in the face of Robert asking for further input. So I say, 'When I come on Thursday, I'll bring the toys... even if you cannot play much, we'll see what you can manage. Goodbye.' Mrs Campbell thanks me. (I leave wondering if perhaps I should have brought the therapy box this time.)

I think back upon his condition today: he is invaded by tubes, thermometers, needles, swabs, and now he pokes into most of the orifices of his body. I wonder if this is an attack on himself, or an exploration at a more infantile level? Perhaps some of his exploration would not be noticed and would be a 'normal' part of his life if he were well, and not being scrutinized and monitored. He has scarcely any privacy left. Whose body is it now?

I also wonder about his self-image now. He still looks grotesque. I hope he has not seen himself in the mirror, but he is, of course, aware of the great changes to his body and limbs. In a sense, an infant sees him- or herself reflected in the mother's eyes. 'What does the baby see when he or she looks at the mother's face? I am suggesting that, ordinarily, what the baby sees is himself or herself. In other words the mother is looking at the baby and *what she looks like is related to what she sees there*' (Winnicott, 1974, p. 131). I feel that the foregoing applies to the older child as well, especially to one who has regressed to a more infantile level and finds him- or herself utterly dependent upon mother and other care-givers.

I then think about Kohut (1977, p. 76) who writes about the parent, usually the mother, who responds to the child who 'seeks confirmation by the mirroring self-object'. The child may then encounter a 'joyful, prideful parental attitude' or, if not experienced as an aesthetic object, a rejecting one. This inability to respond to the child as a whole or even as a collection of part-objects leads the child to feelings of fragmentation and depletion.

This leads me to wonder further about the serious disease which invades Robert's body and makes it impossible for his parents to have a positive attitude towards his whole self. Winnicott (1972) uses the term 'personalization' to describe the existence of a satisfactory working arrangement between mind and body: 'Healthy feelings of personalization have their origins in, and are based upon, positive parental attitudes towards the child's body. When these are not present, the child's resultant attitude toward his own body will be critically impaired.'

Therefore one can see how both parents and child have to keep in mind the healthy body that once was, in order to retain hopefulness for a return to that state.

So I wonder what Robert sees now when he looks into his mother's eyes. We know that, understandably, his father avoids being in his room for long, as he seems to find the sight of him too painful. How difficult it must be for either parent to feed back anything optimistic in their eyes, especially when they try to use denial and yet their underlying feelings show through.

As well, he is draining his mother with demands, thus contributing to a vicious circle of a depleted 'breast' or mother which cannot satisfy his needs. This perhaps symbolizes what the whole of life has become for him.

23 October (Thursday) 10.00 a.m. Peter (the paediatric social worker) and I meet. He has talked to Mr Campbell about the possibility of Robert dying. Apparently the parents cannot talk to each other or share any of this. Mr Campbell cannot look at Robert and cannot realize that it is the same child. He prays a great deal. Later, one of the ward sisters describes Mrs Campbell praying to St Rita, the Patron Saint of 'desperate cases' and Mr Campbell saying, 'Oh well, sister, God wants him.'

We go off to the ward together. The 'protective isolation' sticker has been peeled off the door. Masks, gloves, etc., are no longer outside the room. So Peter's discussion with the doctors on barrier-nursing being lifted was effective. We wonder, though, if the parents (and possibly Robert) will read this as a sign of the hospital giving up.

We enter the room. There is a peaceful atmosphere: as it is a dull day, a sombre light pervades the room. There is a sense of normality about seeing both parents sitting in the room, and both without masks. Mr Campbell is sitting in a chair where his view of Robert is obscured by the locker. Mrs Campbell looks very thin.

Robert seems to be sleeping. They tell us that he is much better: they are pleased with the blood count – the platelets are helping. Mr Campbell will be donating more platelets on Saturday. They say Robert is brighter in himself too. Peter says, 'So he's better in himself, even if his body isn't very well?' Mrs Campbell says, 'Yes – and the blood count *is* better – let's hope he'll be able to start making platelets himself now.'

Robert half opens his eyes. Mrs Campbell goes up to him. He opens his mouth. 'Drink?' He nods, and sips the chocolate milk, struggling to swallow. 'Enough,' he says. He tells Mrs Campbell about a 'kind of little bottle ... in the advertisement'. His voice is as clear as a bell. Mrs Campbell listens attentively.

Peter invites the parents to have a coffee and a chat. Mr Campbell accepts, while Mrs Campbell says she would rather stay with Robert.

Robert requests the bedpan. He leans back on strong arms. His enormously swollen, shiny, distended belly appears to me to be almost obscene on this little boy.

I think I am momentarily in touch with a deep instinctual biological reaction to the trauma or shock of what I see: to withdraw, avoid, or shun that which seems to have gone beyond a reasonable chance of survival. This brief awareness is in conflict with a predominantly nurturing instinct, and may indeed be felt by most of those who encounter the severely ill or profoundly disabled. It is an aspect which may be less shameful if more openly shared and understood.

Mrs Campbell then decides to go and have some lunch – so Robert requests, via his mother, that I read him a story. He specifies *Snow White*. Mrs Campbell leaves.

He seems to listen intently, even though his eyes are shut. The story seems particularly poignant – the drops of blood on the snow are the vital fluid which create Snow White – and seems to link with the emphasis on blood in Robert's illness and treatment.

The 'mirror, mirror on the wall' aspect of the story reminds me of my earlier thoughts about mirrors and mothers' eyes. Robert looks into his mother's eyes/mirror. Can Mother reflect back, and if so, what? And, of course, this is a story about the extreme and destructive envy of the wicked step-mother Queen, when Snow White is aged seven – exactly Robert's age. I wonder to myself about Robert's possible underlying anxieties and phantasies: of his infantile wish to have Mummy all to himself, leading to fears of an attack or retaliation for such phantasies by his mother or father in the form of this illness.

I pause, and ask him if he wants me to continue reading. He nods. I say, 'Seven years old, like you. And you made a little white figure in plasticine, perhaps like Snow White.' I take it out of the box. Robert doesn't want to look at it. I say, 'Perhaps you don't want to think about when you were able to do more.' His breathing is laboured.

Nurses pop in and out throughout. Some seem puzzled about who I am and what I'm doing there.

I ask Robert if it's difficult to breathe. He nods. There is a long silence. He is struggling, giving little moans, his eyes closed.

I say, 'I wonder if there's anything you want to try and talk about... any worries you might have.' There is a silence. I go on '... about where this is going to lead?' He doesn't respond. I don't know what he's hearing. He makes little twitches and occasional grimaces. I find myself having to summon courage to put thoughts into words beyond the point of comfort. I continue, '... whether there may be things you can't talk to Mum or Dad about, because you don't want to worry them, or upset them.' He nods. Further silence. Then I say, 'You must sometimes wonder how long this will go on for, and if you *are* going to get better.' He gives another little nod. I feel immensely sad.

I stroke his forehead for the first time. It's so soft and silky and warm. He seems to like it. I feel relieved that we no longer have to wear gloves. Dispensing with this rubber barrier parallels what feels like the more important removal of an emotional barrier between us.

I stay a little while quietly by him and then have to go, and put the bell by him. He has hardly opened his eyes since Mother left. I feel he reserves that way of actively 'holding on' with his eyes for when his mother is in the room.

I say goodbye, and mention to him that we can carry on with the story book next time if he wants. I tell him that the bell is by him.

I leave, and tell one of the nurses that Robert is alone.

Later, in talking to one of the sisters in the corridor, she expresses her upset at the 'grotesque appearance' of Robert. 'Bloated, absolutely awful, absolutely horrendous', she says. 'And he's conscious of what's happening to him, and looking at it, and so aware that his body is not functioning properly', she continues. I feel relieved that this sister, with her many years of experience of this work, including similar leukaemic cases, is also in touch with what we agree is 'torture'.

I come across a saying by Hippocrates: 'Extreme remedies are most appropriate for extreme diseases' (c. 460–357 BC). I wonder about that. Perhaps that attitude, which still seems to be around today, needs to be re-appraised.

That evening, on the telephone, Peter tells me that Robert's lungs are in a bad state. Apparently, the medical team is surprised by the improved blood count.

I have the fantasy of cooking wholesome soup for mother and bringing it to the hospital. They must be tired of the hospital diet. But, of course, I am prompted by my feelings of frustration and impotence: if I cannot 'feed' Robert more, perhaps I could concretely nourish his most important care-giver.

25 October (Saturday) I telephone the ward to ask how he is, and hear that he has been moved to the intensive care unit, mainly because of difficulty breathing.

27 October (Monday) I hear that Robert is back in his own room.

28 October (Tuesday) 2.00 p.m. I go to the ward, and on my way to reading his medical notes, I hear terrible yelling coming from Robert's room. I ask Carol, his special friend (an auxiliary nurse), who is walking by, if Robert is alone. We both go in. Robert is alone, and he's screaming, *'Mummy!'* His bloodshot eyes look redder than ever and are *wide* open. Robert seems caught in the grip of severe anxiety – possibly separation anxiety. Underlying the fear of separation in a young child is the fear of complete abandonment and thence of being left to die, as I explain in Chapter 2. I feel that Robert's terror at this moment has the raw primitive quality of a fear of death.

Carol countermands, 'What are you screaming for? What do you want? Why don't you use the bell? You'll hurt your throat. Want the bedpan?' Robert nods. So Carol helps him; now Robert hangs around Carol's neck, as he's no longer strong enough to support himself on his arms.

While in this 'embrace' Carol lovingly caresses Robert's swollen body, calling him 'Little Prince'. Then she wipes him, asking each time, 'Enough?' Robert says, 'Not quite', each time. Carol seems amused and continues until Robert is content. Carol is also Scottish. This seems to contribute to a special closeness with the family.

Then she covers Robert who says he is cold. Carol says she will fetch another blanket.

Robert is now less red, and looks less swollen than previously. He has an oxygen supply, pumped out in puffs near his face. Carol asks Robert if he would like toast and he nods. 'With marmalade?' He nods again.

While Carol is out I ask Robert if he would like to see the box of toys. He nods. I take out the family he has used before, with the pram and the baby. I feel he is too weak to play actively, but he looks at it with great interest.

Carol brings the toast, and Robert nibbles tiny bits. He seems to dislike the marmalade, so Carol says, 'OK. I'll get you jam', and leaves.

Robert tries to spit out the shreds of marmalade. He accurately eliminates the lumps one by one for me to wipe off his tongue. I am reminded of an infant who has not yet accepted lumpy food. Moreover, I have the increasing impression that symbolically Robert is pushing out 'dirt', or bad stuff, or the illness, at others, as his way of actively trying to spit out or evacuate it.

We continue with the toy family. Robert seems to look intently at the baby. I talk about previous times when he more actively created the play: how he had said this was the strong Mummy who helps the Daddy and the baby, and how he must feel like that baby now that he feels weak. I begin to explore this further with him: about him needing Mummy so much, and crying out for her. At this point Mrs Campbell arrives.

She seems bright and well, and immediately shows interest in a letter that has arrived for Robert from their doctor in Scotland. Mother says that she must try and telephone the doctor as she finds it hard to write. She asks Robert if he would like a drink. He shakes his head. I fill Mrs Campbell in a little about Robert calling out for her, needing the bedpan, and getting toast from Carol.

Mrs Campbell senses that we are busy, so says, 'I'll leave you.'

I get out the box of assorted animals. Robert seems particularly attentive to the baby kangaroo that fits in the mother's pouch. I refer to him being in a sort of pouch, or inside-place, now: the bed, being fed by tubes. He looks at me and then handles the two baby lambs. There is a pause. I ask him if he remembers playing with them before. He shakes his head. I leave his possible defence against remembering that the baby doll had thought these lambs were 'horrible' and frightening in a previous session. He picks up the hippo, as he calls it (which is really a rhinoceros). I say 'This is the animal that was angry before...and perhaps you too feel angry at all that is happening to you.'

He picks up the white plasticine little figure he had made before, and stares at it. I say, 'Perhaps you're remebering how we talked about this little boy that you made not having hair, like you?' He nods.

He asks for the hospital set of figures. We put the other toys away. But he doesn't play with the hospital set. I become aware that I might be feeling that I have to inject life into him – sensing an over-energetic streak in me that *wants* him to play.

So I sit quietly. After a while I talk to him about him having some worries and some questions that he might not want to talk to Mum or Dad about. He nods. There is quite a long silence. I say that it seems hard for him to talk, so does he want me to ask the sort of questions that I think might be in his mind? He nods. I go on, 'Perhaps, you wonder if you *will* get better.' He nods, opens his eyes more fully, and looks at me. I say, 'Of course, no one can know the answer to that.' He tries to say something, but cannot manage it. His tongue is moving against his teeth. I go on, 'These are big questions in your mind. Rather than you feeling all alone with them, we can share them.' Again he tries to talk. (I wonder whether his brain is affected by the stress or the drugs. The teacher had said that Robert couldn't talk easily. How much of his inability is emotional? Perhaps, the dread and anxiety is too much for him to formulate?)

His tongue movements, and failure to enunciate, lead me to feel that there is a 'nameless dread' I have to try to talk about. Robert is now very still, his eyes closed. Carol comes back with the requested jam. Robert opens his eyes. Carol leaves.

Robert asks for the *Snow White* story again, so I continue with that. He seems very interested in the illustrations. I think to myself about the sensory privation of being in a hospital bed, in a small room, for so long, and how his eyes seem to feed on the extended vistas opened up by the pictures and the story.

When we reach the part of the story where Snow White recovers a second time from near-death, I pause to say that perhaps Robert wants to hear this story because it is about a child like him, who nearly died three times and then gets better each time. He seems to listen to what I am saying, but does not react.

Soon after that I have to go. I show him the bell. He is very still and quiet as I leave.

30 October (Thursday) 10.30 a.m. I see from the medical notes that Robert's blood pressure was considerably raised the day before.

I go into the room. There are fresh flowers in a vase for the first time. This is one of the advantages of him not being barrier-nursed, as flowers were not allowed then. (Besides the restrictions to normal life I have already mentioned, before the platelet level has risen and therefore while there is a strong risk of infection, leukaemic children cannot eat anything that is not sterilized by first being put in a microwave oven. Chocolate is not allowed at this hospital because it cannot be sterilized. Animals or pets would certainly not be allowed. The danger of infection being transmitted by pets is considered by most hospitals to be serious enough to recommend that when the patient goes home, they are not brought into contact with pets for a while.)

Mrs Campbell tells me, 'I don't think he'll be up to much. He's been awake all night. The oxygen kept him awake.'

Robert looks grey now that he is less red and purple. I ask Mrs Campbell if she too was up all night. She nods. Yet, surprisingly, she looks pretty and bright today.

Mrs Campbell asks Robert if he wants to be more upright? 'No.' So Mother leaves the room, telling us where she will be.

The television is on loudly. Robert seems to be avidly watching a programme about a child flying a kite. We watch together. I ask him if he has ever flown a kite? 'No.' 'Has Julie?' 'No.' I suggest that by watching this, maybe he'd like to be able to fly high in the sky like the kite, and in that way get right away from all his worries, away from the hospital and from being ill.

He nods, looking serious. When the programme ends he asks me to make him higher, so I crank up the back-rest, thinking that he has thus perhaps affirmed my interpretation.

He asks to play with the hospital set. I get it out. But as he seems too weak to play actively, I ask him if he wants to tell me what to do with the figures. He instructs me to put the doll's tiny hat in the locker. This is something he had done the first time he played with the set. I say that this seems to be his way of making sure that the little boy doll and he, himself, would get better: if the outer clothes are kept in the locker for when he can leave the hospital. He then designates the lady doll as the mother and the man as the priest. He denotes the latter by turning his collar round.

I comment that he doesn't want him to be the Dad, perhaps because he feels angry with his Dad.

He places the little boy in the bed, and tiny plastic flowers in a vase by the bed. Meanwhile, he is picking his nose, and shows me brownish stuff in his mouth. He grunts as if to tell me to do something about it. I mop up his mouth with tissues. He grimaces. I ask if it tastes awful. He says, 'Yes', and fiddles with the mucus on his hands from his nose.

Again, I feel he tries to project into me his disgust with his illness. He seems to act out a phantasy that the whole of his inside is full of dirt and contamination – which is not far from the truth.

I comment on his feeling so full of so much bad stuff coming out of his nose and mouth, and I wonder if it comes up now when I talk about his not wanting the Dad in the play. 'You can keep the Dad out of the play, but you can't help what's happening to your body.' He continues to fiddle with the mucus. I say, 'Perhaps, it's important for you to be able to do this, when you have so much done to your body . . . *this* is something you have control over.'

He seemes disinclined to play further with the toys. I ask him if he wants plasticine? He nods. I ask him what colour? He says emphatically, 'Dark pink.' He first uses one hand, then both, and soon has fashioned a shark. I ask him what thoughts he has about this shark? He seems too exhausted to contribute more. So I say that a shark is fierce and biting. He nods. I say, 'Maybe you feel like a red angry shark, wanting to bite: angry about not being well for so long . . .' (At another level perhaps Robert feels at the receiving end, assaulted by the shark/illness.)

He then asks me to make something. I comply, although I think to myself that I probably would not do so in a 'normal' psychotherapy setting, where it may be preferable to avoid adding my own fantasies or creations, as this could complicate what the child is bringing. Am I, like Carol, wanting to grant him any wish? This feels very understandable if someone's life is limited. I make him a tiny yellow bear, like his special 'Sunshine', and ask him if he knows who it is. He guesses correctly.

He requests more of the *Snow White* story. We carry on from where we left off. Again he is very interested in the illustrations. Meanwhile, nurses pop in and out, taking blood-pressure, etc. One of them seems very interested in my role and later wants to share thoughts about Robert.

I have to leave. He asks me to call his mother. I leave my version of Sunshine with him, and he agrees to my packing up the shark in the same little box where I kept his previous plasticine model.

Later, I see Peter, who has spoken to the parents while I saw Robert. He says they are 'poles apart': Mrs Campbell is talking along the lines of, 'What if Robert dies . . . what if I saw him in a coffin . . . what would it feel like . . .', while Mr Campbell is unable to listen and distracts with his conversation. However, Mrs Campbell says that over-riding *hope* has kept her going.

Now that Robert has survived the intensive treatment crisis and is a little better, perhaps Mrs Campbell can now talk about her fears. And perhaps, simultaneously, she is distancing herself somewhat from Robert – preparing herself for his death – for she seems to be in Robert's room less.

I talk to one of the ward sisters, who feels that Robert picks his nose for attention: the resultant bleeding creates the fuss he wants. She says all leukaemic patients do this. I put forward my thoughts about the nose-picking, and the other intrusive things he does to other parts of his body, as perhaps the result of frustration and anger that he feels about being ill and in such a closed-in world, where the only outlet, and way of mastering and controlling the situation, is his own body. She seems interested in my thoughts.

We talk about Mother seeing less of Robert these days. Sister says that, nevertheless, Mother is still doing most of the nursing. She adds that she is very aware of Father hardly being there, and that it is a pity that Mother and Father do not share much with each other.

4 November (Tuesday) I hear at a meeting how much better Robert is, in spite of frequent profuse nose-bleeds even when nose-packs are in.

2.00 p.m. I go in. Mrs Campbell is reading letters and cards to Robert who is *sitting* up in bed, wearing over-large hospital pyjamas. The play leader has apparently been in to see him earlier: a large dressed-up teddy is on the bed. Robert sits on his bent legs beneath him. Mrs Campbell hardly says 'hello', and carries on reading. Again, I feel she resents my visit, especially after I've not seen Robert for four days. Robert too barely acknowledges me.

Robert complains about his eyes, so Mrs Campbell gives him a tissue. Robert is then busy fiddling with a loose tooth. I comment on what he is doing and Mrs Campbell tells me that the tooth is hanging on a thread. I think about all the normal bodily processes that seven-year-olds go through and which, of course, are still happening to Robert in spite of everything.

Mrs Campbell says she has to see Peter about a refund on a plane ticket (this was intended for Mr Campbell to fly home to fetch Julie, but Robert's recent crisis forced a cancellation). Robert whines, 'Don't go.' Mrs Campbell suggests Robert plays with the toys I've brought, and tells him to be a good boy. She leaves, Robert waching her with bated breath.

I say, 'It's difficult when Mum goes out . . . when you need her so much . . . and perhaps you don't want me in here?' He shakes his head. I say, 'I'm not sure what that means. Perhaps I talk about things you don't want me to?' He replies, 'No . . . you don't.' Meanwhile, he is poking into his nose, examining smears on his fingers.

I talk to him about how busy he is with his nose, and how important it must be to be the one who decides now about poking in, when doctors and nurses have to poke in a lot these days, in different ways. (Later, I think that my arrival in Robert's room probably felt similarly intrusive to Mrs Campbell and possibly to Robert.)

The drip suddenly makes a loud gurgling noise. I say, 'The drip is deciding to feed you. Even your tummy isn't deciding when it's hungry . . . It's being automatically fed every few minutes.' He nods.

After a pause, I ask him if he would like to do a drawing (see p. 000). He nods. I get out the thick felt tip pens, and he non-verbally asks for help with the stiff lids.

He draws a layer of sky, then the sun, and then six big birds, like the letter 'm', forming a further layer. Then a purple figure, smiling. There is no ground line. He adds orange hair. I wonder to myself about the purplish skin he has, but only comment on the hair being like the hair Robert had when he was well. He nods. I go on, 'And like the hair you'd like to have again.' He nods again. He leans back and looks at the picture. It seemed quite an effort. I ask him if he wants to tell me more about it. He is quiet. I comment on the birds being like 'm' for Mummy, forming a sort of blanket above the little boy Robert, 'protecting you, like Mummy does'. I tell him that I will keep the drawing safely in the box. He agrees.

And then he blurts out, 'I want my Mummy. Will you ask her to come here please?' I say that he seemed to want her when I talked about the mummy birds. I then ask if there is any particular reason why he wants her (thinking it may be a need for the bedpan). Robert says, 'I just want her.'

I go out to find Mrs Campbell and discover that she is meeting with Peter, so I return and explain to Robert that she's busy talking to Peter but will be back in a little while.

He begins a second drawing, now sitting up much more. He seems more able to express himself through drawing than through talking. He draws a blue neat sky, filling in any spaces assiduously. A nurse comes in to take his blood pressure while he is drawing and Robert reluctantly allows her to interrupt. He suddenly asks me in a shrill voice, 'Can you leave the pens here with me?' I say, 'Yes, of course . . . and the pad of paper. You may want to draw when I'm not here, and you could show me your drawings, when I come again.'

The nurse leaves. I expand further to Robert that the drawings he does with me we are understanding together, so it is important for us to keep them in the box to look back on – whereas, of course, it's up to him what he does with the drawings he produces when I'm not here. He nods emphatically in agreement.

He then draws green grass, and a careful row of eight trees or plants. He inserts a smiling figure between the sixth and the seventh tree.

I think to myself about the eight trees, about him being eight next birthday, and about him becoming ill between six and seven. I ask him who the person is. He says, 'You!' I ask what I'm doing in the picture. 'Playing.'

I ask if he has any thoughts about anything else in the picture? He doesn't respond and seems tired. We look at the two pictures, side by side. I say that he made one of himself and one of me, perhaps telling us about his times with me being a time to look back to when he was well, to remember the fresh air and the green grass and the trees in these summer pictures, and all the things he misses. I comment on this second picture perhaps showing him, too, as he was, playing and happy. (I think to myself that perhaps this too is an attempt to integrate his present state with his pre-illness state, as well as a representation of a Mrs Judd who carries on living after he dies.)

He seems to want to stop. As I put the tops back on the pens he tells me in his characteristically emphatic way that grey is his favourite colour. I say,

'Mmm ... it's very different from a bright colour, like red ... perhaps you're saying that grey is more like how you feel now ... sort of sad or dull.' He nods.

We sit in silence for a while. I say, 'You've shown me often how much you notice colours ... how they can fit in with what you feel ... like ...' and I show him the white plasticine figure he had made. 'Your skin was white then.' He nods, making direct eye contact with me. I then talk about the red shark he made, when his skin was looking red and angry, and perhaps he felt angry.

There is a silence. I say, 'You're letting me know that you don't feel like being happy, or smiling. You feel fed up much of the time. Perhaps it's hard for you to be cheerful and smiling for other people.'

He nods meaningfully.

I say that I have to go now, and that I'll be back the day after tomorrow. I tell him that I'll try to find his Mum. I forget my handbag – this obvious reluctance on my part to leave is no surprise – and return. He is fingering the box of felt-tips, and seems to be taken by surprise at my re-entering.

Later, I look back on those pictures, and have further thoughts: in the first picture, the layer of birds not only adds to the encapsulating quality of the hair and purple head but also keeps the sun and sky away. It seems to reflect the present hospitalization as well as, possibly, echo the previous well child aged six (the six birds). The lack of a ground-line suggests a feeling of not being held, echoing his earlier play with the toppling vase of flowers. Perhaps this is exacerbated when his mother goes out.

In the second picture the firm ground-line possibly conveys a feeling of now feeling held by my attention. Again the *six* trees are emphasized by the positioning of the figure – registering the onset of the illness – and although he designates this figure as 'Mrs Judd playing' it embodies Robert in protective identification with a living, playing me. In other words, he wants to put himself into me and thereby be saved and go on living. I think the years stretching ahead are my years, not his. Perhaps – if these *are* trees – the larger-than-life figure reaching upwards to the sky conveys an awareness of his impending 'journey' to heaven, which may be his way of conceptualizing death. (Indeed, his little plasticine figure also had upstretched arms.) (See Appendix 1 for further analysis of these drawings.)

6 November (Thursday) The playleader tells me Robert enjoyed squirting 'silly string' all over the room the night before, as it was Bonfire Night, and he had made 'hair' for himself. I notice that the medical notes state a marked improvement: his blood-pressure is more stable, and the bruising is described as 'old'. Sister tells me that Robert has a mouth infection.

I ask sister about the possibility of some undisturbed time with Robert with perhaps a sign on the door – except, of course, for really necessary medical procedures. Sister is dubious and suggests I ask the doctors.

10.30 a.m. When I enter the room, two radiographers are just leaving with their equipment, after taking X-rays. Robert is intently watching a television drama about boys and girls. He remains absorbed, while I sit by him, and watch it with him. Nurses come in and out. Robert seems to be vicariously joining in their lives of gardens, boy- and girl-friends, and dancing.

When it ends I suggest I turn the sound off. He nods. He has been busy pulling at scabs on his lip. I comment on what he is doing. He nods and continues. His fingers look bloodstained.

We are both silent. I notice some drawings he has done in my absence – and ask him if I can look at them. He nods. One is very colourful, of the sun, coloured birds, a big tree, and a row of flowers. Another is a night sky with coloured shapes in it, and the third is of a big black cloud, with grey sky, rain, and lightning. I describe them aloud. He nods. I ask him if he has further ideas about these pictures? He looks at me and then at the pictures. I ask if perhaps the happier one was before he was ill? He nods. I suggest that he sometimes feels fed up and very unhappy, like the black cloud in a grey sky, and perhaps angry like the flashing lightning – but that he has also shown a brighter colourful side, with the sun shining.

He asks for the box. I open it, and he takes out the box of animals. He examines the crocodile's opening and closing mouth avidly, opening the jaws as wide as possible. Then he inserts the foal's legs, and closes the jaws on them, thus lifting the foal; then feeds the giraffe to the jaws as well. I talk to him about the crocodile's biting teeth and jaws being like his own angry and biting feelings, like the shark he made before. He repeats the scene, perhaps needing to repeat because he has not fully understood. I suggest that when he picks at his lip he is attacking himself rather like this crocodile attacks the helpless baby horse, and at the same time he feels rather like the helpless foal, being attacked by the illness. He leans back and seems to relax. We are silent. Then I say that he seems to feel tired, that playing takes quite an effort. He nods.

He looks down at the Hickman catheter that enters his chest. I ask him if he can feel it. He says, 'No.' (I think to myself that at this moment he is calmly acquiescing to the treatment.)

He seems to be listening to all the sounds . . . of voices, footsteps, other TVs, machines, his drip machine. He turns to look at the door when footsteps approach. I ask him what he is listening for? 'Mum.' I say, 'You feel you need Mum almost all the time?' He nods in a rather desperate way, and then rubs his eye. I ask if it's itchy. 'Yes.' I think to myself about the irritable eye as a reminder of a needy uncomfortable part of him. There is silence. I talk about

Robert feeling 'grey', not wanting to be cheerful. He nods, looking very depressed.

I say, 'We can share your sad feelings. Perhaps you're not only sad about being ill, but also sad about being away from home, away from Julie... I wonder what you miss most... Now that your body seems a bit better, it seems you feel more fed up than when you were really ill, and sleeping a lot.' He seems to take all this in.

He then looks at me beseechingly and says, 'You tell Mummy I want her!' I say, 'Yes... but I wonder why... is it a feeling that you need something special, or what?' 'No, I just want her!' he replies desperately.

I think to myself that Robert feels that his mother is distancing herself, leading to fantasies that he is abandoned or unwanted. Perhaps my emotional availability stirs up this pain in him. Again, this is so unlike an 'ordinary' psychotherapeutic relationship where I may have stayed with the child's anxiety in order to understand it further, rather than rushing to relieve it.

I go to find Mrs Campbell. She has her coat on, ready to go out, and comes back to Robert's room, with Mr Campbell. Mr Campbell asks Robert how he's feeling. 'Leave me alone!' he growls. Father sits down and reads the newspaper.

Mrs Campbell decides not to go out. There is an exchange between mother and son about mayonnaise making him sick the night before, while Mrs Campbell spreads cracker-biscuits with mayonnaise and Robert devours them hungrily.

Meanwhile, Mr Campbell talks to me about Peter being away this week, adding that he was always very busy anyway. (Doubtless, Mr Campbell has a great need to talk to someone about Robert's rejection of him.)

He asks Robert if his legs still feel weak. He snarls, 'Leave me alone!' I comment on seeing this anger directly for the first time, and suggest that Robert needs to put bad feelings into his father, but that it's hard for him. Father nods feelingly while making a pretence of reading the paper.

My understanding of this process, in more detail, is that Robert is at times overwhelmed by death anxieties. These are not necessarily conscious, or clearly formulated, but perhaps more akin to Winnicott's view that the infant is 'all the time on the brink of unthinkable anxiety', relating to an innate awareness of a potentially annihilating force. If this is part of normal experience (Likierman, 1987), Robert's actual illness would surely exacerbate this fear. In order to relieve this unbearable state, he expresses it through destructive behaviour towards his father. Thus, through attempting to expel the experience, or to project it into his father, he becomes bad in Robert's eyes. Mr Campbell's actual avoidance of contact with Robert must be contributing to this view of father.

With Peter away, I feel I have to try to address the family difficulties further. I say something about it not being surprising that Robert *does* feel fed up and angry. Mrs Campbell interjects that Robert used to talk to the doctors, to *tell* them what was wrong, but now they can't get anything out of him. She continues insightfully, 'Perhaps that's understandable, because I think he wants to *control* what people say or do to him - and if you think about it, he hasn't much control over things at the moment . . .' gesturing towards the drip. I agree with Mrs Campbell and say that Robert and I sometimes have a quiet time together, where nothing is expected of him. Mrs Campbell says, 'I don't say much to him - I just do things for him.' I acknowledge this, and then add that of course it *is* difficult for Mr Campbell to know what to do when Mum has the job of looking after Robert.

I have to leave. I feel inadequate and wish Peter was around to provide family therapy.

I leave a note for Peter, for his return from leave, putting him in the picture and hoping he can address the problems of Robert's rejection of his father, of Mrs Campbell not seeming able to facilitate a role for Father, and telling Peter of my anxiety that if Robert were to die now, there would be *so* much unfinished business!

Later in the day, driving around, I find myself taking the wrong road - back to the hospital.

11 November (Tuesday) I gather he was worse over the weekend, with the doctors saying that maybe the transplant had not taken, and that he had the last rites administered. Mrs Campbell was apparently in a bad way yesterday, saying Robert should have died three weeks ago. Clearly she cannot, at times, bear the fluctuations of his condition. There is a possibility that the blood count is not good because of infection, so there is a decision to return to barrier-nursing. I hear from one of the teachers that before the weekend he was 'very bright' and was busy on the computer. The medical notes mention that he is very withdrawn and not eating.

2.00 p.m. I put on mask, apron, and gloves, wondering to myself if this is emotionally a retrogressive step, in the sense that we are returning to further barriers between Robert and the people who are important to him.

He is alone, lying on his back, playing with his fingers. His hands have a marked tremor. His face looks swollen. I say, 'Mrs Judd is here again. I've brought the box of toys. I don't know if you want to see them, though.' I sit by him. A nurse enters to check the drip, and then leaves.

After a silence, I talk to Robert about our being back to wearing masks, gloves, and aprons, and ask him if he knows why? He nods. He is fiddling with a finger-nail very intently, pulling at any rough bits. 'Your illness must feel like one big rough bit . . .' He seems to listen, looking straight ahead, and continues to pick at his fingers. I comment on his shaking fingers making it harder for him to manage to do delicate things. He seems very tense. I comment on that too, and then gently hold his arm. He seems to relax, and stops fiddling with his nail. He gently strokes his own bare neck and chest with his free hand. I comment on him now seeming to find his skin soft and comforting.

Nurses come and go. Dr Fish comes to take blood via the catheter. Robert seems to breathe more quickly as he comes in.

When he leaves, I talk to him about seeming sad today. He is lying very still. I talk about him feeling fed up... perhaps wondering if he *is* going to get better... how long this will go on for. He listens to me. He seems to feel deflated, and I wonder if he is discouraged perhaps by the recent relapse and return to barrier-nursing. I say that I wonder if he feels he is going to die. He looks at me with wide eyes and nods slowly.

A nurse pops in, asks Robert where his Mum is. Robert shrugs. She goes out.

There is a silence. I hold his hand. I comment on the rubber gloves between us. I say, 'We can share feeling sad.' I feel both a heavy sadness, and yet loving towards him. I long to kiss him as one would one's own child. He coughs. His eyes look frightened. 'And frightened,' I add. He seems to agree. I feel that at that moment he is frightened of dying.

He asks for the toys, and takes out the box of animals. He finds the crocodile, and makes it bite the foal, as he did last time. This time I feel that there is a different communication: I suggest to him that the crocodile is killing the helpless foal, and that perhaps Robert feels like the helpless little foal being attacked by death – the illness.

He lies back, coughing. After a silence he asks me to go and find his Mummy. I talk to him about being angry with his Dad last time. I suggest to him that he feels that Daddy is all bad, like a dustbin, to put all the bad feelings in, and that he seems to feel Mummy's all good. 'Pehaps that way you can feel there's a place for all your bad feelings to go...' (With hindsight I think my comments were not on the right wavelength at that point. I think his coughing again leads to a fear of dying there and then, perhaps choking to death, and he needs his mother to be with him.)

I say I will try and find his mother and then come back to say goodbye.

I find Mrs Campbell in her private room. She comes along with me, and I ask how Robert has been today. '*Fed up*. Terrible over the weekend – it was bad news – but now we're holding thumbs... He's just fed up.'

A nurse is taking his temperature and blood pressure when we return. Robert indicates non-verbally to his mother his wish to use the bedpan.

He sits on it for what seems like a very long time, leaning back on strong arms. He looks like a statue. I am becoming more used to his large hairless head, purplish skin and frail limbs.

I say goodbye, and that I will see him on Thursday.

13 November (Thursday) 10.15 a.m. Peter is still away. I look through Robert's door. Mrs Campbell shakes her head at me. I had heard from the play leader that Robert (and therefore his mother) had a bad night.

Perhaps Mrs Campbell feels that I'm only there to 'play' with Robert and if Robert isn't well enough, there is little point in my seeing him. Again, I wonder if she resents my reappearance after two days away, while she has to do *so* much. Nurses and doctors can be seen to be helping in a practical way all the time, unlike psychotherapists.

Mrs Campbell comes to the door to tell me that Robert is very unwell, and that they are busy changing the bed linen. I say I will come back in a little while.

I return half an hour later. Two doctors and several nurses are in the room. Robert has just had a body-scan, and is due to have more platelets as soon as possible.

I stay in the background, after greeting Robert and watch *so* many procedures. His temperature is taken; the fluid in his chest is measured twice; nose swabs and throat swabs are taken; he urinates in the special bottle; Mrs Campbell washes and dries him after he has vomited; his bed linen is changed; he is weighed by being lifted into a special chair (he weighs 19 kilos); he has his mouth cleaned with mouth-wash and swabs; cream for his sore dry lips is applied; his blood pressure is taken; his Hickman site is cleaned and the dressing changed; drips are checked; the bed is lowered and raised; clean pyjamas are put on him; new student nurses come and go – and all this within the space of half an hour!

It all seems a considerable ordeal, except that he cries out for more mouth-wash swabs as he finds this procedure very satisfying. He is remarkably tolerant of all that has to be done, only complaining once or twice while shivering at being washed.

I comment to Mrs Campbell on her expertise (for she is the one who carries out most of the nursing). She tells me that she is used to it, as she's been doing it for the past two years, on and off. Mrs Campbell does indeed have a competent way of doing everything conscientiously and sensitively for Robert.

I notice how skeletal his limbs are. His puffy face and swollen abdomen belie the shrunken state of his limbs. I gather he has a temperature and has been vomiting since midnight.

During one of the complicated procedures to measure the fluid in his chest, during which he has to hold up an arm for a long time, he complains that his hand feels cold. Suddenly he calls out, 'I want Mrs Judd to hold my hand!' Sister says, 'Who's that?' I stand up and step forward, and hold his little hand. He calls out, 'And stroke my forehead!' Mrs Campbell stands on the other side of the bed and holds Robert's other hand. Robert seems to calm down and stop shivering. I feel gratified at his ability to ask for me, and my ability to give the warmth of physical contact, albeit through rubber gloves. As I have taken 'a back seat' during all these procedures I feel especially touched by his acknowledgement of something I can offer. I then reinforce Mrs Campbell's contribution when Robert clamours for his Mum to clean out his mouth again, by saying, 'Yes, your Mum knows just how to do it.'

I think to myself that there comes a time when words are not enough, and where physical contact is the most helpful contribution.

Mr Campbell appears at the moment when his son is sitting shivering in a chair while his bed is being made. Robert brushes his lips along the red dressing-gown over his bent knees, seeking comfort. To my surprise he beckons his father to him, with raised eyebrows and a slight tug of his head. Upon his third gesture, Mr Campbell notices, responds, comes across the room, and kneels by him. Rather guardedly, Robert requests, 'I want you to go and buy jellies: orange and lemon jellies.' Mr Campbell agrees. He tells father to hurry up. Sister jokes about Father being given his orders. Mr Campbell's forehead, pouring with sweat, conveys his anxiety.

I pop out of the room to speak to him briefly about Robert's angry feelings. He says, 'It's much better since you talked about it on Tuesday, and the wife's been helping... Oh, it's not so bad now! Much better...' I suggest to him that it was easier for Robert to feel that his father was bad, including the marrow and platelets he had donated, rather than that Robert had made them bad or useless and was then full of badness. I also refer to the loving feelings for him that he still has underneath the anger, and which seem to be surfacing again now. He says he knows about the loving feelings, and understands that he's serving a useful, but difficult function. He goes off on his errand.

I return to the room. There is a new Paddington Bear from Carol, the auxiliary nurse. Mrs Campbell tells me, 'If Robert picks his nose and makes it bleed, Paddington Bear goes back, back to darkest Peru, doesn't he, Bobby?' Robert nods seriously.

Carol arrives with a big box of ice lollies which she has brought, and which she will freeze. She calls Robert 'Prince' as usual, and seems to personify my instinct to indulge Robert's every whim. She also brings orange and lemon jellies, duplicating Mr Campbell's order. She asks Robert for a kiss and bends down, bestowing kisses and being kissed, and then leaves.

I say to Robert that I should go now, but could stay a little longer. He shakes his head. I say I'm not sure what he means. He says, 'Stay here.' I say, 'Fine. I'll stay for another quarter of an hour.'

Once all the procedures are over, Mrs Campbell and I step back, thinking Robert is dropping into an exhausted sleep. He grimaces. Mrs Campbell immediately interprets this correctly, fetching a vomit dish, into which Robert is copiously sick. Mr Campbell arrives and holds a new bowl while Mrs Campbell disposes of the first one. He seems at last to have a nursing role, and to be as involved as his wife. Eventually, Robert lies back exhausted.

He then begins to shiver dramatically, because platelets are being given in the drip. Apparently this is a usual reaction. His father covers him with two blankets. Mrs Campbell briefly disputes this as too many, and then concedes.

Meanwhile, I have decided that Thursday to Tuesday is too long a gap (from my point of view anyway) and that I will visit on Saturday or Sunday. I tell Robert that I will be working on Saturday or Sunday, and will see him then. He nods. Mr Campbell says, 'That will be nice – thank you. See you then.'

Later I wonder if my proposed extra visit is a response to his more apparent appreciation of me. Am I becoming an 'auxiliary' mother to Robert, in order to spare his own exhausted mother?

He feels perhaps that I can acknowledge his sadness and his anger, and therefore feels me to be more resilient at the moment. Hopefully this, plus Mr Campbell's increased involvement, could spare Mrs Campbell from having to bear everything alone.

Mr Campbell's previous distancing himself is not unusual. The tendency for fathers to abandon the family psychologically during serious illness, by spending increased amounts of time away from home, is reported by Lansky (1974). 'The more a father is separated from the situation... where the mother may shut him out emotionally, the more a father may feel jealous, threatened, and certainly unprepared for a possible death' (Elliot, 1981, p. 117).

16 November (Sunday) I gather from sister that Robert has had a severe nose bleed earlier today from picking his nose, but that he is not so ill and is accepting his drugs more easily.

When I enter the room, Robert is watching *Worzel Gummidge* on television. He seems very withdrawn into a world away from the hospital and away from me as he watches with big eyes and furrowed brow. He is sitting up in bed, his knees up. Characteristically, he is fiddling with his fingers.

He virtually ignores me. Perhaps he needs to reject me; perhaps he is letting me know about *his* feelings about when I go away and 'reject' him.

The only time he talks is to ask his mother plaintively for a nail file. In spite of his trembling hands, he uses it deftly to poke and scrape at his nails and cuticles, his mother meanwhile warning him to be careful. I feel aghast at Robert's ferocity in this activity.

Suddenly, Mrs Campbell calls out, 'Robert!' in a pained panic. He has pulled off a big chunk of dried skin from a finger tip; his mother holds this bit of discarded skin, saying, 'You'll go septic!' and then gives up and goes back to her chair.

I think to myself about the removal of *rough* bits again: his wanting to rid himself of the roughness of illness and to find an inner undamaged unblemished smoothness; wanting to feel some physical sensation, even pain, which *he* can control; wanting to attack the surface of himself to mirror the disease deep inside, possibly as a way of externalizing it. He cannot or does not attack his father any longer – so where is all the 'bad' now situated? I also think about the apparent conflict in Mrs Campbell between (predominantly) a fight for life and (to a much lesser extent) resignation about impending death, in her brief reaction to this incident.

A nurse comes in to make the bed, bribing Robert to co-operate with an ice lolly. Robert watches the bed-making avidly from the chair even though he must have seen it countless times. Of course, he is constantly wired-up to the drip and has to be carefully lifted in and out of the chair. His blood pressure is then taken. He seems to examine his painfully thin arms after the pressure cuff is removed.

When I leave I say, 'See you on Tuesday.'

Outside the room I look at his weight charts. He is steadily losing weight. I think about his quietness: it seems he is conserving his energy for vital (in the true sense of the word) matters only.

18 November (Tuesday) 2.45 p.m. When I arrive Robert is on the bedpan. The television is on, showing a programme about plastic surgery, which he seems to be watching.

Mrs Campbell says she is going off to do various things. Robert makes a slight protest, but allows it. We watch television for a few minutes, and when the programme ends I say, 'We could do something now – can I turn the TV off?' He nods.

I show him a new set of a family of little soft dolls in his box. He seems to feel helpless about relating to them. I ask him if he wants to do anything with them. He shrugs.

Then he asks, 'Can we play with the hospital?' So I pull up a table and he gets the set out, meticulously setting up first the food trolley, with tiny plates and cutlery, then the little boy in bed, then, significantly, he changes the priest-collar on the man so that he's a Daddy again.

He sets up the vase of flowers and hat in the locker, and then spends a long time fixing crutches on the man, as well as a plaster cast on his leg and his arm. He makes the little boy similarly attired with plaster casts and stands them both up. At that point a nurse comes into the room to check Robert's drip, and he seems to freeze, and to proceed with the activity the moment the nurse leaves, conveying, I sense, that he feels involved in something significant.

He tells me the man is Daddy, and looks at me. So I say, 'It's like Robert and Daddy – Daddy when he gave the marrow and the platelets, and perhaps wasn't very well.' I see him give me the first glimmer of a smile that I have seen since knowing him. I smile too, under the mask. He looks hard at my eyes. I ask him if he can tell I'm smiling. He shakes his head. I tell him that I was smiling just then.

He sets up the tiny toy television and radio, and then slumps back. He removes the plaster cast and crutches from the little boy and the man and starts to pack up. I comment that today the Mummy was not in the play. 'Perhaps she's resting, like Mummy can rest now when I'm seeing you.' I go on to talk about him seeming pleased just now to make a scene with the Daddy and the little boy in hospital together, both not well – 'Perhaps, you feel a little happier when you think of your Dad really sharing all this with you, even sharing being unwell.'

I think to myself about Mr Campbell showing considerable emotional pain and distress and wonder then if the analogy is therefore at an emotional as well as a physical level.

He clearly does not want to play with anything else. Then, in a little voice, he says, 'Feel sick.' I quickly get the vomit bowl. He is copiously sick: a bloody and mucus-like substance. He seems *so* resigned and stoical. I wipe his mouth. Then he calls out, 'Want bedpan!'

I quickly fetch it, and propping himself up on his arms he produces dark blood-coloured diarrhoea. Characteristically, he sits there for a long time. His limbs are so thin that I am reminded of concentration camp victims, and I feel angry that this can happen to anyone.

He tells me he has finished. I wipe him repeatedly as I've seen his mother do. He gets off the bedpan. His undersheet is stained. I ask him if I should change it. He nods. So I do. He is very co-operative throughout, and I feel somewhat clumsy.

He lies back on his pillows, exhausted. And then the relentless nausea causes him to ask for the bowl again, and he vomits again.

When this is over he asks me to read him a story. I ask which one, and he shrugs, so I pick up the first book that comes to hand, which is *William Tell*. He listens to the whole story, looking at the pictures. I ask him if he thinks that the people in the castle should have been killed and he nods. He also seems to agree with William Tell slaying the cruel governor.

I am aware of feeling some resistance to reading to him. My reasons are complicated. Partly, I feel that the story is a defence against any spontaneous talking we might do. Mrs Campbell, as well as the teacher and play leader, all read to Robert, so I feel that my professional role is being blurred. I ask myself if this is rigidity on my part. I remind myself that this is one of his coping mechanisms (and is not being used to the exclusion of all else). But the weight of awareness of our limited time together is nevertheless a continual pressure on me – a pressure which I try to resist – to use each moment for 'important issues'.

He leans back, his eyes closing. I stroke his forehead, and ask him if he wants the bed lower. He nods. He wants it right down. I rest my hand on his shoulder. He seems to drop off to sleep, opening his eyes the moment I remove my hand. I tell him I will stay until his Mum returns. He then falls into a deep sleep. Mrs Campbell returns ten minutes later.

Looking back on the present situation, I think about Robert once again rallying, playing with the toys. After all the critical phases of the illness which he has endured, I find it difficult to know what to think or feel. Is he dying? He probably is, but of course in an unpredictable pattern. I sometimes long to talk more to the doctors, in an attempt to have some answers about his physical state, even though I know the fallibility of prognoses. The medical notes are helpful. I feel I have to remain in touch with the probability of him dying and, at the same time, the hope of remission.

Robert himself seems to bob up repeatedly after being punched down by the illness. What can this feel like to him? It seems he has a very powerful life force which continues to resurface, like a cork on a stormy sea. I feel that this is reinforced by his parents' love, concern, and attention. Yet, at times, he has seemed so exhausted and unwell that this life force seems to be wearing very thin. I am reminded of Shakespeare's:

Vex not his ghost: O, let him pass! he hates him
That would upon the rack of this rough world
Stretch him out longer. (*King Lear*, V, iii)

Throughout I have to continue to remain *emotionally present*, through the reverberations of the buffeting of the illness which I feel. I see this as my main task. At times it seems incredibly difficult to continue, especially when my role is not clearly understood by some of the other professionals, nor, perhaps, by the parents.

I wonder about Robert's fortitude, which seems to appear alongside his resilience and life force. The stoical resignation with which he appears to tolerate so much, repeatedly – interspersed with some angry protests – may be a result of his keeping his limited energy for basic survival tasks. But I feel this tacit tolerance is more of a helpless depression, a withdrawal, in the face of such overwhelmingly unpleasant experiences.

20 November (Thursday) When I arrive the notice about protective isolation has (again) been removed from the door. The television is on and Robert seems half asleep and his mother is in the room. The notes had said that he was a little better. I wonder why the doctors have decided upon this shift from barrier-nursing.

He opens his eyes and looks at me. Mrs Campbell says she is going to do a few things. I sit by the bedside. Robert opens his eyes and looks hard at me. I talk about not having to wear a mask, and his being able to see my face now. I turn the television sound off.

We sit quietly together. After a while I say, 'Perhaps there's something you would like to talk about?' He looks at me expectantly. I say, 'I wonder what you think about during the long hours that you're lying here... do you dream... remember your dreams?' He shakes his head. I say, 'I wonder if you feel lonely sometimes... I know your Mum is nearly always here, and Dad, and the nurses... but I wonder if you sometimes feel that you're all alone in being ill... no one can really know what you're thinking and feeling. Do you know what I mean?'

He gives a little nod and closes his eyes, lying very still. Then he opens his eyes, tries to speak, and then says, 'I feel sick.' I fetch a vomit dish, and lying weakly on his side he brings up two bowls full of what seems like mucus, blood, and bile. And then he requests the bedpan, which I help him onto, again producing some blood-like substance. He seems weaker. After wiping him and tucking him up I comment on how tiring this must be for him.

As Robert talks so little with me, I often feel there is a danger that I, in putting forward what I feel he is thinking or feeling, may be colouring the picture with my own fantasies and emotions. His nods or shakes of the head are a helpful guide here. Nevertheless, I worry about becoming too much of a thinking or feeling part *for* him. Being appropriately sensitive to him is an integral part of the present relationship. I can only attempt to monitor if and when I am projecting too much of my *own* feelings through self-analysis.

He lies there, soon requesting the bedpan again. While he is on it, his mother returns, with the haematology consultant and the senior registrar. Mrs Campbell, who has been anxiously awaiting this ward round, exclaims, 'You *would* be on your throne when they come in! They'll come back later', as they withdraw for a moment. Mrs Campbell wipes him and I report to her about the vomiting.

Soon the consultant, senior registrar, and sister return. The consultant is very friendly; he seems not to know what is causing the vomiting and diarrhoea. More platelets are due. Apparently, Mr Campbell cannot donate platelets at present, as he has a cold and has been ill in bed for two days. It seems the blood count has gone up and both sister and the consultant refer to this as 'good news'.

Robert is passive while being examined: neither co-operative nor unhelpful. The consultant's comment upon leaving is, 'Try and get some weight back on you!'

Robert looks hard at me after they have left. I feel his searching eyes are saying, 'Why is he talking about things getting better when I feel weaker and weaker?' I do not address this searching look, perhaps because Mrs Campbell is in the room. I just say, 'He's going to try and help the vomiting. And the blood count *is* up.'

Mrs Campbell reinforces this, and says, 'And we could do with some platelets... been waiting since Tuesday... I suppose it's not an emergency.'

Robert grunts, looking at his mother. Mrs Campbell says, 'Bobby, I know what you want, but you can tell me, can't you? Is it the bedpan?' Robert nods. Mrs Campbell says, 'Really Robert, you're just getting lazy about talking!' as she fetches the bedpan. Robert seems less ready to make the effort to get onto it, so we both help him.

Then he lies back, half asleep. I tell him I can stay for another quarter of an hour. He nods. Mrs Campbell and I sit quietly: I sit by Robert, Mrs Campbell behind me on her bed. After a while, Mrs Campbell talks about the cold weather and the dark evenings. When I leave, I say 'Goodbye, see you on Tuesday', to both of them. On this occasion Mrs Campbell seems warm and friendly.

There was a new drawing by Robert on his wall this time: of a smiling little boy holding a red balloon. He is encompassed by big 'm'-shaped birds, and a layer of colour in a cocoon shape around him. I feel it conveys his feeling encapsulated by the hospital, the bed, and particularly his mother, like a young baby. The red balloon may signify many things. It may have unconscious associations to a placenta – linking with Robert's regressed and dependent state; or the redness can reflect, as Bach (1969) states, 'an acute... consuming state of illness, or psychologically, a "burning" problem'.

I wonder about his mother's understandable attempt to resist some of the regression (for example, in requesting him to speak up more) and how this may represent a necessary part of the fight for life, growth, and development, in spite of such a grim situation. And yet Robert's utter exhaustion may make it very difficult for him to make the effort to talk.

25 November (Tuesday) At a ward meeting before I visit Robert, I gather that he has had a very severe nose bleed the day before. The charge nurse really thought he was dying. The nursing staff seem to be questioning the fact that the care of Robert is not *terminal*, and are wondering what is best for Robert and for his parents. It seems that there is a lack of communication between the nursing staff and consultant: the nurses wishing to indulge Robert more and make this a more positive phase in the sense of acknowledging openly that he is dying, and that, therefore, everything should be as pleasant as possible for him - possibly withdrawing drugs which cause vomiting. However, the doctors' approach seems to be 'Where there's life, there's hope', right until the patient draws his last breath.

2.30 p.m. I go in to see Robert. The television is on extremely loudly. He is sitting up, for once unsupported by pillows, slowly eating a dry cracker-biscuit. He looks at me, and then ignores me. Mrs Campbell says that she is going now, and does Robert want anything from the shop? Robert does not answer, for he is busy poking at the back of his throat to remove bits of biscuit. I comment on his red nail varnish and ask who painted his nails? I speculate to myself that it is an attempt to stop Robert from picking at his nails. Robert says, 'It's a secret.' As his mother leaves Robert tells her not to be long.

Robert agitatedly picks at his teeth. I comment on him seeming to want to poke into his mouth, as he did his ears and his nose before, and that he seems very busy, perhaps to let me know that as I have not been here since last Thursday he wishes to keep me out.

I ask if I can turn the television sound down. He nods.

I bring up a chair. Now he is picking his fingernails, and trembling. Suddenly he blurts out, 'Can you get me a gum in the back of my locker?' At first I do not understand his pronounciation of 'gum'. Then I ask if he is allowed to have it? He nods. Eventually I find it. He unwraps it with some difficulty, curling it into a roll. His lips are scabby. He bites into it as if it is too big for his mouth, totally absorbed in the experience.

He suddenly asks for the bedpan. I fetch it, commenting that perhaps having the gum, like an enjoyable feed, makes him want the bedpan. He produces blackish diarrhoea. I wipe him and wash my hands. I like the smell of the hospital liquid soap, so I hold out my soapy hand for him to smell, responding to an impulse to increase his range of sensations. 'Yuck,' he says. I say 'I like it ... you prefer your spearmint gum smell.' He nods.

And then he asks me to read him a story. 'Which one?' *Paddington Bear*, and he directs me to the last story in the book. I feel a pang when I see its title, 'The Last Dance'.

I read to him, battling with a sudden headache and a feeling of exhaustion that I didn't have before reading. I feel that I am carrying the threat of death alone today - a threat which Robert with his bizarre scarlet fingernails and mouth full of sweet gum is pleasantly denying. He seems to scan my face avidly as I read, as if devouring the details, especially my mouth, with his wide eyes.

He asks for a tissue, to dispose of the gum. After a while I say that the story is very long, and I cannot read all of it – so I mark the page and talk to him.

I ask him if he has seen his Dad lately? He shakes his head. I ask if he wants to? He nods. I say, 'It's because of his cold . . . but it's important for you to see him . . . even if he stands by the door, with a mask. I'll try and arrange something.'

I ask him if there's anything else he would like very much. 'For Julie to come over,' he states emphatically. I acknowledge this, saying I will speak to Peter and to Mum and Dad, to see what we can arrange, 'Because, of course, it's important for you to see her, and for her to see you.'

His eyes begin to droop. I ask if he would like to lie back. He nods. I remove a pillow and make him comfortable. After a quiet time I say, 'I'm thinking about you not being so angry with your Dad these days, about things being better between you and him, and also your need for him to be here to share things with Mum, and to give Mum support.' He gives the most emphatic nod so far, and closes his eyes.

I ask if he wants me to stroke his forehead. He nods. As I stroke his forehead and his slightly furry head, he relaxes more. Occasionally his mouth turns down at the corners, or his brow furrows, or he suddenly grimaces.

I think to myself about him dying, about how he would look – perhaps peaceful like this. I feel we are understanding each other, perhaps he knows I am acknowledging a moment of peaceful acceptance of death, without fear or tension.

I stop stroking his head and rest my palm on his head. He seems to fall asleep, then half opens one eye. I tell him I will have to go soon, but I'll be back as usual on Thursday, and would do what I could about Daddy visiting, and about Julie.

I leave the bell by his pillow, and leave.

Later, in a workshop, we discuss Robert, and it is decided that Dr Green (the consultant child psychiatrist) will see the haematology consultant, to discuss the nursing approach to Robert, including whether Mr Campbell should be allowed in even if he has a cold.

It is also decided that I am to discuss with Peter the possibility of arranging for Julie to come over. There is a strong feeling that I should do all I can to sort out these practical things as well as to sense what is best for Robert as regards talking about death: how explicit to be. Everyone is very supportive, especially Dr Green.

Later, Dr Green hears about another dying child I may be taking on and asks me if I am sure I can take it. I say, 'Just about.' She says, 'You have got some healthy patients somewhere, haven't you?'

Their difficulties seem momentarily insignificant.

27 November (Thursday) I receive a letter from Dr Green letting me know that Robert's consultant is abroad, so it is hard to gauge Robert's medical condition and the overall approach to him. Dr Green says that she visited Mrs Campbell, who seems optimistic about Robert's condition.

I see Peter, who reports that the senior house officer is trying to get Robert to eat more; his liver is functioning badly and he has a temperature. Apparently, Julie cannot come over because she has been in touch with shingles, and there is a danger that she may import chicken pox to Robert. Peter says that he gathers that Mrs Campbell was surprised by Dr Green talking to her about the possibility of Robert's dying.

I enter Robert's room. Mrs Campbell gives a little nod of acknowledgement at my arrival. The television is on loudly as usual. Robert sits in the chair while his mother makes the bed. I sit quietly by Robert for a while. He is busy picking his lips and trembling grossly. He requests to return to bed, so Mrs Campbell puts slippers on him. I see Robert 'walking' the few aided steps to his bed for the first time since before the transplant.

Mrs Campbell then helps him to rest his head back on the pillow as one would a young baby whose neck is not yet strong enough.

Robert lies on his side and seems cold. He asks for a bedpan. Mrs Campbell helps him onto it. He produces diarrhoea and then wants to be sick. We both help him. He vomits dark slimy stuff. Mrs Campbell rubs his back seemingly roughly throughout. (Tropauer *et al.*, [1970], writing about children with cystic fibrosis, found that parental hostility was conveyed to the child by the strength of the mother's pounding during physiotherapy sessions.)

I hold his forehead and the bowl. His mouth is then full of mucus. I ask him if he wants a mouth wash. He nods. Mrs Campbell resignedly fetches a sterile mouth wash kit. Robert cries out in pain at the substance being rubbed on his gums: his mouth is full of ulcers. This is the procedure that he used to welcome. Finally, Mrs Campbell puts ointment on his very sore lips. He lies back, exhausted. And then needs the bedpan again. Mrs Campbell seems fed up. This time Robert does not produce anything in the bedpan.

I talk about the problem of Julie coming over. Mrs Campbell says categorically that she cannot, and that she does not want to plan ahead, because the last time they bought air tickets for Mr Campbell to fetch Julie, he could not go (because Robert had suddenly deteriorated). She says that perhaps, with Christmas approaching, the planes would all be booked up anyway, and adds, 'Everything is against us.' (I think to myself about her determination *not* to make plans for Julie's visit, and feel that it is part of her denial that her son is dying.)

Eventually, she leaves the room. I turn the television sound down, with Robert's permission, and sit by him. He seems to be looking intently at my silver bracelet, and shivering, as he has a temperature. He then concentrates on his hands and nails, picking at them. I say, 'You're busy with your fingers... perhaps because they don't go away, like Mum, or Dad, or Julie, or Mrs Judd... they're always there.'

He is focusing on them at close range, picking at the dry skin, and rubbing the dead bits on the sheet. I repeat what I have said to him before, about being ill being like the rough bits...'You know, people say, "I feel rough" when they're not feeling well.'

He starts to poke his cuticles with his nails. I say, 'Perhaps you're poking into yourself, when you're fed up, and cannot poke into anyone else.' There is a silence. He looks hard at me.

Then his mother returns. I say to Mrs Campbell, 'It seems Robert would like his Dad to pop in more, to see him, if possible.' Mrs Campbell says, 'Well, he was in here yesterday, wasn't he, Robert?' And then she tells me how much her husband hates the hospital air-conditioning, how he gets claustrophobic, phobic about hospital proceduress, and how she used to be too, 'about sick, and drips... I used to feel faint... But when it's your own child...'

Mrs Campbell seems, once again, to be bearing all the actual contact single-handed while all the anxieties are located in her husband. I wonder what Robert is making of this conversation.

He is lying passively on his side. He asks his mother for a nail file. She gives him one, saying, 'If you've got any nails left to file!' I notice Robert sticking it far up inside his cuticle, and feel appalled. I find myself stopping him, by clasping his hands in mine. I worry that it will bleed and bleed; I also worry that by talking about his depression and hopelessness, he is feeling more self-destructive than ever. His mother dismisses what he is doing by saying, 'Oh, he's just getting off the old dry skin.' Again Mrs Campbell and I seem to be responding in an oscillating and polarized way: previously she was appalled at the implications of some of Robert's activities while I resignedly tried to accept or understand them. Perhaps, the acknowledgement of an impending imminent death is often something that is so awesome and overwhelming that we shy away from it if someone else can be felt to be carrying some of that awareness for us. I also feel that she is showing me *her* anger at having to go through all this.

It is time for me to leave. I say, 'Goodbye, see you on Tuesday', feeling helpless. Mrs Campbell, as usual, is more friendly when I leave than when I arrive. Is she pleased to see me leave? Or can she only value me when she re-experiences me as helpful and involved? I feel that in my absence, I become remote and useless to her.

2 December (Tuesday) Robert is in the chair, the television is on loudly, and the play leader is reading him a story. I say, 'Hello', and that I'll return in a little while. While I'm looking at Robert's notes, the play leader comes to tell me, 'He's all yours'.

I go in. His eyes are glued to the television. Nurses come in and out. I ask Robert if I can turn the sound down – he nods – adding that it seems I am to feel left out, especially when it feels to him that I've been away for a long time and have been ignoring him.

He seems to look a little better, his colouring seems more normal, and he is calm. But he does not look at me. I ask him if the programme is important to him. He says, 'No!'

I talk again about it seeming like a long time since I was here, and wonder what he's been doing? 'I guess lots and lots of nurses have been in and out . . . and doctors . . . and Mum . . . What about Dad?' He nods. 'As much as you wanted him to?' He nods again.

His eyelids begin to droop. I ask if he wishes to return to bed? He shakes his head. His eyes are still fixed on the television. I think to myself about watching television being a necessary defence. We sit quietly together. More nurses come in and out.

After a while, I say, 'Last time you felt really fed up . . . and now, again, perhaps you just want peace. Your body seems more comfortable today.'

He then asks if he can go back to bed. I carry him, with his arms around my neck. He seems so light (17 kilos now); I worry about the many tubes getting in a tangle, but we manage. He lies back, seeming comfortable. I cover him up and stroke his forehead. His eyes droop. And then he opens them, and looks hard at me. He grimaces slightly as he moves his tongue around his mouth. I comment on him having had such a sore mouth last time, and ask if it is still so sore. He nods. I say, 'That must be awful – I guess every time you eat or drink it stings.' He nods. I say, 'Mouths should be places that feel nice and comfortable, where food tastes good.' He nods.

His eyes close, and he falls into a deep sleep with my hand on his head. Nurses come in and change the drip, talking very loudly. He does not seem to stir, but I wonder about this restless atmosphere.

I notice a new photograph on the wall, of Julie and Robert taken perhaps a year ago, each holding a little puppy. Robert wears a peaked cap (perhaps to hide his hair loss) but looks well and happy.

4 December (Thursday) I go into the room, to find that the bed and drip are not there. Mrs Campbell is asleep in the chair. I feel shocked. Has it happened? Has he died? His toys are still around the room. Bundles of dirty linen are in plastic sacks on the floor.

I go out and find sister, and gather that Robert is in theatre, having a bowel biopsy under general anaesthetic. She tells me that the anaesthetist insisted upon a venous injection when he could have given it via the Hickman. Robert had protested. Sister had felt very upset.

I wait a while. Sister goes back into the room to tell Mrs Campbell that Robert is on his way back from theatre. Mrs Campbell seems displeased to see me, but perhaps is just sleepy. However, I go in and talk to her about Robert. She seems to take this new procedure of the anaesthetic and biopsy in her stride, saying that she didn't feel Robert really minded the injection.

Soon Robert is wheeled in, in his bed, asleep, and apparently all right. Mrs Campbell gets up to see him, strokes his head, and Robert half awakens. Mrs Campbell seems very pleased to see him. The nurses take his blood pressure, pulse, and temperature, all of which are normal.

Mr Campbell comes in, and there is no exchange of words between husband and wife. He looks extremely anxious as he looks at Robert. I tell him that apparently he has taken the operation well.

He asks me how I am. I say, 'Well, how are *you* is what I was going to ask!' He sits by me on the spare bed, seeming very keen to talk. He says he's fine. I ask about the hospital atmosphere. He says he doesn't want to complain. He feels Robert is much better. He tells me about Robert hugging his old doctor from Scotland who visited him recently. I acknowledge that he does seem more comfortable in his body.

He then tells me that Robert cried for Julie, but that they don't want to risk chicken pox. They feel it would be a 'marvellous tonic' for Robert if Julie visited. He goes on to talk about him anecdotally: about his liveliness, his always putting Julie first when he was well. (I think to myself that he is mentioning the qualities that Robert is so markedly deprived of by his illness, and therefore perhaps it is all the more understandable that he should want us to remember them. This idealization of Robert seems akin to the frequent idealization of someone who has already died.) Mrs Campbell interjects that all leukaemic children in remission are hyperactive, thereby dismissing Mr Campbell's appreciation of his son's lost liveliness. I ask if he has always been active before he was ill? He says, 'Yes... never needed much sleep... even now... it's 11 p.m. before he settles down.'

Meanwhile, he is sleeping deeply. Nurses come and sort out the drip and Mrs Campbell helps. Her husband comments, 'She could have been a nurse.' Mrs Campbell denies this, saying that she is still squeamish, unless it is her own child.

I leave soon after.

9 December (Tuesday) 2.30 p.m. For a reason I do not understand I do not bring the therapy box to Robert's room today. I enter his room, where the television is on loudly, and Mrs Campbell looks very drawn. She greets me and tells me that 'Robert won't be up to much today . . . he is asleep.' I notice that Robert's hands are covered in large bandages, like boxing gloves. Mrs Campbell says it is to stop him picking his lips, since this morning.

He sleeps peacefully, breathing deeply, his 'paws' up near his head. Mrs Campbell says that things have been much the same, but they are trying to get a new antibody from Birmingham. The biopsy confirmed that he has graft-versus-host disease, and Mrs Campbell thinks that this new antibody is, possibly, to combat this condition. I ask Mrs Campbell how *she* is? 'Oh, all right.' She looks pale and exhausted. She tells me that she has had disturbed nights as usual.

She goes to the hospital shop, leaving me with Robert, who continues to sleep for about twenty minutes. In his sleep he repeatedly feels his swollen sore lip with his tongue. Then he groans, opens his eyes which are filled with tears, looks at me, frowns, moves his position, and goes back to sleep. He is half awake again, busy with his tongue.

I stand by his bed, stroke his soft forehead and bald head, notice his lack of proper eyebrows as well, and say hello. I quietly tell him that I saw him last time, asleep, after he had the anaesthetic. He looks at me, then closes his eyes, and opens his mouth, revealing a yellowish substance. I talk about him seeming to be uncomfortable. He sticks out his tongue, as if to request help for the stuff on it. I wipe it with a tissue. Even his tears are yellowish.

I talk about his bandaged hands – that it must be very uncomfortable. He nods. I say, 'I guess you know why . . . to stop you picking at your lips and nose . . . making them bleed.' He nods. I acknowledge how fed up he must feel, though, to have bandaged hands, 'Because when you're lying in bed for weeks and weeks it seems one of the few things you *can* do is to use your fingers.' He nods.

I hold the bandaged hand, and say, 'It's not the same as holding your hand.' He nods again. I go on to say, 'But I can still stroke your forehead.'

His tongue is busy. Then he tries to say something. I don't understand. I ask him if he wants a drink? He calls out, 'Bedpan!' I quickly fetch it. This time he has difficulty in sitting on it in his usual way by supporting himself on his arms, because the bandages prevent him from bending his wrists. I lift him, but cannot get the bedpan beneath him. Fortunately, a nurse appears at this moment and helps. He has diarrhoea again. 'Finished,' he tells me. I wipe him. He lies down on his other side.

I wash my hands, and then come over to talk to him – and to tell him that I will have to go soon. I tell him that on Thursday, the day after tomorrow, I'll be back. I stroke his forehead. I say, 'I know it's difficult to talk, but is there anything you want to say, or to ask me. . .?' He is silent, perhaps asleep. Then he says he's cold. I find an extra blanket. He appears so tiny when I cover him. (I wonder how much the coldness is part of his physical condition and how much a response to my leaving.)

I put up the cot-sides of the bed, which is what the nurses and Mrs Campbell seem to do. He asks for his mother. I say that she will be back soon. Robert seems half asleep. I realize that with his heavily bandaged hands he cannot ring the bell. So I try to rig it up with tape so that he can push it with his 'paws' but I don't know if it will work.

3.00 p.m. I attend the haematology meeting. Dr Fish is there, talking about the consultant's approach to Robert, 'Where there's life there's hope.' Apparently, they always go on to the bitter end with transplant patients. He explains that the awaited antibody is to counteract something in Robert from his father's marrow. His transplant has taken, but there are now these complications. He admits he *is* dying but cannot say when. The nursing staff express their feeling that there is a lack of communication between them and the doctors. They feel that, in their ongoing nursing of him, it would be more appropriate to acknowledge that he is dying and to alter some of the nursing – perhaps disturb Robert less, in order to make him more comfortable. Sister even wonders if Robert and his parents should be flown back to Scotland for Robert to die there. Dr Fish acknowledges the lack of communication, but feels the doctors cannot alter their attempts to fight for Robert's life.

This situation leads me to think further about the issues around home care. While active treatment is still being given, home care could not really be considered. It is this switch to palliative care that is the crucial and difficult decision, especially for the doctors. Home care for dying children has been advocated by some authors (Lamerton, 1973; Lauer and Camitta, 1980; Martinson, Armstrong *et al.*, 1978). The advantages of home care are summarized by Martinson *et al.*, where they describe the child receiving the security and love he needs that can usually be found in the home environment: 'The parents may derive satisfaction in fulfilling their child's wishes to remain at home. This may help allay the sense of guilt that frequently follows death.' Recent research shows that, through home care and therefore improved family satisfaction, the child's psychological state is improved. At home there is often less confusion, less pressure, and fewer negative stimuli on the dying patient and his family. Psychiatric symptoms in parents are then often reduced (Lauer and Camitta 1980; Stein and Jessop, 1984). Home care enables the parents to be essential and active in aspects of their child's care, and not observers. Although Mrs Campbell is very active in nursing Robert in hospital, and this can deepen the relationship, this is not always the case. The experience can be terrifying for the parents if there are unexpected medical crises. Clearly, expert emergency medical help has to be readily available. 'Because serious childhood illness is rare, GPs are not that comfortable about offering support,' says Dora Black (personal communication).

It is characteristic of this phase that the transition to a terminal state is not recognized simultaneously by all those involved. In this hospital it is often the doctors who are last to give up hope for the child. This conflict between members of the team signifies the differences in role, style, timing, and emotional response. As nurses are most constantly physically in touch with the child, and with the suffering, it is not surprising that they are often keen to prevent unnecessary suffering if it is indeed unlikely for a child's life to be saved through further efforts. This is not always the case, though. (For further discussion on this see Chapter 10.)

To return to the story: after the haematology meeting I meet a volunteer who has just met Mrs Campbell. She tells me that Mrs Campbell is devastated at finding a leaflet in the hospital chapel which states that Robert has died, and that the community should pray for him. Apparently, Mrs Campbell is being comforted by Carol, to whom she is very close.

At Dr Green's workshop which follows, for those working with terminally ill children and their families, we relate this appalling mistake. She asks Dr Simmons, the child psychiatrist, to find the chaplain, and says she will bring the matter to the administration, in order to try to prevent unvetted literature entering the hospital. Apparently the leaflet is produced by a local church.

I talk to the workshop about Robert again. They feel that the family should be helped to bring Julie over, in spite of the anxiety about chicken pox.

I talk about the bandaged hands. They feel that cotton gloves would be better. The meeting confirms my feeling that this is the removal of one of the few sensations left to Robert. I agree to try to talk to the nursing staff about alternatives.

Dr Simmons returns to join us, telling us that the chaplain has apologized to Mrs Campbell.

I feel greatly encouraged and supported by this workshop in confronting some of the issues more actively, as well as in carrying the pain of Robert's condition. I go and see sister about Robert's hands. She feels he picks at his lips and nose as a way of getting at his mother. He seems to do it all the more when Mrs Campbell asks him not to. I say that I still wonder about cotton gloves - so he can use the bell, for instance. Sister suggests I speak to Mrs Campbell about this.

I go to see Robert and his mother, and find him sitting up, being fed marshmallow biscuits by his mother, because, of course, he cannot hold anything with bandaged hands. His eyes are half closed. I say that I have been wondering about the bandages, and whether Robert could perhaps wear gloves instead. Mrs Campbell replies, 'No, he'd still pick at himself. It will be just for a few days, until his sores have healed. Already, after *one* day, it's a bit better.'

I comment then to both of them that perhaps it helps for Robert to know that the bandages will come off soon. Mrs Campbell interjects, 'Oh, he knows that all right! Last night we bought him this robot-car, which he could have if he didn't pick, but he didn't keep his promise.'

I say that I don't think he means to pick at himself to be naughty. Perhaps when he's frustrated, his body is all there is to have a go at.

Mrs Campbell says that he never used to, when he was ill before. (She is not prepared to realize that this time the illness is different, more serious.) I comment that the nurses have said that picking at the body is very common among leukaemic patients.

(Repeated picking of the nose and cheek was observed by Bowlby, Robertson, and Rosenbluth (1952) as characteristic behaviour of a two and a half-year-old hospitalized girl. Anna Freud suggested to them that that behaviour may have been connected to the child's attempts not to cry and to wipe away her tears. The authors conclude that while face-fingering may be connected with attempts to control crying, nose-picking appears to be more of a masturbation equivalent.)

Mrs Campbell has left the new remote-control robot-car by Robert on the bed. He looks grotesque: like an injured boxer, with half-closed eyes, sitting up, trying to push the button of this new toy through heavily bandaged hands.

I leave.

11 December (Thursday) His notes say that he has deteriorated generally over the past thirty-six hours. He has a persistent fever and a chest infection.

10.30 a.m. I arrive, to find the blind on his door closed. I tentatively enter the darkened room. Robert is sitting in the chair while Mrs Campbell is busy cleaning the room.

I say hello and go to him.

His eyes are closed. I tell him I am here. There is silence, except for Mrs Campbell vigorously wiping everything she can reach in the room with sterilizing fluid. I talk to him about having his eyes closed for much of the time these days.

Mrs Campbell says, 'Oh, it's because of the eye ointment – since last night.' But I think to myself that he has been increasingly withdrawing for many days. There appears to be an actual eye infection as well.

His hands are not bandaged. His eyes are running, and I do not know if they are sad tears or simply watering eyes. He begins to drop asleep, his head drooping. I ask him if he would like to return to bed? He nods, so I ask Mrs Campbell who replies briskly, 'Oh, he must sit up ... mustn't be in bed the whole time.' Robert seems to accept this. (Mrs Campbell is clearly making a great effort to get Robert back on the path towards health, and her cleaning activities seem to be her way of wiping away the illness.)

Eventually, Mrs Campbell comes to transfer Robert to bed. He seems too weak to push his feet into the slippers which mother holds out. At this point a nurse comes in to weigh Robert who is transferred to the weighing chair. He then 'walks' backwards to the bed, Mrs Campbell supporting him, and telling him to 'straighten up'.

In bed he lies on his side in a foetal position with eyes closed, seemingly exhausted.

Mrs Campbell is still bustling about the room, and comes to bandage Robert's hands, who passively accepts this. Robert half opens his eyes, to say, 'Read me a story.' I say, 'Sure, which one?' He does not answer. I fetch *Snow White* and two others, and read the titles to him. He shakes his head with tiny movements, as if economizing on the effort. I then fetch the story of *Thumbelina*, to which he nods. His eyes are closed throughout: he no longer seems willing or able to make the effort to see the pictures, as he used to.

As I begin to read it to him, Mrs Campbell leaves the room. I find the story increasingly poignant. Thumbelina is nursing the swallow:

As she covered him up, she felt his heart still beating.

The swallow was not dead. He was still alive but very weak.

My voice trembles, but I carry on until the end. Robert seems to be asleep.

I sit quietly until his mother returns. A nurse takes his temperature, which is quite high, so she uncovers him except for a sheet. Robert continues to sleep.

Mrs Campbell returns, saying that he sleeps on and off all the time because he is always disturbed by medical check-ups during his sleep. She tells me that her husband is still asleep.

I say I will pop back later.

I think about the burden Mrs Campbell is carrying, and how it is not surprising that she should be using so much denial.

I pass the auxiliary nurse, Carol. She beckons me, to talk with her. We go into the milk kitchen for a brief chat. She tells me that Mr and Mrs Campbell had a row last night in front of Robert and Carol. Mrs Campbell impatiently asked her husband to leave Robert alone when he was busily trying to do things for him. Carol feels awful about the fact that she is going on holiday on Monday. Apparently Mrs Campbell and Robert are both very upset about this. Carol feels Robert to be worse. Carol tells me that Robert has pleaded with her to try to arrange for Julie to come over, and that Robert has said to Carol, 'That's why I'm fighting.' We both share our feeling that he may indeed be holding on for Julie – and what if she does come over – will he then give up?

Later I return to the room. Robert is vomiting lots of mucus into a bowl, while his mother is patting and rubbing his back (perhaps too hard?) Robert needs the bedpan at the same time. It is awful to witness his extremely weak body being wracked by the violent muscular spasms of his stomach, his throat, his bowels.

Eventually, he is finished. Mrs Campbell leaves the room. Robert looks at me more penetratingly than he has done for weeks. I stroke his forehead, and try to talk to him about how awful he must be feeling. Tears stream out of his eyes. I say, 'Watery-eye tears, and sad tears.' He begins to feel sick again, and to cough. He chokes. I fear he will die there and then, and sit him up. He vomits a little. He feels hot. He complains with a weak moan and then lies back.

Again he starts to cough. He looks at me with startled eyes beneath their swollen lids. I say, 'Perhaps you're frightened that you'll choke, that you won't be able to breathe.' He nods, holding on to me with staring eyes.

A nurse comes in, so I explain to her about Robert choking. She tries to get Robert to sit up, but Robert complains, and will not, or cannot, co-operate. The nurse gives up and leaves.

Mrs Campbell soon returns. I tell her about the choking – she says she knows and that they are going to give him medicine for his chest.

Sadly, I *have* to leave him. I talk to Mrs Campbell and to Robert about Carol being away from Monday, and how difficult it will be for them. Mrs Campbell replies matter-of-factly, 'Oh, yes, indeed.'

I go and see Peter to brief him. He's been snowed under with other urgent cases. He agrees to see the parents about Julie coming over. I tell him I'll be 'on call' over Christmas, if necessary.

15 December (Monday) The first good news for a long time! Peter rings me at home in the evening to say Julie came over on Saturday. This arose out of a meeting Peter arranged on Friday between the parents, Peter, and one of the doctors who informed the parents of the grim outlook.

16 December (Tuesday) 2.00 p.m. I go into the room and find Robert alone. I turn the television sound down. He is lying on his side, propped up on pillows, picking relentlessly at his bottom lip, which is a dark purply red. Bits of skin and blood are on his fingers and on the pillowcase. A medallion of the Virgin Mary is pinned to his pillow.

I say hello, and sit by him, taking the cot-side of the bed down. His eyes are streaming with yellowy liquid. Again I say that I am not sure if they are sad eyes, or watering eyes, or both. He looks at me, continuing to pick and squeeze his lip with trembling boney fingers. I tell him I did not bring the box, as I thought his hands would be bandaged. (This is not the only reason. The truth is that I thought he would be too ill to take an interest in it.)

I talk about him picking his lip, and wonder aloud if it is his way of getting at something, when all he can attack is himself. He nods slightly. I continue to say that I've heard the news about Julie being here. He nods. I ask if they are all having lunch at the moment, and he nods again.

I talk about this being what he has wanted so much for a long time. I ask if Julie has spent a lot of time with him, and he shakes his head. I say, 'Perhaps you pick your lip all the more when Mum, Dad, and Julie are out, and you want them here with you?'

I try to hold his hand to calm him down. He allows it, but then carries on picking. I say, 'You're hurting yourself. Perhaps you feel you have to be punished... that it's your fault you're ill?'

He looks hard at me and nods. I ask him in what way he thinks he has caused it. He does not answer. I say, 'People often wonder, "Why me, why am I the ill one, why not my sister, or someone else", and they think it's because they've been bad.' He gives a hacking cough, and cries a little.

I say, 'You feel you're full of bad stuff, but you know, it isn't anyone's fault when they are ill – and no one can know why it happens to you...'

He is picking and pulling his lip in an awful way. I say, 'Your're wanting me to know what it's like to see you pulling at the rough skin. The roughness is like the illness. This way, by showing me, I can share it with you. But you may make it bleed a lot – shall I read you a story, or tell you a story, instead?' He blurts out, 'I want the box!' 'The box with the toys?' I ask. 'Right... I'll get it. I'll be a little while... have to go in the lift.' I put up the bedside bars.

I dash off, cursing myself for not bringing the box, but pleased that Robert so actively requests it.

When I return, a few minutes later, he is in exactly the same position, picking at his lips. I make a little table out of the box lid, and hold up the various collections within. Animals? He shakes his head. Hospital set? He shakes his head. Soft little dolls? He nods.

I put them out. He seems unable to play with them, so I hold them up, and ask if this is the Mummy, Daddy, and so on, to which he nods each time, correcting me that 'Granny' is 'Nan'. He agrees that the little boy is Robert and the bigger girl, Julie. I ask if Mum or Dad are busy with the children? He shakes his head. I say, 'So are they like this, busy with each other?' He nods to my positioning the parents as if talking to each other. I interpret his wish for Mum and Dad to get on well together. I go on to talk about this little boy doll being left out now, now that Mum and Dad are busy...'perhaps how you feel when Mum and Dad and Julie go out and leave you? And now that Carol has gone away, it must be very difficult.' He looks at me. (I do not interpret his feelings that I too come and go, and leave him, like they do. I'm not sure why I avoid saying this. Perhaps the imminent death is like an inevitable sudden separation or ending which makes me instinctively avoid the impact of *my* close relationship with him. But for whose sake? Mine or Robert's?)

I ask him what he wants me to do with the dolls now? His face puckers. 'I want Mummy!' I stroke his forehead, saying, 'Mummy will be back soon. You feel upset when I talk about Carol going away.' Then, feeling bolder, I say, 'And I go away too, between Tuesdays and Thursdays and Thursdays and Tuesdays.'

'Bedpan!' he blurts out.

Just as I am about to lift him onto it, his sister Julie and his parents walk in. I say, 'Your Mum is much better at this than I am', and hand over the role to Mrs Campbell. Mr Campbell helps too. Robert suddenly cries, as if in pain. Both parents expostulate about his lip, especially Mr Campbell, saying that it is much worse now. Apparently, they had asked a nurse to sit with him. Mrs Campbell clears up the mess impatiently, but is verbally resigned, for when Mr Campbell continues to complain about the state of his lip, she says philosophically, 'He won't stop... no point in going on about it... nothing we can do... even if his hands are bandaged, he'll rub the bandage against it.'

Meanwhile, I talk to Julie for the first time. She seems a pleasant, polite, sensitive girl. She appears rather plump, but perhaps that is simply in contrast to the state of her brother.

Suddenly Robert calls out shrilly, 'I want Mrs Judd to lie me down!' His mother seems to show some difficult feelings about this in her way of saying, 'Oh, all right.' Doubtless, they feel angry with me for 'allowing' the lip-picking. I step forward to help Robert, saying, 'Well, you don't see much of me.' Feeling rather guilty about the lip-picking, I say to the parents that perhaps he feels fed up and feels he has to pick at *something*.

Robert asks for the bedpan again. Mr Campbell tells me he wants it thirty to forty times a day. I comment on how exhausting this must be for him and for them.

Mrs Campbell continues about the picking, 'We can't stop him... if he doesn't want to take his tablets now, I don't force him.'

I wonder to myself about the extent to which Mrs Campbell has given up the struggle. She talks with slight bitterness at times, exhaustion at others. Her shift of attitude does not seem one of a peaceful acknowledgement of the inevitable, a wish to make it as calm as possible. Perhaps not surprisingly, after the months of an agonizing struggle on her part, she cannot give in gracefully at this point. As part of her acceptance there seems bound to be some outrage at what is happening. (This links with my comments on the phases people approaching death go through in Chapter 5.)

Julie's arrival seems to be an appropriate gratification of Robert's overriding need to see her, and Julie's need too to see Robert. The family unit is completed at this point of crisis. But, in a way that I had not anticipated, it seems to stress the situation further. The parents are more anxious and exhausted than I have ever seen them. I feel this is mainly their response to Robert's deteriorating condition, but Julie's presence must lead to conflicting pulls in them to protect the older child on the one hand from the dreadful situation, while, on the other hand, to help her prepare for Robert's death. But can they manage any of the extra parenting Julie requires when they are both so fully stretched by Robert?

Mr Campbell and Julie then set off for a walk. Robert calls out to me, 'I want the hospital set!' I am supposed to attend a meeting at this point, but I decide not to. So I set up the table over his bed and take out the hospital set. He is propped up on pillows, and, in spite of his heavy-lidded eyes, he appears interested. Mrs Campbell leaves the room. I tell Robert that I will just pop out to tell people that I am not going to a meeting and that I will be back soon.

I return very quickly. He seems to expect me to somehow facilitate his play, so I ask him how I should arrange the little figures. He wants the little boy on the bed, the mother and father by his bedside, the hat in the locker (as he himself has arranged it previously). He seems to appreciate my talking about the things *he* did with all this when he was not so ill. I wonder aloud if the hat in the locker is for when the little boy goes home. He wants the little boy to get up and have food at the table, and to then go back to bed. I do not talk to him about his need to experience the normal aspects of life through play, as his way of re-living and re-gaining a lost, dormant or dying aspect of himself. The mere enactment of a more well little boy seems sufficient.

Mrs Campbell returns, and Robert requests the bedpan. While he sits on it he says his back aches. His mother gives him a close cuddle while rubbing it, and then leaves again.

Robert requests the little family of soft dolls. Again, he seems too weak to play with them himself, so I ask him what he wants me to do with them for him. I make the mother doll cuddle the Robert doll, describing the actions, and ask him if that is what he wants me to do. He nods. I ask him, 'And the Dad? To cuddle too?' He affirms, so I do this. I then enact Dad and the Julie doll going off for a walk and talk about Robert struggling here, for such a long time, to get well, while the others can go out for walks.

He blurts out, 'Want plasticine.' His requests today have an almost feverish quality, as if he wants to play with everything for the last time. I wonder if this is the efflorescence that can precede death. I ask him what colour he wants? 'Pink.' So I soften some for him. He tries it out and asks me to make something for him. I remind him that I will have to go soon, and make him a little car, perhaps connected with my coming and going, but more consciously because of Mrs Campbell often telling me about Robert's liking for toy cars. He watches my hands intently as I work. I put it in front of him. He asks me to make something else. I ask him what? He says, 'You choose.' I tell him I will make something for him to guess, and fashion a little mouse. He shakes his head at the finished product. I am not sure if it's a poor representation, or if he has a block to knowing what it is. Anyway, I tell him what it is, adding that perhaps he reminds me of a little mouse today: quiet, but busy. I put the mouse and car on the little shelf with the plasticine Sunshine (teddy bear) I had made before.

He asks for the urine bottle. After using it he lies back, exhausted.

Mrs Campbell returns. I pack up the toy box and say that I have to go now. For the first time he cries out plaintively, 'Don't want Mrs Judd to go!' I stroke his forehead, and say that I will be back on Thursday, the day after tomorrow.

This turns out to be a false promise, as I *am* back on Thursday, but not to see Robert. I find myself holding out the expectation of the usual pattern of visits even though I know that this may well be broken by his death. I continue to hope that there will be another day – even though, in a way, Robert himself seems to have reached a stage where he needs peace above all.

(Robert seems to be showing a growing attachment to me, as someone important to him. Needless to say, the corollary to this is that he occupies a central position in my thoughts and feelings. The volume of painful feelings which I carry reinforce my awareness that I have to try to keep a balance in my life between this kind of work and other work.)

Mrs Campbell comes and stands by Robert's bedside, sympathetically. I say to both of them, 'Robert feels upset at my going, especially after Carol left to go on holiday yesterday.'

Mrs Campbell nods, adding, 'But Carol is going to send you a card, your own special card, isn't she?' She continues to stroke Robert's forehead as I leave, as if to facilitate my going. Later I try to arrange for someone else in the department to see Julie on her own. I realize that today is the only day that I have 'forgotten' to write a note on Robert's ward file about my session with him.

17 December (Wednesday) 12 noon. I receive a phone call at my other place of work to phone Miranda urgently, the head of the hospital school. I do so. She says, 'I have sad news for you. Robert died this morning.' Apparently, it was at about 10 o'clock, and she recounts to me that the parents are weeping, wandering around the hospital looking very lost; everyone is relieved that Julie is over here. She says they are going back home tomorrow or the next day. I tell her that I will try to arrange to come to the hospital today.

Fortunately, a colleague agrees to see a family without me, so I can leave the clinic. The intervening meeting and interaction at the clinic have a strange, unreal feel. Later, I realize that I was in a state of numbness. I feel some conscious relief as well. I have an oppressive headache which lifts soon after I arrive at the hospital.

I think about Robert dying only four days after Julie's arrival. It seems that he really was 'holding on' until seeing his sister again. (Kübler-Ross (1987) writes about similar situations of dying people, beyond the point where they can be helped medically: not letting go until some crucial issue has been resolved. Recent research by the University of California bears this out: it suggests that dying patients enter a 'bargaining' phase in which they ask their god to allow them to survive until the arrival of an important occasion (Brindle, 1988).)

3.20 p.m. I arrive at the hospital and go up to the children's ward. Straight away I see Peter with the parents and Julie in the parents' lounge, talking to them with another Scottish couple. Mrs Campbell is crying, pale, and red-eyed. Mr Campbell immediately comes up to me and blurts out how much he had tried... everyone had tried... how we all did what we could. His speech flows on in a stream: 'Everyone gets impatient sometimes... fed up... I know I did... feel I could only give so much...'. I try to talk to him about Mrs Campbell having a definite role with Robert and that it was hard for him not having this clear role. I also talk to him about him feeling *so* much, right from the start, and that perhaps because he felt so upset, and felt it so strongly, he had to go away a little each day.

I notice Julie sitting there, crying. So I go and put my hand on her shoulder, and say how important it is for her to be here. She nods.

Peter has to go with Mr Campbell to sort out the death certificate and then to arrange tomorrow's journey with the undertaker. The plan is that after all the arrangements have been made, we will go and see Robert's body. I decide to wait with Mrs Campbell and Julie, and then to go with them, for my sake as much as theirs, to see the body.

The Scottish couple are, apparently, from a charity that helps to raise money for leukaemia, and they seem to be here to befriend the parents. Tonight the parents and Julie will sleep at their flat, and the next morning they will fly up to Scotland.

I take them down to the hospital canteen for tea. (I sorely feel the lack of a more private place to be together.) The visiting Scottish lady seems to counter my attempts to allow Mrs Campbell and Julie to cry, with comments like, 'Robert wouldn't want you to cry. He's happy now, in heaven. He's up there', pointing to the ceiling. Mrs Campbell and Julie, though, seem very open in their feelings of loss and utter misery. Mrs Campbell cries, and talks copiously about Robert's special qualities.

Mrs Campbell tells me that this morning he had been breathing with difficulty since about 5.00 a.m., so they provided oxygen. At about 10.00 a.m. Robert asked for the bedpan, but for the first time was too weak to lift himself up, and soiled the undersheet. Mrs Campbell tells me how he held out his little arm, which mother took, 'And it felt strange. He just looked at me with those great big eyes. I rang the bell. Mike [the charge nurse] came, and then I went to get my husband. I think he was "gone" by the time we got back.'

Mrs Campbell reproaches herself for the times she has been impatient with Robert in the middle of the night, saying, 'Not again, Bobby!' when Robert wanted the bedpan for the umpteenth time. I notice that she is wearing Robert's little blue watch. Apparently, Mrs Campbell had asked Julie to put it at the right time earlier today, before the death. Robert has not worn the watch since he has been in hospital.

Mrs Campbell eats a sandwich slowly, as if force-feeding herself. She chokes on it once. Julie begins to cut away at the table top with a plastic knife, so I acknowledge her feeling so angry that this has to happen. More tears spring to her eyes, prompting the Scottish lady to ruffle her hair and tell her that Robert would not want her to cry. I put forward my belief in the value of crying, as a very normal and healthy response. This is risking the alienation of the Scottish lady, but my main concern is clearly with Robert's family.

Mrs Campbell then cries desperately at the prospect of going back home without Robert, going into Robert's room, seeing his little bed, and wonders what to do with all his toys and possessions. I talk about her doing it in her own time. She says she has decided to give the hospital all the toys that are new here, and to take Robert's little Communion Book, and a neck chain with a cross, which she is going to put with Robert. She also has two little bottles of holy water from Lourdes, and 'relics'.

Eventually, Peter and Mr Campbell return. Mr Campbell is extremely agitated, and cannot bear to sit with us while Peter telephones the undertaker. The husband of the Scottish lady rejoins us.

After a long delay, we all go down to see Robert in a strange underground – or should I say underworld – part of the hospital, through various locked doors, escorted by a young man.

Robert's body is in a little room, lit only by a candle-bulb. An iron cross stands next to it. He is covered up to the neck in a blue shroud. His bald head rests peacefully at last. His eyes are closed, behind pinkish lids. The rest of the face is pale, except for dark red lips. Are they painted, or is it the purplish bruising? He wears the smart striped pyjama top he wore before he became desperately ill.

His parents touch his forehead. Mr Campbell exclaims, 'How cold he is!' as if he should warm him or do something to remedy it. Mother is overcome with crying, touches Robert, hugs Julie, who cries too. The blue shroud becomes stained with their tears. Peter and I stand back a little.

I say, 'How peaceful he looks.' Father readily agrees. I touch Robert's forehead and am shocked at the coldness. I remember my father's dead forehead: that lifeless quality. I cry too.

Mrs Campbell searches frantically for Sunshine, the teddy bear. It does not seem to be there. Julie joins her in the search. They then find it, tucked far down. Mrs Campbell adds the mementoes she has brought. Mrs Campbell's desperate need to place Sunshine with Robert seems to be her way of easing the separation between Robert and herself. Sunshine represented mother for Robert in the past and now Sunshine once again is to bridge Mrs Campbell's separation from her son. Similarly, Robert's little blue watch on Mrs Campbell's wrist may help to ease the separation.

> This small forgotten object, that was ready to signify everything, made you intimate with thousands through playing a thousand parts... This Something, worthless as it was, prepared your relationships with the world... you experienced through it, through its existence, through its anyhow-appearance, through its final smashing or its enigmatic departure, all that is human, right into the depths of death.

Thus Rilke (1914, *Gesammelte Werke*, IV) described the importance of that which Winnicott (1951) much later termed a 'transitional object'. In describing its symbolic potential Rilke encompasses the possiblity of including the 'depths of death' in its range. Although Rilke did not mean it literally, it serves to illustrate what he describes in his Fourth Elegy as 'the gap left between world and toy': the significance of this toy/doll/teddy bear/object which usually represents the absent mother.

I am reminded of hearing from a health visitor about the death of a young baby. The mother wished to place some of her breast milk on the baby's lips, as her last gesture, when saying goodbye to her baby. This seems to epitomize the wish to continue to provide for the baby after death and to ease the separation for the mother. And, as we know, the ancient Egyptians attempted to assure the happiness of their dead children in the after-life by burying with them the toys with which they had played (Puckle, 1926). Similarly, another mother insisted upon changing her dead daughter into a new track-suit, after the child had already been laid out.

Peter asks about the holy water which Mrs Campbell has not used yet. She makes the sign of the cross on Robert's forehead with it, and on his chest, and gives some to Julie to do the same, then puts the bottle of holy water with Robert.

The Scottish lady says, 'He's not there, that's not Robert, he's in heaven.'

The parents look at his seemingly long limbs stretched out under the shroud as if to take stock, before leaving. Mrs Campbell kisses him, saying, 'Good night, my pet.' Afterwards, she says, 'I kept wanting him to open his eyes.'

Julie and Mrs Campbell are crying as we walk along the corridor away from the mortuary. I put an arm around them, feeling helpless, saying, 'It's awful for you. Robert had a few happy years, and lots of love...'

We all go up in the lift, to the children's ward, for the parents to pack their bags. I say goodbye to them, and Mrs Campbell begins to cry again. We hug each other, and she thanks me. I say that I will be thinking of them, and that I feel grateful to have known Robert. Mr Campbell and I shake hands warmly. I say goodbye to Julie, and shake hands with the Scottish couple. Mrs Campbell's eyes follow me beseechingly to the lift, as if searching for her son through me.

Outside the hospital, the darkness of the night is regaled by the Christmas lights. I curse the Christmas trees and the Christmas lights. I feel so angry with this season of jollity. I can now fully understand why the word 'Christmas' had made Mrs Campbell cry earlier today.

Tomorrow they fly home 'with' Robert.

Later, at home, I feel the need to care physically for my healthy seven-year-old. I look at him, stretched out in the bath, and gain succour from his health, while feeling a shiver of shock at the coffin-like surround of the bath. I have to begin my own process of mourning Robert.

18 December (Thursday) I go into the hospital as usual on Thursday. I feel deeply touched by the warm support I receive from colleagues. Robert's family will not need to return to the hospital today. I go up to the children's ward to add my last notes to Robert's medical file.

I read the medical notes for yesterday. These are some extracts:

7.15 a.m.   Very weak
7.30 a.m.   Fairly rapid deterioration. Pneumonia
9.30 a.m.   Very unwell. Morphine prescribed
10.10 a.m. No spontaneous respiration
             No pulse
             Certified dead (by the Senior House Officer)

I wander into Robert's empty room, feeling that if I postpone this step it will become more fearful. The door is wide open for the first time. And the room is indeed empty. Very empty. Some of the posters are still on the walls. I find the little plasticine version of Sunshine I had made for Robert still sitting on a shelf. I feel irrationally hurt that it has been left there. I remove it.

At a staff meeting the next week, one of the staff nurses who knew Robert tells me that she and the other nurses were 'really pleased' when Robert died. At first I think I have misheard her, and ask her to repeat herself. I then realize that she does mean what she says, and that she is referring to the relief the nurses felt that the long and painful struggle was over. Nevertheless, it leads me to wonder about some of the nurses' difficulties in really feeling *loss* at Robert's death. Their training and work, with its emphasis on nursing people to health, does not seem to have sufficient place for thinking about, and staying with, the pain of terminal illness. But then, can anyone repeatedly *experience* this in an exposed way?

I realize I have to spare myself too frequent encounters with death through my work: to balance it with all the other work as a way of gaining equilibrium. To really share the process with the dying and their families, I have to find a balance: somewhere between the raw pain that they are feeling, and the defended state of some of the medical team, in order to be most useful to them.

Without the suppport of colleagues, of Dr Green's fortnightly workshop for those working with terminally ill children and their families, as well as that of my husband and analyst, I probably would not have coped.

Weeks later, I go back to Robert's medical file, and see that someone has written in the date of his death under the 'date of discharge' column, and then inscribed, in big letters, 'R.I.P.'.

Chapter Eight

Postscript

> ... the emotional pain of loss, the pain that
> has broken a heart. Such pain fills the space
> of an entire life. It may have begun with a
> single event but the event has produced a
> surplus of pain. The sufferer becomes
> inconsolable. Yet, what is this pain, if it is
> not the recognition that what was once
> given as pleasure or happiness has been
> irrevocably taken away?
> John Berger, *And Our Faces, My Heart, Brief
> as Photos*

Five months after Robert's death, I heard from Peter, the paediatric social worker, that Mr and Mrs Campbell and Julie would be revisiting the hospital in a few days. This seemed to be in order to see the hospital staff again and to go over some of the events by re-experiencing the place.

I left a note for them, so that they could contact me if they wished. Mrs Campbell telephoned, sounding jovial, and I arranged to meet them at the flat of Carol with whom they were staying.

I was warmly welcomed by Mr Campbell who seemed to have put on weight and looked extremely well. He told me how the airline company had – after Mrs Campbell had complained – offered them free tickets as compensation for the two-hour delay they had endured at Aberdeen airport when they were taking Robert's body back home. Julie, now in the same room as her father, continued with her absorption in a television computer game, barely acknowledging my visit. Understandably, she had more engrossing matters to attend to.

Mrs Campbell then came in to meet me. She looked pretty and delicate, her gentle manner harmonizing with the pastel shades of her jumper and make-up, reflecting the warm early summer weather. I felt relieved at the apparent health of all three of them, and moved by the keenness and openness with which both parents talked about their feelings upon revisiting the hospital. It seemed that through this nostalgic, painful, and pleasurable journey they were sharing memories with the many people who knew Robert. It seemed a very understandable part of the mourning process: to face the hospital ward (and most of the people involved) which had been the centre of their life for three months, to express gratitude for all the concern and care Robert had received, and perhaps to begin to work through some of the agonizing questions, particularly in Mrs Campbell's mind. She conveyed that she repeatedly questioned every aspect of the past few years, feeling guilt and self-reproach at some decisions and ways she behaved.

Julie continued to play with the computer game throughout my long visit, interjecting with occasional comments. I gathered she had had an outing the day before, alone with Peter, so I felt her avoidance of me now may have been her way of giving her parents, and particularly her mother, their 'turn'. Her manner was pleasant and calm, and she was looking forward to a shopping trip that afternoon.

A very detailed account was then given to me of the three years since Robert's diagnosis: from the initial tummy pains, to the sore throat, to the numerous copious nosebleeds, to the body rash – until the diagnosis was made. And then the first treatment, followed by several healthy months in remission, then an ominous nosebleed and the realization that he was relapsing. This time Robert was very close to death, and yet, with the chemotherapy, he re-emerged for a further remission; and then began the final phase at the hospital in the North of England.

Mrs Campbell showed me an album of photographs of Robert, from babyhood onwards. He did indeed seem to have been an active, spirited, and robust child. It is hardly surprising that the home was described as being very quiet and empty nowadays. It seems that the remaining family members were very conscious of the gap left by Robert. Mrs Campbell found it difficult to enjoy her increased leisure now that she did not have a boisterous little boy – nor an ill little boy – to care for.

Mrs Campbell recounted how Robert, even as a very little boy, had a precocious awareness of death. She gave several examples of her son's down-to-earth (if I may use that expression) understanding of the process, including the three-year-old Robert's own word for coffin, which was 'bury-box'.

Mrs Campbell cried freely at many points in her story. Both parents were still raw in experiencing their pain. It seemed that now their religious beliefs were helping them in their mourning: some feeling of a divine being that has an all-powerful plan seemed to help them to reliquish Robert.

I felt there was a possibility that this tragedy of Robert's death could actually leave them with a greater awarness of life's pleasures as well as its pains. 'The deeper that sorrow carves into your being, the more joy you can contain.' (Gibran, 1926.) They seemed to have so much humility, love, and compassion, in their accounts of their son and of their involvement with others who had helped them. Although there were reproaches, mainly self-directed, but also towards possible delays in the doctors diagnosing the illness, there was no bitterness.

Mrs Campbell said that she had one or two further administrative matters to sort out regarding Robert's death, which she was consciously postponing. It was as if she did not yet wish to complete the 'burial'. Yet, of course, this child will live on in the minds of many of us.

We talked about the many times that I sensed Mrs Campbell's ambivalent and, at times, negative feelings towards me. She acknowledged that this had indeed been the case: she had often had appallingly disturbed nights with Robert and then the next morning they would be in the midst of various medical procedures, when I would arrive. Of course, my appearance with a box of toys for Robert, who could barely move, seemed singularly inappropriate! Mrs Campbell felt, moreover, that I would be judging her if she felt exhausted and did not face Robert's demands with resilience. However, she warmly conveyed that she now saw it all differently: 'You were there for Robert, and he valued you. That's the important thing.'

Chapter Nine

Brief retrospective analysis

> ... but I think people always die alone...
> with or without relations. I was a little girl
> then... And I remember asking her one
> time... how does it feel to die? - Only a
> little girl would ask such a question... She
> said - It's a lonely feeling.
> Tennessee Williams, *Orpheus Descending*

R eflecting upon my inhibition in really using the transference in my work
with Robert, I now feel that it would have been more useful to him if I
had 'gathered' it more fully. Limitations within the setting and my own
countertransference responses, at times, of overprotectiveness played a part
in this. Eissler writes 'It is conceivable that through the establishment of
transference, through an approach which mobilizes the archaic trust in the
world and reawakens the primordial feeling of being protected by a mother,
the suffering of the dying can be reduced to a minimum' (1955, p. 119). I
would add, however, that equally the transference relationship would be the
place wherein anxiety, grief, anger, guilt, and other painful emotions can be
experienced - once the 'archaic trust' is established.

Given the widespread anxiety about facing death *alone* - alone externally
as well as internally - an established relationship with a therapist can
provide a sense of inner 'holding' which mitigates the pain, fear, and
impending loss. This is something that has rarely been established, owing to
the unusual time commitment and flexibility required on the part of the
therapist. In situations where there are emotionally available family or
friends it is less necessary. I would argue that as family and friends have,
understandably, a greater emotional vested interest in the survival of the
patient, even when medical science appears to have little further to offer, the
therapist, although still struggling with his own inner feelings of grief,
anxiety, guilt, and anger, may be better able to *facilitate* (and I do not mean
instigate) a process of anticipatory mourning in the patient (Eissler, p. 181).
Thus, as we often see, the patient gradually detaches from his loved ones
before death, as a way of easing the separation. A transference relationship to
the therapist can then provide a substitute arena for the relinquished ties.

I feel that my ability at times tacitly to accept Robert's impending death (even though part of me railed against it) was probably of considerable benefit to him. To sit with him, quietly, but thinking about him and his situation, seemed to give him the opportunity to 'be'. There is an irony in a situation which, by allowing the child to be dying, actually seems to validate him and in that sense allows him to be alive. The alternative would be to deny him the life he is still living, albeit a dying life, by attempting to force him backwards towards health, or by denying his sadness. Winnicott (1972) writes: 'it is not unhealthy, but indeed a sign of health, that the child can use relationships in which there is maximal trust, and in such relationships at times disintegrate, depersonalize, and even for a moment abandon the almost fundamental urge to exist and to feel existent.' Although here he is not necessarily writing about a child with a terminal illness, his comments describe the way in which Robert and other dying children can use trusted relationships.

As the reader will have noted, I hardly spoke to Robert directly about death. This was, sometimes, the result of my own inhibitions; at times the parents' denial made it difficult to really pursue this; and, at other times, Robert and I seemed to communicate to each other non-verbally that he was dying. In fact, generally, he was very communicative in his nods and facial expressions.

I do have some regrets about the lack of communication between individual members of the team. This problem ties in with the other main difficulty: that a clear decision to switch to palliative care was not made. Therefore Mr and Mrs Campbell did not have a final stage of relative acceptance (admittedly with a dying child it would be rare for there to be absolute acceptance) and thus Robert did not have the opportunity of sharing his *dying* with anyone other than myself and possibly Carol (the auxiliary nurse). Above all, he may well have suffered unnecessarily with various treatments right until he died.

I need to add that Peter (the paediatric social worker) was considerably over-worked during those three months owing to an unusually heavy and demanding work-load, partly as a result of a curtailment of social services resources. This led to less contact between him and the family, and between him and myself and the rest of the team, than he, or we, would have liked.

Each of us who is closely involved with a dying child has to negotiate our own individual sense of guilt and failure. This arises not only out of understandable regret at not having somehow increased one's efforts to save and repair the child, but also out of feelings that we have played a part in bringing about this death. For we have underlying primitive phantasies: when frustrated we tend to hate that which frustrates, leading to aggressive impulses to destroy the 'breast' or mother (Klein, 1937). These basic conflicts unconsciously colour the emotional life of adults: not only may we feel at times that our anger may have caused this death (see the Freud quotation in Chapter 2, 'children... unashamedly threaten one another with the possibility of dying...') but past impulses of hatred towards someone we love contribute to our now feeling guilty when faced with death.

In a case with which I have been involved, the parents of a five-year-old girl, Polly, became emotionally unavailable to her owing to their uncertainty about her survival. Polly became increasingly rejecting of them when they did appear. The hospital staff attempted to encourage them to participate more in the everyday care of Polly, but did not have much success.

However, Polly was then seen twice weekly by a child psychotherapist, to whom she developed a very strong positive transference. Although Polly showed considerable distress at the gaps between the therapy sessions, the therapist was able to use this positively by helping her to get in touch with her anger at her parents' frequent unavailability. The parents were able only up to a point to use the support of a social worker: they found it difficult to remain present as much as possible and to bear and survive Polly's onslaughts. They were helped, separately, to express some anxiety and grief.

Until her death five months after her BMT, Polly continued to use the therapist as a reliable and resilient figure, finally mourning her too by becoming very detached from her and from everyone else in the last week of her life. She seemed to accept and appreciate the therapist's calm presence as sufficient.

The psychotherapist's work generally goes against the grain of this process of detachment. Therefore, the distancing mechanisms can be talked about with the patient: 'How painful it feels to get attached at such a time.' This ability to *stay with* the detached patient (contradictory though that sounds) and survive the apparent rejection is important.

Perhaps in the light of having looked at the death of a *child* any discussion about an acceptance of death, or a working towards death, seems inappropriate. Perhaps some readers feel that they (or I, if it were my child) would rail against death until and beyond the last breath, and possibly for ever. I feel that this *protest* does and must exist, but that alongside, or interwoven with this, the therapist, in the special position of being both involved yet not totally personally immersed, can at times swim with the patient who is being carried along by the tide of the illness.

Part Three

Survival or death

Chapter Ten

Prolonging dying

... the doctor should obtain the patient's
freely given consent after the patient has
been given a full explanation. In case of
legal incapacity consent should also be
procured from the legal guardian...
  The doctor can combine clinical research
with professional care, the objective being
the acquisition of new medical knowledge,
only to the extent that clinical research is
justified by its therapeutic value for the patient.
Wolstenholm and O'Connor, *Declaration of
Helsinki Code of Ethics* of the World Medical
Association

In considering the complex and controversial issue of sustaining the life of a dying child, we need to approach the dilemma from the points of view of all those involved: the patient; the patient's family; the medical team, which includes doctors, nurses, students; as well as the paramedicals, such as social workers, teachers, psychotherapists, clergy, and others.

Firstly, in defining 'terminally ill', we mean a state of disease which is characterized by irreversible and progressive deterioration. Inevitably therefore there are varying degrees of impairment of function, and the patient's survival is severely time-limited. With modern technological developments and new therapies, life for the terminally ill can be prolonged. However, looked at from a slightly different angle, *dying then becomes prolonged*. Therefore there is an increasing need to concern ourselves with the moral and ethical implications of prolonging dying: the quality of the remaining life and dignity of the patient needs to be considered.

Ethical committees of professional and lay people are attached to all National Health Service teaching hospitals in Britain. They are actively debating these issues, often in a thoughtful and caring way. Their main role is to consider all proposals for clinical research, thus providing peer-group supervision. Clinicians submit their protocols, and although the committee's approval is deemed important, there is no legal obligation to respect it. The basic guidelines are the Nuremberg Code (1947), which, prompted by Nazi medical crimes, lays down ten standards to which physicians must conform when carrying out experiments on human subjects; the Declaration of Geneva (1948), which is a modified form of the Hippocratic Oath; as well as the Code of Ethics of the World Medical Association Declaration of Helskini (Wolstenholm and O'Connor, 1968). There are also guidelines published by the Royal College of Medicine. (See Appendix 2 for extracts from the Nuremberg Code.)

Some of the research proposals include plans for trials of new therapies or drugs for children which may affect the life (and death) of the terminally ill. I gathered from Reverend Peter Speck (Chaplain at the Royal Free Hospital, London and Honorary Senior Lecturer in the Department of Clinical Epidemiology and General Practice in the School of Medicine there) that at the Royal Free Hospital, in respect of every protocol, the clinician responsible writes a one-page synopsis in lay terminology, which is attached to the protocol, and which comes before the Ethical Practices Committee. This synopsis is supposed to carry details not only of potential therapeutic benefit, but also of possible side-effects and risks.

The British Medical Assocation's ruling states that from the age of sixteen a child's informed consent must be sought. However, some physicians and some ethical committees respect the involvement in the decision-making process of some fourteen- and fifteen-year-olds. In Speck's experience, below those ages it seems that *parents'* decisions are sought. The BMA, in its attempt to clarify this grey area, adds the proviso that if the consent of under-sixteen-year-olds is sought, you have to demonstrate that the child is capable of this decision. This seems to lead to a further grey area: how do you prove this kind of capability? I explore this further under 'Children's consent' (see pp. 158-9).

In parallel with the work of ethical committees, individual consultants have to make clinical decisions about, for example, the shift from cure to palliative care. These are decisions which do not depend on committees. It is here that there is an attempt to teach medical students through the involvement of clinicians in the teaching programme, thus hopefully opening up a dialogue on issues such as when to pursue *cure*. Speck says (personal communication) that students' questions during 'ethics seminars' within a clinical attachment can be useful as part of a self-questioning process for doctors. Inevitably, the majority on ethical committees are doctors, and they are deeply committed by their training and vocation to *save* people's lives and primarily to *cure* illness. This may be an obstacle to the objectivity required, and the same reservation applies to the consultants who, against the background of ethical committees, are making major decisions.

However, Judith Chessells, Professor of Haematology and Oncology (Hospital for Sick Children, Great Ormond Street), herself a chairman of a joint ethical committee, says (personal communication) that her unit does not find problems in switching its emphasis from cure to care; nor, in her experience, do patients always opt for treatment. She explains, 'In our institution, when treatment has failed, there is a very open discussion with the parents involving various members of the caring team, and we try to reach a communal decision about what is the right thing.'

In discussing these concerns there seem to be two separate problem areas: one of economic moral questions (considerations of financial cost) and the other of non-economic moral questions (the quality of life and human dignity). The former inevitably becomes a political issue, with governments primarily deciding upon the allocation of resources. The moral approach to this is that the decision as to who should be kept alive and who should die should not depend on governments, for it runs the risk of creating situations of totalitarianism. Therefore these decisions should be part of non-political health councils, ethical committees, and medical research councils.

Looking, then, at the non-economic issues, there are those who believe that there are situations where death can be hastened – not just allowed to run its course. Those who believe this are not denying the value of medical intervention to prolong life where it is meaningful (and this needs very careful definition) but are saying that there are times when the vitality, purpose, and meaning of life have broken down, cannot be repaired, and life becomes non-life. They are not in favour of killing, but, as Phillip Miller (1987) writes, on occasion willing 'to take an active role in the process of death'. He continues that they must do this 'to stop suffering... to protect autonomy, and to replace technology by real people in dying situations'. He writes that, if he were breathing his last breath, he would prefer to be 'touched by a hand than violated by a tube'. However, in attempting to define 'suffering', and the issue of the dignity of the patient, we are up against the differing perceptions of the patient, the observer, the family, and the professionals. (These issues reflect the similar debate between those who wish to 'unmedicalize' birth and allow it to be more natural, and those who favour technological innovations.)

The conflicting view of, on the one hand, those doctors who believe in a compassionate easing of dying or, at least, in an allowing of dying, and, on the other hand, those who believe in a sustaining of life, are expressed in these two quotations (Crispell and Gomez, 1987):

> It should be stressed that treatment that prolongs pain and suffering by patients and relatives and only prolongs the physiologic process of dying benefits no one, least of all the patient.

While another doctor says:

Perhaps philosophers and theologians can resolve these perplexing problems, but the medical profession must follow a one-track course favouring life with a humane and sensible therapeutic approach.

I do not for a moment propose that there is the intention on the part of those who wish to prolong life at all costs to undermine the patient's dignity or autonomy. I believe that they are acting to the best of their knowledge to do all that they can for the patient. *However, a distinction needs to be drawn between that which is therapeutic and that which becomes research.* By 'research' I mean trying some new method or practice in order to gain knowledge and in the long run hopefully benefit other future patients. This is an important issue, which needs to be openly debated between the parents of a child, different members of the professional team, and possibly the child himself, depending on his age, understanding of the situation, and physical and emotional state. The issue of whether or not a child is capable of giving informed consent is crucial to this debate.

As stated previously, all this is complicated when considering the ethical issues around sustaining the life of a terminally ill *child*. In this area we are not considering someone whose life has run its course. We are up against a tragic curtailment of life and many other issues mentioned in Chapter 1. This makes any moral or ethical debate more fraught, and makes the polarized views expressed above perhaps even more opposed.

When considering the issue of when the medical team switches from treatment to palliative care, the paediatric sister quoted earlier, Dorothy Jordan, made the point that this decision is more readily and easily reached in a specialist children's hospital than in a paediatric ward of a general hospital. This is because the doctors in a general hospital are not necessarily *paediatricians*, and therefore find it more difficult to embrace the child's emotional state. She describes the situation in a general teaching hospital:

> It's because the doctors are so dynamic. You can understand, going to the bone marrow transplant meetings, listening to those doctors, and their fight to get a cure for leukaemia – you can only feel admiration for them. But if the white-cell picture looks good – it doesn't matter what the child looks like – they think they're better, and you know, it's taken a while for them to understand, to begin to understand what the child *really* feels like.

I talked to her about the difficult position she, and other nurses, are in, as somebody who is closely involved with the child on a daily, indeed hourly, basis: who is in touch with the child's distress, and who then is told to administer a drug that will actually make the child feel worse. I asked her how that left her feeling?

Obviously you do feel frustrated, but also don't forget that when the doctors are saying there's this new drug to try, they've got the consent of the parents, and the parents are desperate. One mum said to me she'd go to the top of this hospital and jump off the roof if that would make her child better from leukaemia. So, if we're saying, which we have done, that we've got this new drug, it's still on trial, but we're willing to try it, of course the parents want to try that...

I questioned this statement about parents always opting for treatment. She replied that in her experience in this particular hospital, over the past nine years only two parents have taken their children home. 'And that was very early on, probably about 1980, when of course the treatment wasn't as good as it is today. There was a two-year-old with myeloid leukaemia, and the parents took him home without treatment. And, sometimes, we are in a situation where we have no treatment to offer the children, and the parents then take them home.'

Many of the issues around current guidelines for research on children in Britain, and some of the moral dilemmas arising, are delineated in the detailed report of the Institute of Medical Ethics working group, on the ethics of clinical research investigations on children (Nicholson, 1986). Important distinctions between therapeutic and non-therapeutic research are explored, as well as between invasive and non-invasive treatments. They conclude that: 'the distinction has to be that *therapeutic research* is research consisting in an activity which has also a therapeutic intention, as well as a research intention, towards the subjects of the research, and *non-therapeutic research* is research activity which has not also a therapeutic intention' (p. 33).

When considering the problems of using 'controls' for the purpose of comparison, their committee examined the extent to which a control group should be subjected to non-therapeutic research in order to benefit at least some of the children in the project. They quote the example of the treatment of acute lymphoblastic leukaemia, or ALL, where the control children may receive what is considered to be the best treatment regime, while the subject children receive a new regime which *might* be an improvement. As the cure rate for ALL is greater than 50 percent (and is in fact now around 70 percent), one could conclude that both groups are receiving therapeutic benefit. This trial could be considered to be therapeutic research. However, twenty to twenty-five years ago, when the cure rate for ALL was less than 10 percent, a trial of treatment regimes often led to death before the trial was finished. Therefore those children in the trial did not benefit, but future children with ALL may have benefited. It is this type of issue which is still relevant to children with other cancers today, especially those with poorer prognoses.

Some research projects question established treatment, and can lead to a re-evaluation and a change. For example, children with ALL were routinely given three-monthly bone marrow examinations while in remission in order to detect relapses. A research programme (by Watson *et al.*, 1981) established that the incidence of unexpected relapse was only 0.4 percent. Therefore, as this is a traumatic procedure, it was concluded that it was unnecessary, and it was abandoned.

CHILDREN'S CONSENT

Whether or not children can or should give meaningful, informed consent to treatments which are proposed is another issue debated by the Institute of Medical Ethics.

Basing their research on studies by Piaget (1932), Kohlberg (1976), Weithorn and Campbell (1982), and others, they conclude:

Before the age of seven years (by which is meant the developmental age of an average seven-year-old, rather than a precise chronological age that would apply to all children equally) attempts to obtain a child's assent (by which is meant the permission given by the child that does not, however, have the legal force of consent) are likely to be meaningless, and it is more important simply to tell the child, as much as possible using his level of language, what is going to be done. From the age of seven upwards, it becomes important that an investigator should try to obtain the assent of a child subject. The nearer the child is to fourteen years old, the more important does his assent to a research procedure become. (Nicholson, 1986, pp. 150–1)

They add, however, that, as the young person between seven and fourteen will still have an immature moral judgement, in some instances refusal of assent would have to be overridden. They conclude that over the age of fourteen young people are as competent as adults to decide, and that therefore their views should carry as much weight as those of their parents. A refusal to give consent should, therefore, be binding – whether to therapeutic or non-therapeutic research procedures.

I asked Dorothy Jordan to what extent she thought that the children themselves should be brought into the decision-making process about continued treatment?

It depends of course on the age of the child. You can say to the four-and-a-half-year-olds and the five-year-olds, 'We're going to do this, we're going to do that' and they can say 'Yes, that's all right'. Then when you come to it, they change their minds. I don't know how much we should be saying to them, 'You're going to die if you don't have this treatment'. But I think maybe the twelve-, thirteen-, and fourteen-year-olds should be consulted. But then you've always got this horrible feeling that they are going to say 'Yes' but when they have all that chemotherapy that makes them so ill, their hair falls out, and so on, then they might change their minds. It's a terrible dilemma.

Of course the parents also have to give their consent. She emphasized the importance of this, and how the haematology consultant is adamant about this, 'because we've had situations where a child has had a bone marrow transplant and it's gone wrong, and the parents then say it's our fault. So the consultant makes it quite clear to parents that their *consent* is sought.'

She continued:

However, although parents are told what the chances are, what they *hear* and what they *retain* are often very different things. If you say to them we are offering you 75 percent for a lymphoblastic leukaemia, 75 percent chance of becoming disease-free, but 25 percent die because of the bone marrow transplant – they don't hear that. They don't hear that, about the 25 percent who die. Maybe it's just human nature, maybe you don't want to listen, do you?

In considering what we mean by 'informed consent', therefore, we find it difficult to arrive at a proper evaluation when, understandably, parents' decisions and consent are so coloured by their emotional state. It seems that one way in which parents manage to continue to opt for treatment, even when this is extremely unpleasant if not horrendous, is by distancing themselves from their own child and from what is happening to him or her. Sister Jordan confirms this: 'Looking back to all these deaths, and all these children, I think nearly all the parents say, *that's not my child.*' This denial seems especially understandable in the light of the external, visible signs of the illness, or the reaction to the drugs, altering the child's appearance dramatically.

Yudkin, speaking from the point of view of a doctor, pleads for the dying child to be allowed to die peacefully:

I am not, of course, referring to an acute crisis in illnesses which can perhaps be cured but, when the end is inevitable, although we feel the death of a child to be out of time, must we rush around with tubes, injections, masks and respirators? Someone said recently that no one nowadays is allowed to die without being cured. Perhaps we do it only for the parents' sake; but perhaps we ourselves cannot accept our limitations. (Yudkin, 1967, p. 40)

Chapter Eleven

Those who survive

> In order to arrive at what you do not know
> You must go by a way which is the way of
> ignorance...
> And what you do not know is the only thing
> you know...
> T. S. Eliot, *Four Quartets*

As increasing numbers of children *survive* treatment for life-threatening diseases, we need to consider the physical, psychological, and social effects on these children, and on their families – who often live under the shadow of the possible return of the illness. With many ill children the quality of life inevitably suffers in a major way. In the following pages the main focus continues to be on leukaemia.

PHYSICAL SIDE-EFFECTS OF BONE MARROW TRANSPLANTATION

In this chapter I shall briefly describe some physical side-effects to be borne in mind, as a background to, firstly, the psychological effects of cancer, and then, specifically, of bone marrow transplantation.

Among the restrictions upon remission and discharge from hospital is a prohibition upon going into crowded public places. The depression of a child's immune responses presents a constant concern because of the greatly increased susceptibility to all kinds of infections (Koocher and Sallan, 1978). Hygiene between members of the family would have to be strictly observed. Over-exposure to direct sunlight would have to be avoided. Clearly, exposure to common childhood illnesses would have to be assiduously avoided. Special oral hygiene procedures are often recommended, because as a result of total body irradiation the salivary glands have changed and are no longer as effective at washing bacteria from the mouth. Persistent dryness of the mouth is therefore a likely symptom, as well as an increased tendency to develop dental caries and mouth ulcers. Contact with pets would probably not be allowed for a while.

Then there are the long-term possible physical side-effects. These are delayed growth and physical development through receiving total body irradiation; possibly, in younger children, a delay in overall growth. Radiation affects sexual development; the development of teeth; and cataracts, which may be treatable, can form on the eyes. Sterility in both males and females is another inevitable side-effect.

Intellectual functioning seems to suffer from the disease and treatment, although here the research (Cousens, Waters, *et al.*, 1988) on IQ decrement is inconclusive as to the part played by cranial irradiation and that played by the emotional impact of the disease and other treatments administered. However, it does seem that younger children suffer more of a deficit than older children, perhaps because their brains are more vulnerable (Stehbens, *et al.*, 1983) or because their intellectual growth is arrested at a younger age and therefore they have longer to fall behind their non-affected peers who continue to develop (Twaddle, Britton, *et al.*, 1983). I would add that the emotional trauma of the irradiation treatment – as described earlier – must play a considerable part in arresting the child's cognitive growth. This can be assessed through the developmental level of children's drawings, which often become 'frozen' at the age of onset of treatment (Mary Sue Moore, personal communication).

Other problems may include dramatic weight gain or loss, mouth ulcers, muscle spasms, skin rashes, skin discolorations, scars, and, depending on the type of cancer, even organ losses and amputations (Koocher and Sallan, 1978). Psychological preparation is of course helpful for all these, but ongoing problems in adapting to physical changes and treatment arise. Continued loss of hair (including eyebrows and eyelashes) is a side-effect for those children on maintenance chemotherapy. Many children report being teased by other children at school, and being called 'Baldie' or 'Skinhead' (as shown in *I'd Rather Stay at Home*, 1986, a film by the Department of Teaching Media at Southampton University, sponsored by Cow & Gate). One mother said that while the unpleasant side-effects of the chemotherapy do disappear, the baldness remains for a length of time, as a continual reminder of the disease, and makes it very difficult for that child to be treated normally. Eventually the hair does grow back, but sometimes changes in its quality or colour.

PSYCHOSOCIAL FUNCTIONING OF CHILDREN SURVIVING CANCER

Before exploring the psychosocial effects specific to cancer, it is important to remember the possible emotional consequences to a child simply of being in hospital. These have been well documented since Spitz (1945). The early studies by Robertson in the 1950s exemplify the dramatic short-term effects. These influenced the Ministry of Health's recognizing the emotional needs of these children in a special report (1959). Isabel Menzies Lyth's paper, *The Psychological Welfare of Children Making Long Stays in Hospital: An Experience in the Art of the Possible* (1982), drawing upon Robertson and Bowlby, sensitively surveys the attachment needs of children and babies in this context. Her suggestions would form a very useful starting-point for both professionals and parents who wish to provide children with the most appropriate care. Studies by Douglas (1975) show that many brief admissions to hospital, as well as admissions of longer than a week for children under six, were associated with a likelihood of increased emotional problems in later years. However, these findings relate to conditions which had not generally been affected by later, more enlightened approaches to parental visiting and provisions for parents to stay overnight. It is not surprising that a more recent study (Shannon *et al.*, 1984) shows that hospital admissions for six-year-olds do not necessarily lead to subsequent behaviour problems when a progressive paediatric approach is instituted. However, in Britain the National Association for the Welfare of Children in Hospital is still campaigning for these basic tenets of good paediatric practice, which have, after all, been recommended for over thirty years. In 1982 a NAWCH survey showed that only half the wards in Britain to which children were admitted had appropriate settings – that is, for example, facilities for parents to be accommodated at night. Their 1988 campaign was called 'Room for Parents': an attempt to focus public consciousness on the need for making room on the wards for parents to share the nursing, as well as room in everyone's hearts and minds for more than formal facilities for visiting ill children.

The psychological implications of having to be wary of, and vulnerable to, infection, may lead to a feeling that the world is a very hostile and attacking place. In other words, this situation could well accentuate underlying infantile phantasies of persecution. (See earlier chapters on Klein's theories of the development of infants.) Not surprisingly many studies of the psychosocial functioning of children surviving childhood cancer show that they are at an increased risk of developing emotional problems: Koocher and O'Malley (1981) and O'Malley *et al.* (1979) find that the majority of these children develop at least mild psychiatric symptoms, such as depression, extreme mood changes, anxiety, and low self-esteem. However, in differentiating between the well-adjusted and maladjusted survivors, some of the positive variables appear to be a short course of treatment, no recurrence of the disease, a family which communicates openly and is supportive, an early diagnosis, and the onset of the disease at a young age (Koocher *et al.*, 1980). This better adjustment among young children seems to relate to the resilience of younger children (Rutter, 1980) as well as to the fact that the study included types of cancer predominantly found in early childhood which have a good prognosis if detected early. Therefore, although there certainly is an increased risk of children with cancer developing emotional problems, a foundation of good psychological health in the child and in the family would help to mitigate this.

Siblings of children with life-threatening illnesses show more disturbance than the actual patient in some studies (Cairns *et al.*, 1979; Spinetta, 1981). The obvious problem here is that the siblings can easily be overlooked while the ill child receives all the attention: both as the focus of anxiety as well as, possibly, being the one who is over-indulged. Lansdown and Goldman (1988) offer suggestions on the handling of siblings: in particular they firmly state that the siblings' tendency to feel guilty that they have caused the illness through hasty words and aggressive impulses needs to be acknowledged and addressed.

As stated in a survey of the literature on the psychosocial long-term sequelae of childhood cancer by Van Dongen-Melman and Sanders-Woudstra (1986), there appears to be an emphasis on the impact of *loss*, separation, and anticipatory mourning, while scant attention has been paid to the implications of *living* with a life-threatening illness. They suggest that 'a child who will die of cancer will also *live* with illness', while at the same time issues around loss, anticipatory mourning, loss of self-esteem, and loss of control over daily living need further research and understanding.

Now that childhood cancer is not inevitably fatal, and there has been a marked improvement in prognosis over the last twenty-five years, some recent literature does show a considerable shift of emphasis from a position of preparing for death, to one of preparing for *living with* a life-threatening illness. As this is a relatively new field, a great deal of research into the psychosocial needs of children with cancer still needs to be carried out. Spinetta (1977) describes a series of coping tasks (originally described by Lazarus (1976), which are: tolerating or relieving distress associated with the illness; maintaining a sense of personal worth; maintaining positive personal relationships with parents, peers, and care-givers; meeting the specific requirements of particularly stressful situations; utilizing the resources available.

PSYCHOLOGICAL EFFECTS OF BONE MARROW TRANSPLANTATION

Although there are inevitably major psychological effects of BMT, there appears to be a lack of systematic studies on those effects. A pilot study has been undertaken by Pot-Mees and Zeitlin (1987) in London, as a preliminary to a fuller three-year study on the psychosocial effects of BMT. This follow-up is not published at the time of writing. However, the pilot study, which I summarize below, contains some interesting findings.

(Even if readers find some of the following findings predictable, it may be of interest to link these findings with the account of Robert's experiences in Part II. If so many psychological side-effects are widespread perhaps they need to be addressed as part of the overall treatment plan.)

The researchers found that during the pre-admission stage the entire family was affected from the moment a BMT was proposed. Parents were 'severely distressed' and the majority were depressed. Most experienced doubt – as part of their difficulty in comprehending the medical details and the possible side-effects – about this course of treatment throughout the pre-admission stage. Waiting for the transplant added to their distress. Among the patient's siblings, blood typing to choose the donor caused considerable distress; non-donors experienced feelings of relief as well as rejection; while donors felt pride at having been selected, but anxiety about the procedures they would have to undergo.

During the transplant stage, not surprisingly, Pot-Mees and Zeitlin found that the patient's admission to hospital for BMT caused a complete change in the lifestyle of the whole family. The patients primarily experienced a variety of restrictions: being confined in isolation cubicles, restricted diets and activities, and having little privacy. With the treatment, the patient's physical appearance changed (loss of hair), as did their physical and emotional conditions. Side-effects, medical problems, such as graft-versus-host disease (see p. 80), and duration and intensity of treatment also affected their emotions.

Generally, the under-five-year-olds tended to become withdrawn and to regress. Some stopped eating and drinking on their own, lost bladder and bowel control, lost speech and other skills.

The five- to sixteen-year-olds felt more that living in isolation with almost constant medical intervention was an intrusion into their privacy and an attack on their wish to have some control and independence. This often led to frustration, anger, and clashes with parents and staff over issues of medication and eating. Apparently, the anger of some children was directed inward, leading to withdrawal and depression.

Boredom was inevitable. The isolation and side-effects of treatment led to anxieties in all the children. Most children became over-dependent on their parents, becoming much more anxious if the parents left the room.

This research then states that 'the patients who deteriorated after the BMT and finally died usually showed progressive regression and withdrawal. Because of the nature of the problems caused by graft-versus-host disease, infections, or both, some children had extremely traumatic medical and psychological experiences before they died, which created severe guilt feelings in their parents' (p. 79).

Among the effects of the experience on the parents where couples were separated during treatment, the marital relationship was stressed. Not surprisingly, some families experienced increased financial problems. For those parents who stayed in the hospital, most became extremely anxious and distressed at times, and most complained of 'claustrophobic feelings' as well as other psychological complaints.

Many of the siblings developed new behaviour problems, but the distribution of this was, understandably, far greater in the group of donors, as opposed to non-donors.

This pilot-study indicates that BMT temporarily alters the lifestyles and roles of all members of the family, and that further research is needed to ascertain the long-term effects. They recommend that the entire family be assessed – that is, nuclear family plus possibly grandparents – and monitored in order to evaluate the degree to which the patient's emotional disturbance is reflected in the rest of the family.

These preliminary findings are consistent with other research which states that BMT produces severe psychological disturbance, such as Kamphuis (1979), and Patenaude *et al.* (1979). The latter conclude similarly that BMT 'strains the emotional balance in even previously well-functioning families' and stress the importance of psychological services as part of the team provision.

Gordon (1975), in examining specifically the psychological aspects of isolator therapy in acute leukaemia, suggests that psychological difficulties relate primarily to the stress of adjustment to the diagnosis, but that living in isolation can accentuate the disturbance. Although 'isolator therapy' is more extreme than Robert's isolation situation, the findings would still be relevant. Over two decades ago, however, Anna Freud (1965) recognized the psychological meanings for children of isolation: 'isolation because of infection gives substance to ever-present fears of being rejected and of being unworthy.'

Atkins and Patenaude (1987) emphasize that as BMT nowadays often necessitates a move to a regional or other distant hospital, this relocation adds to the stress implicit in the transplant. Therefore they recommend open and frequent communication between medical, psychological, and social services, before, during, and after the transplant period, as well as clear communication with the parents and the mental health professionals to clarify the child's understanding of the complicated procedures and events. If there is not a linking network, differences in technique and approach between what are often three different hospitals leads to mistrust. Finally, they summarize: 'It is important that care-givers from all disciplines and from each institution serve as clarifiers and distillers of the transplant experience and as links from one caring hospital staff to another until the patient and family can resume that protective role for themselves' (p. 252).

The traumatic medical and psychological experiences quoted were certainly part of Robert's experience, as well as his mother's subsequent feelings of guilt, as she later conveyed to me. Her guilt covered many areas, including much questioning of her less than perfect response to him during illness. She reproached herself for leaving him at all during the final months, saying (unrealistic though this was) that if she had known about the ensuing loss she would have been by his bedside twenty-four hours a day.

There seemed inadequate communication, too, on the psychosocial side, between their cottage hospital in the North of Scotland, a hospital in the Lowlands where Robert had been for a while, and the hospital in the North of England where he had his transplant. Although some attempt at communication was made between the various social work departments, this was not carried out very effectively. The medical team, of course, had full and detailed communication over the details of his physical condition pre-transplant, and finally a full medical report was sent to the hospitals who knew him, after his death.

Therefore it seems that as that side of the process indisputedly requires full information, not only from a practical point of view but also as a way of learning about the processes and improving research, so the psychological effects need a more thorough monitoring and sharing. The frequent lack of this aspect seems to result from the view that the psychosocial side is not 'a matter of life and death' in the way that the sharing of other information indubitably is. Despite apparent shortages in staffing and funding on the psychosocial side, an enormous effort still needs to be made to keep the network alive. The family and the patient are the centre of this network, and who more than they require sensitive feed-back and contact with all parts of the network at all times?

Chapter Twelve

After the death of a child

> Why should a dog, a horse, a rat, have life,
> And thou no breath at all? Thou'lt come no more,
> Never, never, never, never, never!
> *King Lear*

Thus King Lear rails against the untimely death of his daughter, Cordelia. He seems momentarily in touch with the finality and reality of her death, and then, almost immediately, he dies too. This may partly be explained by his considerable age, but it serves to illustrate a parent's outrage, despair, and lack of purpose in living, upon the death of his or her own child.

Dora Black emphasizes the need for families to have support after a death. She states (personal communication), 'I like working with the whole family whenever I can, and I'm very keen to see them after a death – to be available. Of course that's very difficult if the family live far from the hospital.'

She continues on a more personal level,

> What I do with friends who have been bereaved is to drop them a card often, saying 'Thinking of you' – because you *do* think of people often and it's always appreciated. One of the problems that people have in our society is knowing quite what to say. There is still the situation that widows report, of people crossing over to the other side of the road, to avoid the bereaved person.

Olivia Cox (1988), whose two-year-year-old daughter died of leukaemia, writes of exactly the same experience:

> Some would cross the street rather than face our pain and though I hold no blame for these people, there were times when such actions compounded my feelings of isolation to unbearable limits.

She continues to describe her struggle during the fatal illness, 'At some of these times there was even an effort on my part to deny the hurt rather than court further rejections.' She writes that she did not want answers, 'just the silent expression of empathy, and perhaps the comfort of a hug'.

Mother Frances Dominica, whose hospice, Helen House, encourages bereaved families to remain in contact for as long as they need, says (personal communication):

We find that, after the death of a child, the first two years are hell for the parents. People don't allow you anything like a long enough time. Many people think in terms of weeks, or 'After three months you surely ought to be back to normal'. Almost without exception we have found that our families fare worse in the second year than they do in the first. The vast majority into the third year do definitely show signs of having made some sort of adjustment. No way can you claim that they've got over it, *because you never do get over it*. Into the third year many of the families have found a different way of living, accepting the fact that the child has died, and that they've got to make some sort of life – facing the reality of that. But of course there are many individuals, and whole families, where that doesn't apply actually, and it's going to be much, much longer, or where the marriage breaks up, or the surviving siblings show signs of disturbed behaviour way past the two years. You can *expect* it for two years, but after that you hope that something would have happened, and they would be able to adjust, but there are always exceptions.

It's interesting – every year we keep a weekend where we try not to take routine bookings here: we keep the house empty if we can, and we invite all our bereaved families back. At least half of them come. It was quite touching last year to hear the parents of the very first child who died here, five years ago, say how much it means to them that somebody still recognizes that they are bereaved, because a lot of people they spend time with now don't even know that she existed. It's important to them that there are some people who still remember.

The contact with the bereaved families is informal – we don't run groups. We have had, from time to time, a little self-help group that's met here for a series of sessions, but the catchment area is difficult, as relatively few of the families are sufficiently local – they're from all over the country. We have sometimes told families about 'Compassionate Friends', and one or two have found that helpful. I don't know of any family who has found it helpful in the very early stages of bereavement. Sometimes a few meetings with other bereaved families are helpful later on. What a lot of them do find useful is the 'Compassionate Friends' Newsletter, when they may not necessarily be able to cope with a *group* of people. I think particularly the fathers find groups difficult – they don't talk so readily as the mothers may. Many parents have found that being able to read about the experience of other people helps, because it's one little ray of hope: you have evidence that other people have been through, or are going through, the same kind of hell, and that you're not mad, sick, or have two heads. So often bereaved families say that one way or another they really feel they have been pushed out of the circle of ordinary human fellowship.

I asked how much this arose out of their own feelings of displacement and collapse, and how much was as a result of society's stigma. Mother Frances replied:

I think an awful lot is society. I guess that some people are predisposed to it, but it is awful how people avoid meeting, avoid confrontation – you know, the example of a mother going to meet her children from school and the other mums scatter as she approaches. People will talk about anything except the one thing you feel like talking about, which is your child and the loss you are experiencing. And the reluctance to comment on photographs of the child. Again it's dangerous to generalize, but many people actually do want to talk about it, don't they, about their child, or relive memories even if it does become very emotional. It is because of this terrific need that they often find that other bereaved parents are the most useful group.

In discussing attitudes to death, Mother Frances commented:

I think that funeral directors have got an awful lot to answer for, and yet they are presumably doing what they feel the public is demanding of them. We've had parents in very real distress, because, without being consulted, the undertakers have sometimes embalmed a child, plastered the child in make-up, done all sorts of things either to hide the truth, or to pretend, or to deceive, and to me that's conniving with the generally held view that the more you pretend, the more you deceive, the faster you get on with it all and get it all out of the way, the better.

We had parents here quite recently – one child had died ten months ago, the other died two weeks ago – and that's quite commonplace, we have quite a lot of families losing two or more children. We weren't really involved in the first funeral because we'd only just met the family, and it was all done at home, but when the second little girl died it all spilt out that they had a horrendous idea of what had to happen the moment the child died: she had to be taken away, and packed, and the cheeks filled out, and made up, and would be unrecognizable, and therefore they shouldn't see their child afterwards. We felt, 'Whatever is this?!' This was the experience they'd had last year, where the funeral directors had said that all these things had to be done to the child, and that, as she wouldn't look at all like her, they really recommended that nobody should see her afterwards. We tried to say that that just isn't right, and it isn't the way we do it, and you can stay here with her after she's died, as long as you want. All we do is wash her and dress her in the clothes you choose, or you can do it if you want to, and she can then lie in our little room here until the day of the funeral, and you can go in and out as often as you want – and the relief! You know, they've talked about it since: the contrast, how bitter they are that it happened so badly the first time. But funeral directors, presumably, are only doing what they feel the public is asking of them.

I discussed with Mother Frances how, as we often find, loss can rekindle earlier losses, and thus the impact of earlier losses is reworked, and I wondered how this continuous process affected those so frequently exposed to death at Helen House? Mother Frances:

We do experience this here, because you've no sooner started to grieve for one child when another child that you love dies – so much unfinished mourning. I find very often at the funeral of, for example, an old person with whom I may not have been very emotionally involved, I suddenly experience an enormous well of emotion, out of all proportion to the grief I am actually feeling for this individual, and it's just the unresolved grief from previous bereavements.

So that therefore I wonder about Third World countries, where there might be an almost continual process of that sort, where death is so much more commonplace, with children dying like flies of gastro-enteritis or measles or malnutrition, and how often, particularly in Islamic society, the phrase you hear is 'It is God's will'. There you are allowed a limited period of grief – forty days and then finish. I wonder, therefore, whether in fact where death is so much more commonplace, particularly with children, the bereavement doesn't go as deep, or whether the limited time-period initiates and in a way brings about a more speedy process, because it is allowed, and tolerated. And what about their expectations? I mean they are almost bound to expect that some of their children will not survive childhood, aren't they? And does that make it easier? I do not know.

We discussed those families whose grief does not really seem to be resolving itself after two or three years, and where they return to Helen House in a distraught state. Mother Frances:

Sometimes, if it really isn't working out, then either through us or their own GP or somebody, they will be referred for professional help. I don't scorn professional help at all, but I think we refer people too readily in the very early stages for professional counselling or therapy. However, one example of where it was very good was where the mother actually started going to therapy a year before her child died, so that she could anticipate the grieving, and then carried on for a year afterwards. That was a marvellous example of good use of therapy.

But I think we too readily turn to experts, because we live in a society which feels we need experts for everything, and where the rest of us easily feel disabled. There's a failure to recognize that 90 percent of what a bereaved person needs is a fellow human to be alongside, not with lots of good advice, not using professional skills, but just ready to listen and absorb. People don't want to be told what to do, or how they should be managing their lives or their grief, do they? So I think, give it time, and then if things really clearly are not coming right, they should seek good professional help. Again we are at a disadvantage because of our large catchment area, and limited number of links with therapists or counsellors with whom we have had personal contact. I can think of three or four parents who really continue to suffer severe bereavement problems several years on. Whether anybody would actually be able to help, I don't know. I think we need to recognize, don't we, that for some individuals it is not actually going to work out. I remember a child psychiatrist saying to us, 'You will, sooner or later, have a parent who will commit suicide, and the most important thing is that you don't feel guilty. You cannot be responsible for another person's life. You can help along the line and do your best, but you are not responsible.'

EFFECTS ON SIBLINGS

All infants and children inevitably experience loss (through weaning, separations, frustration). Some of this loss is in the child's external life, some in phantasy. For example, a child can imagine that its mother will never reappear or is dead, when faced with a separation or in response to the child's aggressive impulses. The child is capable of responding with feelings of grief, and experiencing the processes of mourning (Bowlby, 1960; Erikson, 1950; Klein, 1940) as part of normal development.

As Klein explains (drawing upon Freud): the child inevitably experiences states of mind which are similar to the mourning of the adult, and this is revived whenever loss and grief are experienced in adult life. She terms this sense of loss and grief the 'depressive position', as explained in Chapter 1. Part of the emotional 'work' which the child carries out when negotiating the depressive position - which is never ultimately *resolved* or finally worked through but is a state to which the infant, the child, and the adult, episodically return - is reality testing. In other words, as the child's inner world, when faced with loss, feels in grave danger of disintegrating, he gradually realizes that his destructive phantasies have not succeeded in destroying the 'breast' or the mother (for example, she returns to him after absence) and his despair at the apparent damage is mitigated by his loving impulses and attempts to repair. Thus a gradual distinction between the vicissitudes of the infant's internal world and the external world emerges. Clearly, the way in which the infant negotiates these early experiences will have inevitable repercussions on his later emotional life.

Therefore a major event, such as the death of a sibling, and the extent to which the child can deal with it would clearly depend, among other things, on earlier experiences which are re-evoked. There is a considerable body of evidence to suggest that psychiatric disorder is significantly more common in bereaved children, both during childhood and in adult life (Black, 1978 and 1989), and in the siblings of children who have died (Pettle and Lansdown, 1986). In this latter study of twenty-eight children whose brother or sister had died of cancer between eighteen and thirty months previously, the majority were found to have behavioural and emotional difficulties. Low self-esteem was found to be very common and was not restricted to those with other emotional problems. The dead sibling was, in these cases, often idealized, thus making it seemingly impossible for the surviving sibling to measure up to the dead one. Self-esteem seemed to relate to the length of the patient's illness – the longer the illness, the greater the self-esteem. This is probably a reflection of parents' greater opportunity to adjust to their own forthcoming loss, and then being able to help their healthy children.

The authors of this study acknowledge that the numbers involved were small, thus making generalizations difficult. Nevertheless, they feel that there were sufficient indicators to suggest that, as they studied children who had been bereaved more than two years previously, there were indications that even greater difficulties were experienced in the first year. They suggest that self-esteem is enhanced by the surviving child having experienced all or some of these events: participating in the patient's care – for example, having a helpful role in caring for the sibling; regular hospital visits; being told that death is the likely outcome; having the opportunity to say 'goodbye' near the time of death; being with the rest of the family on the day of the funeral and, possibly, attending the service; being allowed to keep some of the dead child's possessions; and previously having experienced the death of a relative or pet.

There were two further experiences which are of questionable benefit. These are: the sibling dying at home, and seeing the body. Further studies need to be made before these can be truly evaluated. But, as Pettle and Lansdown state, 'Excluding children from information seems to be unsuccessful in reducing their pain, as clearly they sense that something is seriously amiss, and in the absence of age-appropriate explanations, are prone to fantasize.'

Many siblings of dying children convey ambivalence about the amount of parental attention focused on the ill child (*I'd Rather Stay at Home*, Southampton University film, 1986). The infantile part of the surviving child feels jealous and resentful, and this is sometimes complicated by guilt that their own rivalrous and hating feelings have successfully, possibly magically, brought about this illness. The well child may feel that their own safety is threatened by the event: if it could happen to my brother/sister, what is to stop it happening to me? This could be felt to be as a result of the expectation of retaliation or retribution for destructive fantasies, or that the well child identifies closely with the dying or dead child. Young children may perceive their parents as being unable to protect any of their children.

There seem to be sufficient indicators of potential emotional disturbance, over and above the normal process of grief and mourning, in siblings which would warrant early skilled intervention. A grieving parent would probably not be the best person to help the bereaved child. If psychotherapy is available, it would be an opportunity for skilled interpretation of bereaved siblings' sense of abandonment, jealousy, and anger, through the re-experiencing of separation and loss within the transference, evoked by the ending of sessions and the eventual cessation of therapy. Thus the struggles would become more conscious, and their unconscious power to affect behaviour and emotions in some of the ways indicated would be lessened.

On a more positive note, although many siblings report feeling 'left out', they also often describe the experience as bringing family members closer together. This feeling is often also mentioned by parents, who, while acknowledging the considerable stress, observe that it can ultimately strengthen marriages and bring families closer (see *I'd Rather Stay at Home*).

Ailsa Fabian's (1988) book *The Daniel Diary*, a well-written account of her young son's response to the death of his older sister, gives insight into a young child's struggles to come to terms with this death. Daniel, not quite three, shows curiosity and determination to understand the truth.

STAFF INVOLVEMENT AND STAFF SUPPORT

Professionals working with terminally ill children face severe psychological stress. Unlike caring for individuals whose lives are not terminal, these care-givers have to face the reality that, despite their efforts, these patients will die. They have various ways of responding to this work situation. Some shut themselves off emotionally, so that it is 'just another job', and therefore they do not feel so buffeted or upset by the work. Some become so caught up in the distress that the part of their careers spent in this speciality is inevitably limited, they suffer from 'burn-out', and usually leave this area altogether. These are usually people who are unable to express their feelings about treating life-threatening illness (Slaby and Glicksman, 1985). Others find sufficient support from colleagues and/or families to enable them to feel adequately supported, understood, and therefore able to continue. Similar to this last category are those who balance their professional life by working part of the time in less distressing work.

The ways in which nurses cope with stress and anxiety in a hospital setting have been analysed in Isabel Menzies Lyth's seminal paper, 'The functioning of social systems as a defence against anxiety' (1959). (See Appendix 3 for a summary.) Her findings can be, and have been, usefully applied to many other institutional settings. Although she was writing thirty years ago, much of her thinking is still apt today. This is because hospital management and organization has not basically altered, and neither have nurses' roles. However, an important and developing part of the teaching programme for student nurses in many teaching hospitals includes the opportunity to discuss feelings about death and dying. Nurses, if part of a co-ordinated multidisciplinary team, realize that they do not have to provide psychosocial support for their patients. Training in how to work as a team is increasingly being recognized as a necessary part of managing a patient with a life-threatening illness.

I found the hospital staff I spoke to had their own perspectives on these issues. Sister Jordan (quoted earlier), in talking about a death on a paediatric ward and the response of the nurses, says (personal communication):

> First of all we have to remember the student nurses. Although they are at the end of their second year, paediatrics is a speciality, and many of them have never seen a dead person, never mind a dead child. So for them it's a very big ordeal, very traumatic. Their experience is only eight weeks on this ward, so in a way you would think they don't get as involved – but they do, in fact, a lot of the students do, and for them it's difficult. And we do try, on the same day as a death occurs, to get them together and talk about death and dying in children, but it's not always possible. We bring them in here (sister's office) or in the treatment room, and sit and talk about it. I allow them to talk, and then I say what I feel about it. If it's still haunting them, they could bring it up in the monthly support group for student nurses.

This sister then described how doctors can become upset and may cry:

> and that's where you get the situation where we, as sisters, are comforting the doctors, because they feel that they've got nobody to talk to. Remember, we're working with an academic department, where it's all go, go, go, treat, treat, treat, and, as you know, we still have a way to go to get them to understand when *not* to treat these children, and let them die with dignity, and let mum cuddle them.

She summarized the problem of whether or not staff should be allowed to cry:

> As far as not getting involved – that goes back to when I started – I mean I've been nursing twenty-three years, and when I started to nurse you were never allowed to cry. You were never allowed to get emotionally

involved with your patients, but, I'm glad to say, particularly in paediatrics, that's now something that isn't frowned upon. Nursing children on a general ward in a general hospital, you tend to find that your managers (because they're not involved, and they only visit the ward) are the ones who say 'Pull yourself together and don't cry'. Over my eight years here of nursing these children, and with the many deaths that I've been involved in, many of the parents *do* say that to see the nurses crying makes them feel better.

I asked her how she understood that. She continued: 'We understand that they know that we have cared for their child and that we are sorry that unfortunately the treatment that we had couldn't save them. They appreciate our involvement.'

However, these foregoing comments regarding 'managers' reflect the findings of Menzies Lyth cited earlier, in relation to the 'stiff-upper-lip' ethos.

Sister Jordan described the extent to which she becomes involved in her patients, and talked about one little girl whom she says she will never forget:

She was twelve months old when she was diagnosed as having myeloid leukaemia. She was in with us for something like eight months, and she was absolutely delicious, and there was no way that she was anybody else's baby but mine! Her mum and I, we had this 'deal' that when mum wasn't there, I was her 'mum'. She was a delight to nurse. This poor little baby was put through all this treatment, Hickmans, having all these drugs, and she would have been two on the Thursday, but she actually died on the Tuesday morning. It was a shock for us, never mind the parents. Even though we know that these children are going to die, it was still a shock, because we are carried along on this wave of 'it'll be all right, of course we can treat', and she died.

But what happened was that Mum went home that night, for the first time in many months, and at 7.10 in the morning, I was just leaving to come to work and the phone was ringing, and we'd got the alarm on, so it would have meant undoing the alarm which would make me a bit more late, so we just ignored that phone call. My husband dropped me off at the hospital, and I was walking through the ground floor and I saw the mum and dad coming toward me, and she grabbed hold of me and burst into tears and said 'She's dead'. For me, even though I knew she was going to die, it was just awful.

I laid her out, and put her in this little dress, and I took her down to the mortuary. Unfortunately, during that weekend there was a fire and we'd had two children brought in to Accident and Emergency, dead, as well as another child, and as they were going down the porter said 'Ooh, sister, you know three other children died this weekend'. I remember saying 'This one is so precious, don't tell me about any other child who's died'. Because it's a little one, you're carrying her down in your arms, and putting her into the mortuary and leaving her there. Then of course because we knew this family they asked me if I would go to the funeral. Well, oh dear, that was absolutely traumatic, and I remember going home and for about four days I kept saying to my husband, 'Why did the baby die?' I was very upset, and then what actually helped was her mum: she was able to ring me up, and she'd say to me, 'Look, you know, one day's good and one day isn't, but I'm all right and I'm going to have another baby.' She did have another baby, and was very worried about that baby, but he had a blood test, and was all right. Since then she's had another one, and she's moved to Devon, and they have rebuilt their lives quite nicely. But in that room, Room 8, if you look on the door, there's still all these little stickers, from this little baby, and her name, we stuck them on. And you know, that's just one...

That was six years ago, and she still seems to feel raw.

She then described how her work with families involved much more than conventional nursing – for example, after a child had died of leukaemia, she took the parents down to the room where the body was laid out, and described this scene:

Clare's mum touched her, and she exclaimed 'Oh my God, she's so cold!' And I thought, 'Oh gosh, that's something we forget, don't we?' In the midst of all their grief, we just take the child and put them in the fridge, and of course they're going to be cold. For the mum, to see and feel that – to see Clare lying there, and just to touch her, she couldn't believe how cold she was. I very gently had to say, 'Sylvie, this is what happens'. From then on it got worse, because I had to change the child – the mum insisted I put her in a new track-suit – put her back, and then of course one grandma faints, somebody else was screaming. Eventually I got them all sorted out, back up here on the ward, and then I have to take the brother, Clare's uncle, down to get the death certificate, because none of them were in any fit state whatsoever to go. That is a horrendous experience. I mean, I'd known Clare for about five years, and this final thing, for parents, I think is absolutely awful, although the people down there at the Registry Office try to be nice, under the circumstances.

She acknowledged the difficulty in knowing when to cut off from the families, where she feels torn between helping them and leading her own life:

It's difficult, because I find that I want to go, and I want to help them, but I also think I've got my own life to lead. On my days off I've got this to do, and that to do, and to have to say 'Yes, Sylvie, I'll come and see you', when I've only got one day off. I think to myself, why do I say it? Why do I say 'I'm going to go' , when I know very well I've got this to do, that to do. So I've got to ring up and say 'Look, I'm awfully sorry, but would you mind...' And then last time I saw her I said 'I'll give you a ring', but I haven't, and I feel guilty. Now, when I've got a number of days off I'll ring her up.

It must be very hard, I suggested, because she needed time to switch off and get away from all this. Sister Jordan agreed:

Oh yes, where I found it fairly hard was one time, before, when Clare had relapsed, and they sent her home, before she came into hospital and died. Her parents said 'Come round and see Clare'. So I think it was after an early shift that I went round there. I found it particularly painful to go into their playroom, with this little girl and her friend from next door, and they were playing Children's Trivial Pursuit. They were just so lovely, and I thought, 'Oh dear, for the parents it must be soul-destroying, to be sitting, just waiting and watching that little life - you know - go.'

She clearly felt that this visit to the child at home put her more in touch with the parents' plight, and yet overall in a way that she valued rather than avoided. I asked her if in fact she was more open to painful feelings than most people in her profession. She replied: 'I think maybe I'm more open than most, but I think there's a lot more that are - certainly in paediatrics. You can't look after children and not become involved, you can't.'

And this is after eighteen years of working in paediatrics, and twenty-three years of nursing. She added:

I've worked at Great Ormond Street and Guys, and very specialized places where we've had some quite horrendous deaths as well. What makes me want to carry on is working with this team of haematologists, now that we are offering about a 75 percent cure for lymphoblastic (not as much for myeloid). But in the eight years I've been here, the changes in the treatment and the new drugs are so impressive, and they are so dedicated, that if there is going to be a cure for leukaemia, I feel that they deserve to find it here.

She acknowledged that she felt carried along by the dynamic spirit of the department and by its medical successes, and that if leukaemia was still in its earlier less treatable stages she would find it much harder to continue in this work. Moreover, as it is a mixed paediatric ward, where many children come in and get better and go home, a balance is kept.

She wondered whether her degree of involvement meant that she was over-identified with her patients, rather than simply feeling empathetic, but then concluded that working with these children led to her valuing her own life, as well as her own problems then becoming insignificant by comparison.

Speaking from the viewpoint of her work in a children's hospice, Mother Frances Dominica described the support needed for staff:

> I suppose we need different levels of support and ways of recharging our batteries. Every week from just before Helen House opened, we have had a staff support group, which meets for an hour and is facilitated by a consultant child psychiatrist. That is an opportunity for everyone and anyone on the team to share whatever they feel is appropriate, and it's interesting how, to begin with, it was almost always focused on a child or children. Then it went further afield to be concerned with the families, and how the families were or were not coping, and only after that did it feel safe enough to go into how people themselves on the team were feeling, and reacting, and what it was doing to them. That's on one level. Then we have had somebody who's come in at regular intervals and been available for individuals to talk to. Some people have found that useful. But then it comes down to the individual discovering what he or she finds most helpful. It may be an understanding spouse, although many people have found that people who are not actually experiencing the day-to-day happenings in Helen House can't fully enter into it. However sympathetic and compassionate and understanding they try to be, it's not the same as talking to somebody who's actually here. Some people rely on their religious faith for recharging their batteries; some have activities and hobbies. I myself find that if I can go away three or four times a year and be quite alone for a few days, then that's my best way: to listen to lovely music, or to walk. It's the withdrawing and solitude, I think, that I find most helpful.

I asked her if she was then cutting off, or, in fact, going over and digesting the experience. She replied that it was more the latter,

> because you are experiencing one major grief after another. People sometimes say to us 'How do you remain emotionally uninvolved?' Well, it's a non-question, isn't it. You don't. You become very involved, or you can't do the job. In a setting like this, the families really do in a sense adopt you as part of their family; they'll select their own people, on the team, as their 'specials', so there's strength in that, in that you're not always the key person.

So you don't decide who's the key worker, I asked, they choose you? Mother Frances replied:

We try to let them do that, without realizing what they're doing. That person becomes the contact person, and then there's a back-up person. But that doesn't eliminate the other members of the team: anybody and everybody is involved. It happens naturally that people gravitate towards certain people, I think. Sometimes it's the child who says, 'I want to be looked after by so and so', so we encourage that. A recent study of staff distress discovered without doubt that the greatest support came from informal mutual support within the team. Quite a lot of the team have been here since Helen House began, six years ago. We now know each other very well indeed, and have learnt to recognize each other's signs of stress and distress. You learn to know who benefits from hugs and who best benefits from space.

Another thing we have talked about quite a lot is whether we shouldn't introduce into job contracts of new members of staff a possible cut-off point of three years, or that the contract should be for a three-year renewable period. This would give respectable permission for somebody to say, 'Now that's complete, I feel that I should move on to something different'. Otherwise it's very hard, because it's addictive work, and most of the families, most of the time, are 'stroking' you and telling you you're wonderful. There are exceptions, obviously, but ... and you love them, you know, and to move back or to move forward, whichever way you look at it, into a different kind of work, is sometimes very difficult. But there needs to be the opportunity, and if at the end of three years, if that doesn't seem right, then fine, the contract can be renewed. We haven't actually implemented that yet, but it has certainly been discussed.

This degree of emotional involvement recalls that of the hospital sister cited earlier. It seems that both respond to the challenge of the daily confrontation with the reality that some of their patients will die. However, while the hospital sister needs the balance of less seriously ill patients and medical treatment breakthroughs, Mother Frances may be more able to face the existential reality because of the support of her religious beliefs. The mutual support from the care team which Mother Frances values seems also to be the most usual avenue of support for professionals in hospital settings.

Epilogue

As long as I live I shall probably grieve,
even if time makes it more gentle, less
frequent. But in death and grief, because
there is pain, therefore I know there is life,
and life is change and I must set some limit
or I shall nibble at these thoughts and
feelings for the rest of my life.
Mary Jones (1988)

The little boy whom I have described in detail still has an important place in my mind. It was perhaps his tenacity, and his ability to endure, often stoically, days and nights of torturous treament and illness, that I remember above all as his main characteristics. He 'held on' to life as long as he could, surviving several crises. Although I did not know him prior to his last illness, I feel that in health he must have been a passionate child, with a great zest for life, and with an ability to form strong relationships. Even on the brink of death he seemed - for some of the time - steeped in life.

In working with this particular child I had to bear in mind his parents' views about illness and death. I felt I had to try to use the parents' basic strengths, directly, or through Peter, the social worker. My work was inevitably tempered by the extent to which the parents could adjust to his imminent death. Nevertheless, the resourcefulness of Robert's mother was truly impressive. Working with people who are dying is always salutary: it puts into perspective (albeit temporarily) other worries, leading to more tolerance of these difficulties.

Now, reflecting on this experience, the question of the moral and ethical efficacy of keeping someone alive under these conditions arises once more. Most parents *do* opt for the fight for life for their child, even if the chances of success are very slim. Occasionally, some children manage to find a way of conveying to their parents that they do not want to continue with the ordeal. Some parents respect this, and allow the child to die peacefully, preferably in its own home.

Over the past twenty years enormous advances *have* been made towards increasing the survival of cancer patients. In the mid-1960s, 90 percent of children diagnosed with the most common form of childhood cancer (acute lymphoblastic leukaemia) died within three years. Today, approximately 70 percent of children treated survive three to five years after diagnosis without recurrence; the survival rate for AML with the most recent treatment can allow us to push up the traditional 30 percent to 55 percent. Overall 60 percent of children with cancer can expect to reach long-term remission (Morris Jones, 1987). Robert's prognosis was much more pessimistic, especially with the lack of an appropriate sibling donor, and long-term cure is not necessarily the outcome, even if remission is achieved. For some doctors, a sense of involvement is maintained in treating people with terminal illness, such as cancer, through the developments in research. As these developments become more successful, so the doctor's task in relation to individual patients becomes less grim. Nevertheless, some doctors still tend to give the parents a prognosis weighted towards a hopeful outcome, rather than the full truth – however grim – of the situation. It is here that I feel that this 'kindness' towards the family (or fear of being the harbinger of bad news?) is doing a disservice to the whole process of attempting to arrive at the most appropriate decision. There is a possibility that a 'hopeful' (more optimistic than the truth) diagnosis could have a benevolent effect. As I mentioned in Chapter 7, Robert's parents probably were not told the full truth about his chances of survival. However, if there is a foundation of *truth*, those involved can of course view this basic truth according to their own bias. For example, one thirteen-year-old boy, when told he had a 30 percent chance of survival, was sure that he would be 'one of the lucky ones'. A bone marrow transplant may lead to remission, but remission can only be assessed retrospectively, as it is impossible to tell if a few leukaemic cells remain in the body after treatment. Facing a relapse is often worse than facing the original diagnosis, because a relapse suggests that the doctors may not be able to cure the patient. There is also the memory of unpleasant treatments and side-effects which the patient then knows he will have to endure again.

Untreated acute leukaemia would bring an inevitably premature death. The choice, then, of a bone marrow transplant is taking the risk of making that life even shorter, and of a possibly more troubled death. The months of possible 'tortures' and of isolation are part of the price to pay for the possibility of an extra lease of life. These are the factors to be taken into consideration by the parents and by the medical team, and were explored more fully in Chapters 10 and 11.

It is worth asking whether the cases where the child is treated beyond what appears to be the bounds of humanity, where 'torturous' treatment is given even when there is a very small chance of success, are partly symptoms of a lack of an effective multi-disciplinary team. (Depending on the resources available, a paediatric multi-disciplinary team can include all or some of these people: doctors, nurses, teachers, physiotherapists, occupational therapists, social workers, clergy, psychologists, child psychotherapists, psychiatrists, play leaders, nursery nurses, health visitors, speech therapists, community nurses. It is unlikely that anaesthetists, radiotherapists, and other specialists would be involved in the regular discussion of the psychosocial aspects of the child - although that might be desirable.) In other words, a decision to *treat* may, on occasion, indicate a more or less unilateral decision on the part of the consultant.

My hypothesis is that in a divided team where, for example, the nurses (and child psychiatrist, child psychotherapist or psychologist if there is one) are in touch with and are carrying the child's suffering, the doctors in charge of the physical care may not be. The latter may be aware of 'improvements' in the patient, such as a rise in the platelet level, while the patient's overall condition and level of discomfort may be appalling. Thus, they may be only taking into account the patient's *physical* condition, and not the emotional side. This pattern is not inevitable; of course the team can be split in other ways. The function of team meetings is for all these differing views of the patient to be pooled, discussed, and, bearing in mind the parents' wishes (and if possible, the child's), for an informed decision about further treatment to be constantly reviewed. The differing members of the care team would still 'carry' different functions, and this is intrinsically useful and spares individuals from a possibly too onerous task, but these parts of a whole do need to be able to come together in a way that is ultimately humane for the patient. However, all this takes time: people need to value the time spent thinking together as a team for this function not to be eroded by other duties. Hospital doctors in Britain are notoriously over-worked and under considerable stress, so it seems that practical considerations do often prevent them from contributing equally to the psychosocial aspects of the team. This dilemma exacerbates whatever splits are in the team. It is nevertheless an ethical question as to whether doctors should, or could, or want to shift from their position of prime decision-makers to one where they are more a part of a homogeneous team.

A switch to terminal care does not preclude the care-givers being alert to the possibility of sudden recovery. Just as our ancestors were often fearful of being buried alive (Puckle, 1926), so some people nowadays may feel that, in *allowing* someone to die, any diversion from the path towards death will not be noticed or tolerated.

Since there is always uncertainty as to when death will occur, each day can become meaningful and precious if valued in its own right. The focus for patient and family can therefore become short-term, or immediate. A patient, or his family, who is not told as much as possible of the reality - however stark - of the situation can feel cheated of the lost opportunity to use the available time constructively. It is important, in dealing with the dying, that we do not forget that life, even a drastically shortened life, can be worth living, and that remissions, if not miracles, do occur. And just as every child has a right to whatever medical care is available, so it is every dying child's right to have emotional care and support, including the right to express every sort of feeling.

We all have to face death, as part of life. It is particularly difficult in our society, not to see the death of a child as a failure, a breakdown in our attempt to control the forces of mind and body, to equate health with goodness and correct living and illness and death with evil. For those not having to face death and dying as part of their work, or a life-threatening illness in someone close, death can be denied until the day it comes. This may successfully avoid conscious anxieties, but may disturb us more deeply than a more open acknowledgement of our mortality. For example, illness affects most of us at some time. This unpredictable experience – which stirs up associations with death – can be deeply unsettling.

However, those working with the dying or those who face the death of those they love, often find that they gain insight into parts of their psyche that previously were inaccessible; that they can emerge strengthened, 'a sadder and a wiser man' as Coleridge put it in 'The Ancient Mariner', aware of their own vulnerability and mortality, and therefore their own humanity. I think it is this awareness of our own fragility and that of others that can actually enhance, strengthen, and enable us to continue to be sensitive to our patients or our loved ones, for we are not then putting so much of our energy into denial.

'Crisis' means 'time of danger' and it also means 'turning-point'. A crisis in both nuances is what the patient facing death experiences, and is something those close to the patient are also capable of going through. 'The helper and the helped are in a partnership, both often changed by the experience', as Derek Nuttall, the Director of CRUSE, said at a conference on 'Bereavement: Grief and Loss' (Association of Child Psychology and Psychiatry, 1988). There is the danger of a frightening or lonely experience, or the possibility of a turning-point, leading to decisive change and development, for both the dying and the carers.

Within the concept of wholeness there is without doubt a place for death alongside life. If we see, feel, and dwell only upon life, we shall, strangely, not be truly living. To come up against the death of a child forces us to re-evaluate our lives, and thus perhaps become more aware of what it is to be alive.

Analysis of Robert's drawings

Recently, I was fortunate to have the opportunity to show Robert's drawings to Dr Mary Sue Moore, a psychotherapist and psychologist who has carried out considerable research into children's drawings. She gave her comments before I had told her many details, other than the child's age, sex, and the fact that he had a terminal illness. This was in order for us to test whether her observations could be appropriately applied. She clarified my understanding of them considerably.

Moore stated that the first picture we draw in any particular period of time carries the strongest projection of ourself. She commented that the figure in this first drawing has what is sometimes called a 'refrigerator' body: it is squarish in shape, has no shoulders, and is without feet, and the body goes off the bottom of the page. She said that this kind of body is drawn by children from many sub-groups, but frequently the main experience that they have had has been a traumatic physical experience: for example, children with chronic medical conditions where they have had repeated intrusive operations. (Other physical traumas, such as sexual abuse, may also lead to this type of depiction.) The child is warding off any sensations to the body by drawing the body as if it is just a block.

Moore expressed interest in the fact that the head is connected directly to the body without any neck. She says that this is typical for young children, but it also indicates that the child has little cognitive ability to distance himself psychologically from the events he has experienced, whether internal or external. 'Therefore, his impulses are probably strongly felt by him,' she says. He doesn't have the ability that, say, a nine- or ten-year-old child has to *think* about things, and thus separate himself from his impulses and the reality of the life experiences.

Moore then commented on the drawing of birds in the sky, with a heavy layer of sky across it. 'Clouds, rain, snow, and birds have all been interpreted variously to represent a sense of oppression from the environment, from above. This can be interpreted as parental or authority figures to whom the child is closely attached, who are watching over, but also oppressively involved in, the child's life.'

She added that it was very significant that he had placed the sun directly over the figure. Moore referred to research carried out by Mary Main (Berkeley, USA) who found that this positioning frequently occurred where a close family member had died but the loss was unmourned and unresolved and was still actively felt. Then the child often drew a sun over that member of the family. She wondered, therefore, about this positioning (which is not the more typical placing of the sun, in a corner of the picture) over the only figure in the picture and suggests that he himself feels at risk of dying, or is dying.

Moore noticed the little stick-like arms: 'Those are arms that are not particularly useful. Children who have an active sense of control over their environment draw two-dimensional arms – not just one line – which are usually connected to a shoulder. That's where we have our sense of power – in our shoulders. So I guess he does not feel very powerful.'

When looking at the second picture, Moore commented that it was striking that the leaves of the plants stretch upwards. Apparently in the research on the drawings of terminally ill children (Bach, 1969), the leaves of plants often reach upward in some sense of growth. In this research, the number of plants represented was often significant in relation to the duration of the illness or the number of months of life left. Moore observes that he has overlapped himself with one of the plants, so we may wonder what he is saying about his life, his years, his experience of growing.

She continued:

Another conspicuous feature is that although the figure still has the same little helpless arms, these are reaching up. A very young child does these asking-for-help, comfort, needing-to-be-picked-up arms. It's a much more dependent stance. If you put yourself in the position of the child in the drawing, you can see how it feels.

I would say that the first figure represents more an attempt to be grown up, to stand up to things, to present himself with intact defences. My guess is that when he drew this second figure, more of his feelings were showing, about wishing he could be held or comforted.

Moore points out that in this picture, in contrast to the first one, he has shown his legs touching the ground, so that some part of him which is a 'whole, longing, connected self' is being shown. He shows this figure as wearing clothes – unlike the first one, which is a non-sexual rendering.

Both drawings, Moore feels, are inappropriately immature for a seven-year-old child, and would be more characteristic of a four-and-a-half-year-old or a five-year-old. Therefore she wonders at what age the child had had traumatic experiences, and whether something had occurred between the age of three and five which had fixed his emotional development.

Another point to notice, Moore says, is the positioning of figures on the page. The first drawing shows the figure more or less centrally positioned, and therefore suggests the present or the here-and-now, while the second shows the figure right over to the right. This is generally assumed to be a looking toward or thinking about the future. Therefore this suggests that it is more about how he sees himself henceforth, rather than now.

At this point, I gave Mary Sue Moore details of Robert and of my contact with him, including a description of his physical condition. This led Moore to feel that the first drawing conveyed that he had lost a sense of his body: it is swathed in something like a heavy garment. His swollen purple body may have led him to lose a sense of his actual skin, as a container for his body. We agreed that the diagnosis and the ensuing invasive and pervasive treatments that he had undergone could indeed have led to the lack of emotional development which Moore had speculated.

We discussed the positioning of the figure in the second drawing in the light of the seriousness of the illness perhaps having a full impact on him between the ages of six and seven, and how this figure seems to depict both himself and me. Thus, from his comments, it seems that I am this figure, but in embodying both Robert and me, he shows his identification with me. Therein there is a feeling that there is a future, but it is a very short one. Feeling that this was a reflection of the work I was doing with him, Moore said 'There's a real self here that's identifying with you in a positive way.' She agreed with my thoughts about a fantasy of heaven Robert may have had, feeling that this positive reaching upwards may have indicated a hopefulness towards something that could only be better than that which he was currently experiencing.

Finally, Moore pointed out that it has been observed in the drawing of dying children that a halo is often depicted - and we both felt this first drawing could indeed convey a halo.

Extracts from the Nuremberg Code (1947)

1. The voluntary consent of the human subject is absolutely essential... there should be made known to him, the nature, duration... all inconveniences and hazards reasonably to be expected; and the effects upon his health or person which may possibly come from his participation in the experiment.

The duty and responsibility for ascertaining the quality of the consent rests upon each individual who initiates, directs... It is a personal duty and responsibility which may not be delegated...

6. The degree of risk to be taken should never exceed that determined by the humanitarian importance of the problem to be solved by the experiment.

9. During the course of the experiment the human subject should be at liberty to bring the experiment to an end if he has reached the physical or mental state where continuation... seems to him to be impossible.

10. During the course of the experiment the scientist in charge must be prepared to terminate the experiment at any stage, if he has probable cause to believe... that a continuation... is likely to result in injury, disability, or death...

Note on Isabel Menzies Lyth's 'The functioning of social systems as a defence against anxiety' (1959)

This is a summary of a process one sees at work in hospital work with children. Menzies Lyth describes the ways in which nurses are confronted with death and suffering, as well as distasteful and distressing tasks, far more than one would ordinarily come across. They are confronted by opposing sets of feelings in their work: pity, compassion, and love versus hatred and resentment of the patients who arouse these strong feelings. These powerful feelings reflect primitive phantasies (in other words, unconscious phantasies) which are in everyone, relating to infancy. These phantasies are around feelings of omnipotence: where the infant feels that his loving impulses can be life-giving while his aggressive impulses are capable of killing. Understandably, then, the infant's inner world is peopled by damaged, injured, or dead objects (see reference to Witham's paper, p. 14), as well as loved objects and loving feelings.

The stress that a nurse then feels, the argument continues, is influenced by her own inner world and elements remaining from infancy. Unconsciously she will respond in part at least according to her unconscious phantasies. Similarly, patients and their families have an inner world which may well be characterized by violent phantasies with which the adult is not normally in touch. The overt distress or subtle messages from patients or relatives therefore increase the nurses' stress, possibly at an unconscious level. Menzies Lyth summarizes this dilemma thus: 'By the nature of her profession the nurse is at considerable risk of being flooded by intense and unmanageable anxiety.'

She then proceeds to describe the ways in which the hospital situation protects the nurse from this anxiety. This is, for example, through splitting the nurses' duties between several patients, through moving nurses from ward to ward, through depersonalizing the patients, through an expectation of professional and emotional detachment, and through performing ritualized tasks.

Thus, 'this social defence system', as Menzies Lyth calls it (following Jaques, 1955), helps the individual to avoid anxiety, uncertainty, and guilt. As the social system sufficiently matches the individual psychic defence system of the nurses, both continue to support each other through a continuous process of projection and introjection. Menzies Lyth writes that this situation does not facilitate growth or maturation in the nurses, and may partly account for the high level of wastage in the profession.

Glossary

Some medical and psychoanalytic terms used in this book

acute: coming sharply to a crisis.

benign: a lump in the body which does not invade the surrounding tissues nor travel to other parts of the body; not malignant.

biopsy: examination of small piece of tissue from the body; removal of such tissue.

chemotherapy: treatment of disease using drugs or chemicals.

chronic: lingering, lasting, constant.

cytotoxic: cell poisoning.

decathect: (psychoanalytic term) to withdraw the investment of energy, or interest, in *external objects*.

denial: (psychoanalytic term) defence mechanism by which either some aspect of the self is denied, or some painful experience is denied.

dysfunction: not functioning properly.

ego: (psychoanalytic term) the part of the self, or psychic apparatus, which is organized; that which may 'be called reason and common sense, in contrast to the id, which contains the passions...' (Freud, 1923).

external object: (psychoanalytic term) person or thing which is recognized by the subject as being external to himself – 'out there' – as opposed to objects which have been introjected into the ego.

haematology: study of, or science of, the blood.

identification: (psychoanalytic term) process by which a person either borrows his identity from someone else, or extends his identity into someone else, or confuses or fuses his identity with someone else.

internal objects: (psychoanalytic term) mental processes which are located in an inner, or psychical, space, in contrast to their 'external' equivalents; images occurring in phantasies which are felt to be real.

maladaptive: faulty adaptation to, or interaction with, environment.

malignant: a cancer that grows and can travel to other parts of the body.

neuroblastoma: malignant neoplasm, or new growth of abnormal tissue, characterized by immature nerve cells.

object: (psychoanalytic term) person or thing to which feeling or action is directed; that to which subject relates.

oedema: swelling caused by fluid retention.

oncology: the study and treatment of cancer.

palliative: that which serves to alleviate, or bring relief to, disease, without curing.

phantasy (and fantasy): see 'Note on conventions', p. xxi.

platelet: a very small cell in the blood, essential for the clotting of blood.

projection: (psychoanalytic term) process by which specific impulses, aspects of the self, wishes, or *internal objects* are imagined to be located in someone else. This is usually preceded by denial that this aspect is felt by the person who projects.

projective identification: (psychoanalytic term) 'part of the self and internal objects are split off and projected into the external object, which then becomes possessed by, controlled and identified with the projected parts' (Segal, 1973, p. 27).

radiotherapy: treatment of disease by radiation; that is, by electromagnetic waves of energy.

reintrojection: (psychoanalytic term) process by which feelings which had been projected into an *external object* (and which may have been thus modified) are then taken back into the psyche; that which has been reintrojected becomes an *internal object*.

renal: of the kidney.

splitting: (psychoanalytic term) both *ego* and *object* can be split; in splitting of the *object*, the two parts are typically perceived as 'good' and 'bad'.

tissue-type: mass of cells of one kind.

transference: (psychoanalytic term) process by which a patient displaces on to the therapist feelings which derive from earlier relationships (see p. 62 for a fuller explanation).

tumour: lump, growth, or swelling in any part of the body; can be malignant or benign.

venesection: surgical blood-letting by the opening of a vein.

venous: of the blood vessels.

Useful addresses

BACUP
British Association for Cancer United Patients, Families and Friends
  (Offers information, emotional support and advice to cancer patients,
  their families, and friends, by telephone and post.)
  121 Charterhouse Street, London EC1
  Telephone: (01) 608 1661

The CLIC Trust
The Cancer and Leukaemia in Childhood Trust
  (Offers support to children with leukaemia and their families. The
  support is offered in various ways, including accommodation at CLIC
  House which caters for approximately forty people.)
  CLIC House, 12 Fremantle Square, Cotham, Bristol BS6 5TL
  Telephone: (0272) 426217

The Compassionate Friends
  (An international organization of bereaved parents offering friendship
  and understanding to other bereaved parents.)
  National Secretary, 6 Denmark Street, Bristol BS1 5DQ
  Telephone: (0272) 292778

Cruse Bereavement Care
  (The national organization for bereaved adults and children, offering
  counselling and opportunities for contact to people who have lost a
  relative. Offers a wide range of supportive literature.)
  Cruse House, 126 Sheen Road, Richmond, Surrey TW9 1UR
  Telephone: (01) 940 4818 / 9407

CancerLink
  (Provides an information service; cancer support and self-help groups;
  Medical Advisory Board to provide expert information; publications list.)
  46 Pentonville Road, London N1 9HF
  Telephone: (01) 833 2451

Cancer Relief Macmillan Fund
(Macmillan nurses will, if required, help children: either community-based, or hospital-based and/or out-patient. Referrals through GP, district nurse, social worker, or hospital.)
Anchor House, 15 Britten Street, London SW3 3TZ
Telephone: (01) 351 7811

Foundation for Black Bereaved Families
Lorrene Hunter, 11 Kingston Square, Salters Hill, London SE19
Telephone: (01) 761 7228

Helen House
Hospice for children, 87 Leopold Street, Oxford OX4 1QT
Telephone: (0865) 728251

Hospice Information Service
St Christopher's Hospice, 51–9 Lawrie Park Road, Sydenham, London SE26 6DZ
Telephone: (01) 778 1240

Leukaemia Care Society
(To promote the welfare of people suffering from leukaemia and that of their families; also bereavement support.)
PO Box 82, Exeter, Devon EX2 5DP
Telephone: (0392) 218514

Leukaemic Research Fund
(Provides an information service on the different types of leukaemia and the treatments available. Local branches throughout Britain.)
43 Great Ormond Street, London WC1N 3JJ
Telephone: (01) 405 0101

Malcolm Sargent Cancer Fund for Children
(Can provide cash grants to parents of children with cancer; offers other types of support as well.)
14 Abingdon Road, London W8 6AF
Telephone: (01) 937 4548

National Association for the Welfare of Children in Hospital
(Support group for sick children and their families. Provides reading list of the many 'hospital' books specially for children.)
Argyle House, 29–31 Euston Road, London NW1 2SD
Telephone: (01) 833 2041

Parents Lifeline
(Support for parents whose children are critically ill in hospital.)
Station House, 73d Stapleton Hall Road, London N4 3QF
Telephone: (01) 263 2265

United Kingdom Children's Cancer Study Group
(Aims to improve the management of children with cancer and to
promote research. Produces a guide for parents.)
Dept. of Epidemiology and Social Research, Kinnaird Road,
Manchester M20 9QL
Telephone: (061) 4343615

BOOKS FOR YOUNG CHILDREN
Alex, M. and B. (1981) *Grandpa and me*. Tring, Herts: Lion Publishing.
Althea (1982) *When Uncle Bob died*. Dinosaur.
Viorst, J. (1971) *The tenth good thing about Barney*. London: Collins.

FOR OLDER CHILDREN
Little, J., *Mama's going to buy you a mockingbird*. Harmondsworth, Middx:
Puffin.

BOOKLETS FOR CHILDREN
Leukaemia by Allyson Hague;
When your sister or brother has leukaemia by John Silkstone and Allyson Hague,
both published by
Lederle Laboratories Ltd.,
Fareham Road, Gosport, Hants

Bibliography

All works are published in London unless otherwise indicated.

Alexander, I. and Alderstein, A. (1958) 'Affective responses to the concept of death in a population of children and early adolescents', *J. Genet. Psychol.* 93:167–77.

Alvarez, A. (1974) *The Savage God.* Harmondsworth: Penguin.

Anthony, E. and Koupernik, C. (1973) *The Child in His Family: The Impact of Disease and Death*, vol. 2. New York: Wiley.

Anthony, S. (1973) *The Discovery of Death in Childhood and After.* Harmondsworth: Penguin.

Ariès, P. (1974) *Western Attitudes toward Death.* Baltimore, MD/London: Johns Hopkins University Press.

Atkin, M. (1981) 'Fatal illness: how does the family cope?' *Nursing* (March).

Atkins, D. and Patenaude, A. (1987) 'Psychosocial preparation and follow-up for paediatric bone marrow transplant patients', *Amer. J. Orthopsychiat.* 57:246–52.

Bach, S. (1969) *Spontaneous Paintings of Severely Ill Patients: A Contribution to Psychosomatic Medicine.* Basle, Switzerland: J. R. Geigy.

Baldwin, J. (1963) *The Fire Next Time.* Harmondsworth: Penguin, 1964.

Berger, J. (1984) *And Our Faces, My Heart, Brief as Photos.* Writers & Readers.

—— (1988) 'My mother's secrets', *New Statesman & Society*, 10 June.

Bergmann, T. (1965) *Children in the hospital.* New York: International Universities Press.

Bettelheim, B. (1967) *The Empty Fortress.* New York: Free Press.

Bick, E. (1967) 'The experience of the skin in early object relations', in *Collected Papers of Martha Harris and Esther Bick.* Strath Tay, Perthshire: Clunie, 1987.

Bion, W. (1962) *Learning from Experience.* New York: Jason Aronson.

—— (1984) *Second Thoughts.* Maresfield Reprints/Karnac.

Black, D. (1978) 'The bereaved child', *J. Child Psychol. Psychiat.*19:287–92.
—— (1989) 'Life threatening illness, children, and family therapy'. Accepted for publication, *J. Fam. Therapy.*

Black, D., Hardoff, D. and Nelki, J. (1989) 'Educating medical students about death and dying'. Accepted for publication, *Arch. Dis. Childh.*

Bloom, A. (1988) 'My country childhood', *Country Living*, May.

Bluebond-Langner, M. (1978) *The Private Worlds of Dying Children.* Princeton, NJ: Princeton University Press.

Bowlby, J. (1960) 'Grief and mourning in infancy and early childhood', *Psychoanal. Study Child* 15:9–52.

—— (1973) *Attachment and Loss*, vol. 1. *Attachment.* Hogarth.

—— (1979) 'On knowing what you are not supposed to know and feeling what you are not supposed to feel', *Can. J. Psychiat.* 24(5):403–8.

Bowlby, J., Robertson, J. and Rosenbluth, D. (1952) 'A two-year-old goes to hospital', *Psychoanal. Study Child* 12:88–90.

Bozeman, M., Orbach, C. and Sutherland, A., (1955) 'Psychological impact of cancer and its treatment, III: the adaptation of mothers to threatened loss of children through leukaemia', Part 1 *Cancer* 8:1–19.

Brindle, D. (1988) 'Terminally ill "put off death" for a festival', *Guardian*, 23 September.

Brown, H. and Kelly, M. (1976) 'Stages of bone marrow transplantation: a psychiatric perspective', *Psychosomat. Med.* 38(6):339–446.

Burton, L. ed. (1974) *Care of the Child Facing Death.* Routledge & Kegan Paul.

Cairns, N., Clark, G., Smith, S. and Lansky, S. (1979) 'Adaption of siblings to childhood malignancy', *J. Paediatr.* 95:484–7.

Cannadine, D. (1981) 'War and death, grief and mourning in modern Britain', in J. Whaley, ed. *Mirrors of Mortality: Studies in the Social History of Death.* Europa.

Chambers, T. (1987) 'Hospices for children?', *BMJ* 294:1309–10.

Chesler, M. and Barbarin, O. (1987) *Childhood Cancer and the Family.* New York:Brunner/Mazel.

Childers, P. and Wimmer, M. (1971) 'The concept of death in early childhood', *Child Dev.* 42:1299–1301.

Chodoff, P., Friedman, S., and Hamburg, D. (1964) 'Stress, defenses, and coping behavior: observations in parents of children with malignant diseases', *Amer. J. Psychiat.* 120:743–9.

Corr, C. and McNeil, J., eds (1986) *Adolescence & Death.* New York: Springer.

Cousens, P., Waters, B., Said, J. and Stevens, M. (1988) 'Cognitive effects of cranial irradiation in leukaemia: a survey and meta-analysis', *J. Child Psychol. Psychiat.* 29(6):839–52.

Cox, O. (1988) *Sunday's Child.* Bath: Ashgrove Press.

Crispell, K. and Gomez, C. (1987) 'Proper care for the dying: a critical public issue', *J. Med. Ethics* 13:74-80.

Davies, R., Quinlan, D., *et al.* (1973) 'Organic factors and psychological adjustment in advanced cancer patients', *Psychosomat. Med.* 35(6):464-71.

Debuskey, M., ed. (1970) 'Orchestration of care', in *The Chronically Ill Child and His Family.* Springfield, IL: Charles Thomas.

Detwiler, D. A. (1981) 'The positive function of denial', *J. Paediatr.* 99:401-2.

Dominica, F. (1987) 'Reflections on death in childhood', *BMJ* 294:108-10.

Douglas, J. (1975) 'Early hospital admissions and later disturbances of behaviour and learning', *Developmental Med. & Child Neurol.* 17:456-80.

Dunkel-Schetter, C. and Wortman, C. (1982) 'The interpersonal dynamics of cancer: problems in social relationships and their impact on the patient', in H. Friedman and M. Di Matteo, eds *Interpersonal Issues in Health Care.* New York: Academic Press.

Eissler, K. R. (1955) *The Psychiatrist and the Dying Patient.* New York: International Universities Press.

Eliot, T. S. (1944) *The Four Quartets.* Faber.

Elliot, M. (1981) 'Parent care', in E. Kübler-Ross *Living with Death and Dying.* Souvenir Press.

Erikson, E. (1950) *Childhood and Society.* New York: Norton.

Escher, M. C. (1961) *The Graphic Work.* Pan/Ballantine.

Fabian, A. (1988) *The Daniel Diary.* Grafton Books.

Feifel, H. (1962) 'Attitudes towards death in some normal and some mentally ill populations', in H. Feifel, ed. *The Meaning of Death.* New York: McGraw-Hill.

Forfar, J. (1984) 'Demography, vital statistics, and the pattern of disease in childhood', in J. Forfar and G. Arneil, eds *Textbook of Paediatrics* (3rd edn). Edinburgh: Churchill Livingstone.

Freud, A. (1952) 'The role of bodily illness in the mental life of children', *Psychoanal. Study Child* 7:69-81.

—— (1965) 'Children in the hospital', in *Writings of Anna Freud*, vol V. New York: International Universities Press.

Freud, S. (1900) 'Distortion in dreams', in J. Strachey, ed. *The Standard Edition of the Complete Psychological Works of Sigmund Freud.* 24 vols, 1953-73. Hogarth, vol. 4, pp. 134-62.

—— (1905) 'Fragment of an analysis of a case of hysteria'. *S.E.* 7, pp. 3-122.

—— (1915a) 'Our attitude towards death'. *S.E.* 14, pp. 289-300.

—— (1915b) 'Mourning and melancholia'. *S.E.* 14 pp. 237-60.

—— (1920a) 'A psychogenesis of a case of homosexuality in a woman'. *S.E.* 18, pp. 145-72.

—— (1920b) 'Letter to Ferenczi, February 4', in M. Schur (1972) *Freud: Living and Dying.* Hogarth.

—— (1923) *The Ego and the Id. S.E.* 19, pp. 3-66.

Give Sorrow Words

—— (1929) 'Letter to Ludwig Binswanger', in E. Freud, ed. (1970) *The Letters of Sigmund Freud 1873-1939*. Hogarth/Institute of Psycho-Analysis, p. 386.

—— (1938) *An Outline of Psychoanalysis*, S.E. 23, chs II, VII, VIII.

Fromm, E. (1974) *The Anatomy of Human Destructiveness*. Cape.

Furman, E. (1974) *A Child's Parent Dies*. New Haven, CT: Yale University Press.

—— (1984) 'Helping children cope with dying', *J. Child Psychoth.* 10(2):151-7.

Gaes, J. (1987) *My book for kids with Cansur. (sic)* Aberdeen and S. Dakota: Melius & Peterson.

Geist, R. (1979) 'Onset of chronic illness in children and adolescents: psychotherapeutic and consultative intervention', *Amer. J. Orthopsychiat.* 49(1):4-23.

Gibran, K. (1926) *The Prophet*. Pan, 1980.

Glaser, B. and Strauss, A. (1963) *Awareness of Dying*. Chicago: Aldine.

Gordon, A. (1975) 'Psychological aspects of isolator therapy in acute leukaemia', *Brit. J. Psychiat.* 127:588-90.

Gorer, G. (1965) *Death, Grief and Mourning in Contemporary Britain*. Cresset Press.

Greenacre, P. (1980) 'Infant reactions to restraint', in *Trauma, Growth and Personality*. New York: International Universities Press.

Hageboeck, H. (1962) 'Tragic silence', *New York Sunday Times Magazine*, 5 August.

Hoffman, I. and Futterman, E. (1971) 'Coping with waiting: psychiatric intervention and study in the waiting room of a paediatric oncology unit', *Comprehensive Psychiatry* 12:67-81.

Howell, D. (1967) 'A child dies', *Hospital Topics*, February.

Isaacs, S. (1952) 'The nature and function of phantasy', in M. Klein and J. Riviere, eds, *Developments in Psycho-Analysis*. Hogarth.

Janssen, Y. (1983) 'Early awareness of death in normal development', *Infant Mental Health J.* 4(2):95-103.

Jaques, E. (1955) 'Social systems as a defence against persecutory and depressive anxiety', in M. Klein, P. Heimann and R. E. Money-Kyrle, eds *New Directions in Psycho-Analysis*. Tavistock.

Johnson, F. L., Rudolph, L. A. and Hartman, J. R. (1979) 'Helping the family cope with childhood cancer', *Psychosomatics* 20:241-51.

Jones, M. (1988) *Secret Flowers: Mourning and Adaptation to Loss*. Women's Press.

Judd, D. (1988) 'The hollow laugh: an account of the first six months of therapy with a brain-damaged boy', *J. Child Psychother.* 14(2):79-92.

Kahana, R. (1972) 'Personality and response to physical illness', *Arch.*

Psychosomat. Med. 8:42–62.

Kamphuis, R. P. (1979) 'Psychological and ethical considerations in the use of germ-free treatment', in Fleidner *et al.* eds *Clinical and Experimental Gnotobiotics.* Stuttgart: Fischer Verlag.

Kane, B. (1979) 'Children's concepts of death', *J. Genetic Psychol.* 134:141–53.

Kastenbaum, R. (1981) *Death, Society, and Human Experience* (2nd edn). St Louis, MO: Mosby.

—— (1982) 'Dying is healthy and death a bureaucrat: our fantasy machine is alive and well', in M. Di Matteo and H. Freidman, eds *Interpersonal Personal Issues in Health Care.* Academic Press.

Keats, J. (1817) 'Letter to his brothers George and Tom, April', in M. B. Forman ed. (1952) *Letters.* Oxford: Oxford University Press.

Kendrick, C., Culling, J., Oakhill, T. and Mott, M. (1986) 'Children's understanding of their illness and its treatment within a paediatric oncology unit', *ACPP Newsletter* 8(2):16–20.

Keniston, K. (1967) 'The medical student', *Yale J. Biol. Med.* 39:346.

Klein, M. (1932) Preface to 1st edition *The Psycho-Analysis of Children.* Hogarth 1949, pp. 7–10.

—— (1937) 'Love, guilt and reparation', in M. Klein and J. Riviere *Love, Hate and Reparation and Other Works.* Hogarth, 1975.

—— (1940) 'Mourning and its relation to manic-depressive states', in *Love, Guilt and Reparation.* Hogarth, 1975.

—— (1946) 'Notes on some schizoid mechanisms', in *Envy and Gratitude.* Hogarth, 1975.

—— (1949) 'The relations between obsessional neurosis and the early stages of the super-ego', in *The Psycho-Analysis of Children.* Hogarth, 1975, pp. 149–75.

—— (1952) 'The origins of transference', in *Envy and Gratitude.* Hogarth, 1975.

Kohlberg, L. (1976) 'Moral stages and moralisation: the cognitive-developmental approach', in T. Lickona ed. *Moral Development and Behavior: Theory, Research and Social Issues.* New York: Holt, Rinehart & Winston.

Kohut, H. (1977) *The Restoration of the Self.* New York: International Universities Press.

Koocher, G. and O'Malley, J. E. (1981) *The Damocles Syndrome.* New York: McGraw-Hill.

Koocher, G., O'Malley, J., *et al.* (1980) 'Psychological adjustment among paediatric survivors', *J. Child Psychol. Psychiat.* 21:163–73.

Koocher, G. and Sallan, S. (1978) 'Paediatric oncology', in P. Magrab ed. *Psychological Management of Paediatric Problems,* vol. 1. *Early Life Conditions and Chronic Diseases.* Baltimore, MD: University Park Press.

Kübler-Ross, E. (1970) *On Death and Dying.* New York: Macmillan.

—— (1975) *Death: The Final Stage of Growth.* Englewood Cliffs, NJ:

I WB   A K

Prentice-Hall.

_____ (1983) *On Children and Death*. Macmillan.

_____ (1987) *Living with Death and Dying*. Souvenir Press.

Lamerton, R. (1973) *Care of the Dying*. Priory Press.

Lansby, S. B. (1974) 'Childhood leukaemia – the child psychiatrist as a member of the oncology team', *J. Child Psychiat.* 13:1–4:499–508.

_____, Cairns, N., *et al.* (1978) 'Childhood cancer, parent discord and divorce', *Paediatrics* 62:184–8.

Lansdown, R. (1980) *More Than Sympathy: The Everyday Needs of Sick and Handicapped Children*. Tavistock.

_____ (1987) 'The development of the concept of death and its relationship to communicating with dying children', in E. Karas ed. *Current Issues in Clinical Psychology*. Plenum.

Lansdown, R. and Goldman, A. (1988) 'The psychological care of children with malignant disease', *J. Child Psychol. Psychiat.* 29:555–67.

Lansky, S. (1974) 'Childhood leukaemia – the psychiatrist as a member of the oncology team', *Amer. J. Child Psychiat.* 13:499–508.

Lauer, M. E. and Camitta, B. M. (1980) 'Home care for dying children; a nursing model', *J. Pediatr.* 97:1032–5.

Lazarus, R. (1976) *Patterns of Adjustment*. New York: McGraw-Hill.

Levenson, P., Copeland, D., Morrow, J., Pfefferbaum, B. and Silberberg, Y. (1983) 'Disparities in disease-related perceptions of adolescent cancer patients and their parents', *J. Paed. Psychol.* 8:33–45.

Levine, S. (1986) *Who Dies? An Investigation of Conscious Living and Conscious Dying*. Bath: Gateway, 1988.

Lewis, C. S. (1966) *A Grief Observed*. Faber.

Likierman, M. (1987) 'The function of anger in human conflict', *Int. Rev. Psycho-Anal.* 14:143–61.

Liston, E. (1975) 'Education on death and dying: a neglected area in the medical curriculum', *Omega* 6(3):193–8.

McCue, K. (1980) 'Preparing children for medical procedures', in J. Kellerman, ed. *Psychological Aspects of Childhood Cancer*. Springfield, IL: C. C. Thomas.

McKeown, T. (1976) *The Modern Rise of Population*. Arnold.

McNeill, P. (1988) 'The sociology of health', *New Statesman & Society*, 8 July.

Marcus, S. (1966) *The Other Victorians*. Weidenfeld.

Martinson, I., Armstrong, G. D., *et al.* (1978) 'Home care for children dying of cancer', *Paediatrics* 62:106–13.

Menzies Lyth, I. (1959) 'The functioning of social systems as a defence against anxiety', in *Containing Anxiety in Institutions*. Free Association Books, 1988, pp. 43–85.

_____ (1982) *The Psychological Welfare of Children Making Long Stays in*

Hospital: An Experience in the Art of the Possible. Tavistock Institute of Human Relations Occasional Paper No. 3.

Miller, P. (1987) 'Death with dignity and the right to die: sometimes doctors have a duty to hasten death', *J. Med. Ethics* 13:81–5.

Milne, R. (1988) 'Hinkley cancer rate higher', *Guardian*, 19 December.

Ministry of Health, Central Health Services Council (1959). *The Welfare of Children in Hospital.* London: HMSO.

Mitchell-Rossdale, J. (1988) 'Tread softly... some thoughts on creativity', *Brit. J. Psychother.* 2nd Annual Lecture, 23 May.

Morris Jones, P. H. (1987) 'Advances in managing childhood cancer', *BMJ* 245:4–6.

Morrisey, J. (1963a) 'A note of interviews with children facing imminent death', *Social Casework* 44:343–5.

—— (1963b) 'Children's adaptations to fatal illness', *Social Work* 8:81–8.

Munro, A. (1971) *Lives of Girls and Women.* New York: McGraw-Hill; Harmondsworth: Penguin, 1982.

Nagera, H. (1970) 'Children's reaction to the death of important objects: a developmental approach', *Psychoanal. Study Child* 25:360–400.

Nagy, M. H. (1959) 'The child's view of death', in H. Feifel, ed. *The Meaning of Death.* New York: McGraw-Hill.

Natterson, J. (1973) 'The fear of death in fatally ill children and their parents', in E. Anthony and C. Koupernik, eds *The Child in his Family*, vol. 2. New York: Wiley.

Natterson, J. and Knudson, A. (1960) 'Observations concerning fear of death in fatally ill children and their mothers', *Psychosomat. Med.* 22:456–65.

Nicholson, R. (1986) *Medical Research with Children: Ethics, Law, and Practice.* Oxford: Oxford University Press.

Norton, J. (1963) 'Treatment of a dying patient', *Psychoanal. Study Child* 18:541–60.

O'Malley, J. E., Koocher, G. P., *et al.* (1979) 'Psychiatric sequelae of surviving childhood cancer', *Orthopsychiatry* 49:608–16.

Orbach, I. (1988) *Children Who Don't Want to Live.* San Francisco: Jossey-Bass.

Orbach, I., Gross, Y., Glaubman, H. and Berman, D. (1985) 'Children's perception of death in humans and animals as a function of age, anxiety and cognitive ability', *J. Child Psychol. Psychiat.* 26:453–63.

Parker, M and Mauger, D. (1979) *Children with Cancer: A Handbook for Families and Helpers.* Cassell.

Parkes, C. M. (1972) *Bereavement: Studies of Grief in Adult Life.* Tavistock.

—— (1979) 'Terminal care: evaluation of in-patient service at St Christopher's Hospice, part I: self-assessments of effects of the service on surviving spouses', *Postgrad. Med. J.* 55:523–87.

Patenaude, A., Szymanski, L. and Rappeport, J. (1979) 'Psychosocial costs of bone marrow transplantation in children', *Amer. J. Orthopsych.* 49(3): 409–22.

Pettle, M. and Lansdown, R. (1986) 'Adjustment to the death of a sibling', *Arch. Dis. Childh.* 61:278–83.

Pfefferbaum, B. and Lucas, R. (1979) 'Management of acute psychologic problems in paediatric oncology, *Gen. Hospital Psych.* 1(3):214–19.

Piaget, J. (1932) *The Moral Judgement of the Child.* Routledge & Kegan Paul.

—— (1951) *The Child's Conception of the World.* Routledge & Kegan Paul.

Pincus, L. (1976) *Death and the Family.* Faber.

Pot-Mees, C. and Zeitlin, H. (1987) 'Psychosocial consequences of bone marrow transplantation in children: a preliminary communication', *J. Psychosocial Oncology* 5(2):73–81.

Puckle, B. (1926) *Funeral Customs: Their Origin and Development.* Werner Laurie.

Rank, O. (1929) *The Trauma of Birth.* New York: Harcourt, Brace.

Reilly, T., Hasazi, J. and Bond, L. (1983) 'Children's conception of death and personal mortality', *J. Paed. Psychol.* 8(1):21–31.

Richmond, J. and Waisman, H. (1955) 'Psychological aspects of management of children with malignant diseases', *Amer. J. Diseases Children* 89:42–7.

Rilke, R. M. (1915) *Duino Elegies.* Chatto, 1981.

Robertson, J. (1952) Film *A Two Year Old Goes to Hospital.* Tavistock Child Dev. Res. Unit.

Rochlin, G. (1959) 'The loss complex: a contribution to the etiology of depression', *J. Amer. Psychoanal. Assn* 7:299–316.

—— (1967) 'How younger children view death and themselves', in E. Grollman, ed. *Explaining Death to Children.* Boston, MA: Beacon.

Rothenberg, M. (1974) 'Problems posed for staff who care for the child', in L. Burton ed. *Care of the Child Facing Death.* Routledge & Kegan Paul.

Rutter, M. (1980) 'The long-term effects of early experience', *Dev. Med. Child Neurology* 22:800–15.

Sadgrove, J. (1988) 'Electricity and cancer', *Guardian,* 27 July.

Segal, H. (1973) *Introduction to the Work of Melanie Klein.* Hogarth.

—— (1987) 'Silence is the real crime', *Int. Review Psycho-Anal.* 14:3–12.

Shannon, F., *et al.* (1984) 'Early hospital admissions and subsequent behaviour problems in 6 year olds', *Arch. Dis. Childh.* 59:815–19.

Sigler, A. (1970) 'The leukaemic child and his family: an emotional challenge', in M. Debuskey, ed. *The Chronically Ill Child and his Family.* Springfield, IL: C. C. Thomas.

Slaby, A. E. and Glicksman, A. (1985) *Adapting to Life-Threatening Illness.* New York: Praeger.

Solnit, A. and Green, M. (1963) 'Paediatric management of the dying child, II: a study of the child's reaction to the fear of dying', in A. Solnit and S. Provence eds *Modern Perspectives in Child Development*. New York: International Universities Press.

Sontag, S. (1978) *Illness as Metaphor*. New York: Farrar, Strauss & Giroux.

Spinetta, J. J. (1974) 'The dying child's awareness of death', *Psychol. Bull.* 81(4):256–60.

—— (1975) 'Death anxiety in the outpatient leukaemic child', *Paediatrics* 56(6):1034–7.

—— (1977) 'Adjustment in children with cancer', *J. Paed. Psychol.* 2(2):49–51.

—— (1981) 'The sibling of the child with cancer', in J. J. Spinetta and P. Deasy-Spinetta, eds *Living with Childhood Cancer*. St Louis, MO: C. V. Mosby.

—— (1982) 'Behavioural and psychological research in childhood cancer: an overview', *Cancer* 50:1939–43.

Spinetta, J. J. and Deasy-Spinetta, P., eds (1981) *Living with Childhood Cancer*. St Louis, MO. C. V. Mosby.

Spinetta, J. J. and Moloney, L. (1978) 'The child with cancer: patterns of communication and denial', *J. Consult. Clin. Psychol.* 48:1540–1.

Spinetta, J. J., Rigler, D. and Karon, M. (1973) 'Anxiety in the dying child', *Paediatrics* 52(6):841–5.

—— (1974) 'Personal space as a measure of the dying child's sense of isolation', *J. Consult. Clin. Psychol.* 42:751–6.

Spitz, Professor L. (Nuffield Professor of Paediatric Surgery, Inst. of Child Health; Hon. Consultant Surgeon, Hospital for Sick Children, Great Ormond Street, London) (1988) in *Observer magazine*, 17 July.

Spitz, R. (1945) 'Hospitalism', *Psychoanal. Study Child* 1:53–74.

Stambrook, M. and Parker, K. (1987) 'The development of the concept of death in childhood: a review of the literature', *Merrill-Palmer Q.* 33(2):133–57.

Stannard, D. (1977) *The Puritan Way of Death: A Study in Religion, Culture and Social Change*. Oxford University Press.

Stedeford, A. (1984) *Facing Death: Patients, Families, and Professionals*. Heinemann Medical.

Stehbens, J., Kisker, C., and Wilson, B. (1983) 'Achievement and intelligence test-retest performance in paediatric cancer patients at diagnosis and one year later', *J. Paed. Psychol.* 8:47–56.

Stein, A., Wooley, H., *et al.* (1988) 'Imparting the diagnosis of life-threatening illness'. Paper presented at 60th Annual Meeting, British Paediatric Association, New York.

Stein, R. and Jessop, D. (1984) 'Does paediatric home care make a difference for children with chronic illness?', *Paediatrics* 73:845-53 (Paediatric Ambulatory Care Treatment Study).

Thomas, D. (1966) 'Do not go gentle into that good night', in *Collected Poems*. Dent, 1977.

—— (1966) 'Death shall have no dominion', in *Collected Poems*. Dent, 1977.

Tropauer, A., *et al.* (1970) 'Psychological aspects of the care of children with cystic fibrosis', *Amer. J. Dis. Children* 119:424-32.

Turk, J. (1964) 'Impact of cystic fibrosis on family functioning', *Paediatrics* 34:67-71.

Twaddle, V., Britton, P., *et al.* (1983) 'Intellectual function after treatment for leukaemia or solid tumours', *Arch. Dis. Childh.* 58:949-52.

Van Dongen-Melman, J. and Sanders-Woudstra, J. (1986) 'Psychosocial aspects of childhood cancer: a review of the literature', *J. Child Psychol. Psychiat.* 27:145-80.

Vernick, J. (1973) 'Meaningful communication with the fatally ill child', in E. Anthony and C. Koupernik, eds *The Child in his Family*, vol. II. New York: Wiley.

Vernick, J. and Karon, M. (1965) 'Who's afraid of death on a leukaemia ward?', *Amer. J. Dis. Childh.* 109:393-7.

Waechter, E. (1968) 'Death anxiety in children with fatal illness'. Doctoral dissertation, Stanford University, Ann Arbor, MI: Univ. Microfilms, No. 72-26, 056.

—— (1971) 'Children's awareness of fatal illness', *Amer. J. Nursing* 71:1168-72.

Walker, G. (1983) 'The pact: the caretaker-parent/ill child coalition in families with chronic illness', *Fam. Systems Medicine* 1:4, 7-29.

Walvin, J. (1987) *Victorian Values*. Cardinal (Sphere Books).

Watson, D., *et al.* (1981) 'A reappraisal of routine marrow examination therapy of acute lymphoblastic leukaemia', *Arch. Dis. Childh.* 56:392-4.

Watson, M. (1983) 'Psychological intervention with cancer patients: a review', *Psychol. Med.* 13:839-46.

Wells, R. (1988) *Helping children cope with grief*. Sheldon Press.

Weininger, O. (1979) 'Young children's concepts of dying and dead', *Psychological Reports* 44:395-407.

Weithorn, L. and Campbell, S. (1982) 'The competency of children and adolescents to make informed treatment decisions', *Child Dev.* 53:1589-98.

Wenestam, C. G. (1982) 'Children's reactions to the word death'. Unpublished paper, Dept. of Ed., University of Göteborg, Sweden.

Willcock, D. (producer) (1988) *The Facts of Death*, film by Everyman BBC TV, 15 August.

Williams, T. (1957) *Orpheus Descending*. Harmondsworth: Penguin, 1976.

Winnicott, D. W. (1951) 'Transitional objects and transitional phenomena', in *Collected Papers: Through Paediatrics to Psychoanalysis*. Tavistock, 1958.

—— (1954) 'A primary state of being: pre-primitive stages', in *Human Nature*. Free Association Books, 1988.

—— (1962) 'Ego integration in child development', in *The Maturational Processes and the Facilitating Environment*. Hogarth, 1987.

—— (1963) 'The value of depression', in *Home is Where We Start From*. Harmondsworth: Penguin, 1987.

—— (1972) 'Basis for self in body', *Int. J. Child Psychother.* 1:(1):7–16.

—— (1974) *Playing and Reality*. Harmondsworth: Penguin.

—— (1987) *The Maturational Processes and the Facilitating Environment*. Hogarth.

—— (1988) *Human Nature*. Free Association Books.

Witham, A. (1985) 'The idealization of dying', *Free Assns.* 3:80–91.

Wölfflin, H. (1932) *Principles of Art History*. New York: Dover.

Wolstenholm, G. and O'Connor, M. eds *Law and Ethics of Transplantation*. (1968) Ciba Foundation Blueprint. J. & A. Churchill.

Yalom, I. (1980) *Existential Psychotherapy*. New York: Basic.

Yorke, C. (1985) 'Fantasy and the body-mind problem', *Psychoanal. Study Child* 40:319–28.

Yudkin, S. (1967) 'Children and death', *Lancet* 1:37–41.

Zorza, R. and V. (1980) *A Way to Die: Living to the End*. Deutsch.

Index

acceptance of fatal illness/death 30, 56–9, 147–8
acute lymphoblastic leukaemia (ALL) 157–8
acute myeloid leukaemia (AML) 77
adolescents 48, 49, 53
advances in survival times 183–4
after-life, belief in 10, 11, 43–4
aggressive/destructive impulses, fear of 18, 24, 148–9
Alderstein, A. 27
Alexander, I. 27
'Ancient Mariner, The' (Coleridge) 186
anger 34, 53–4, 63, 67, 149, 165
animals, death of 22–3
Anthony, E. 30
antibiotics, discovery of 5
anticipatory mourning 57, 147
anxieties 12, 14, 17, 22, 27, 29, 31–2, 33, 35, 38, 39, 51–2, 62, 165, 186, 193–4
Ariès, P. 6
Asclepius 9
assimilation stage of illness 50–1
Association for Child Psychology and Psychiatry 7
Atkin, Margaret 65, 66–7
Atkins, D. 166
attention, demands for 52
attitudes to death, children's 17–27
awareness of death
  dying child's 29–36
  stages in 19–21

Bach, S. 120
Bacon, Francis 10

Baldwin, James 9
'bargaining' phase of illness 56, 136–7
barrier-nursing 94, 95, 99, 103–4, 111, 118
bereavement 169–81
  and insensitivity of funeral directors 171–2
  and pain of loss 13, 26, 173
  and social stigma 169, 170–1
  children's experience of 24, 25
  counselling/therapy for 172–3
  effects on siblings 173–5
  first months of 143–5
  initial reactions to 137–40
  long-term effects of 170–1
  staff involvement in 172, 175–81
  understanding of 7
Berger, John 23, 143
Bettelheim, B. 58–9
Bion, W. xvii, xviii–xix, 18
Black, Dora 5, 7, 15, 64, 128, 169
Bloom, Alan 5
Bluebond-Langner, M. 37, 43
body image 53–4, 98, 100–1, 162, 189
bone marrow tranmsplants (BMT) 34, 50, 54, 77, 78–9, 80, 184
  donors for 78, 165, 166
  physical side-effects of 79–80, 161–2
  psychological effects of 164–7
  see also chemotherapy; radiotherapy
boredom, of hospitalized children 165
Bowlby, J. 18, 40
Bozeman, M. 65
brain tumours 71
British Medical Association (BMA) 154
British Medical Journal 71
'burn-out' of staff 175

213

This first edition of
Give Sorrow Words: Working with a dying child
was finished in August 1989.

It was set in 10/13 Baskerville Roman
on an AM Comp/Set 560
printed on a Crabtree Sovereign NP56
on to 80 g/m² vol. 18 Book Wove.

This book was commissioned by Ann Scott,
edited by Ann Scott and Selina O'Grady,
copy-edited by Gillian Wilce,
indexed by Peva Keane,
designed by Wendy Millichap
and produced by Miranda Chaytor
and Martin Klopstock for
Free Association Books.